Stormy Outside

The Adventures and Misadventures of a Forester and His Dog

Mark Stormzand

Mission Point Press

Stormy Outside

The Adventures and Misadventures of a Forester and His Dog

Readers are encouraged to go to www.MissionPointPress.com to contact the author or to find information on how to buy this book in bulk at a discounted rate.

MISSION POINT PRESS

Published by Mission Point Press

2554 Chandler Rd.

Traverse City, MI 49696

(231) 421-9513

www.MissionPointPress.com

ISBN: 978-1-943995-84-4

Library of Congress Control Number: 2018953133

Printed in the United States of America.

Illustrations by Nathan Stormzand. Copyright © 2018.

TABLE OF CONTENTS

INTRODUCTION

As long as I can remember, I have loved the outdoors. Not so much for the activities it provides, but I just feel better outside. As a young boy, I would spend countless hours staring out the classroom window. Unfortunately, my teachers did not share my passion for the outdoors, and invariably I was moved to a portion of the classroom without a view (the cloakroom). Upon graduation from high school, I was among just a handful of students who knew exactly what they wanted to do. I wanted to be outside. Did not matter doing what, it just had to be outside. So, with encouragement from my future wife, and to the amazement of my former teachers, I started college and became a forester.

Not everyone is fortunate enough to stumble into the perfect career path as I did. I did not realize it growing up in a metropolitan area, but not only did I like the outside, I liked my outside big with lots of space, lots of trees, and not a lot of people. Short of being a wilderness guide, which was highly unlikely for a kid growing up in the "burbs" in the fifties and sixties, a career in forestry was perfect. I worked alone in spectacular landscapes and with one very wonderful perk: Every day was "bring your dog to work day."

As a forester, I found out that each day was an adventure in itself. Terrain, weather, animals, bugs, and trees could all add or subtract to the day's experience. In addition, I have been privileged to work all the way from a logging camp in Idaho to the wilds of Maine. Along the way I met many a colorful character. For as long as I can remember I had a lot interesting stories to tell. So, in 1991, in complete disregard to what my high school English teacher, Mrs. Stevenson, would have thought, I started writing short stories about my adventures for our local newspaper. One can't work outdoors all of the time. Then, in addition to my forestry escapades, I started writing about our family canoe, kayaking, and backpacking trips—much to the chagrin of my family.

Except for an occasional meeting or trip, I have had the good fortune to have a canine companion, our family dog, with me every day. Over the course of my career, I have had four completely different Golden Retrievers accompany me through the workday. Having shared many experiences with me, they play major roles in my stories. They were all the same, yet each very different. They are all prominent characters in the tales of my life in the bush. I thank them for their perseverance, loyalty, and love

The book is a compilation of those stories of my life's adventures. The reader will see that the tales are not in strict chronological order. I was more comfortable being guided by topic than the clock in organizing the book. But the first essay begins in 1975, the last in 2015. Those were true bookends for me.

I hope you enjoy those . . . and the stories in between. I sure have.

Mark "Stormy" Stormzand
August, 2018

To my loving wife Gail,
who passed away on January 18, 2015.
Without her love and support,
I would have never had the courage
to live my life to its fullest.

Old Man and the Trees

Idaho, 1975

To say I have met many unusual and colorful characters during my forestry career would be a colossal understatement. I have worked with loggers and foresters from Idaho to Maine. And what an interesting mix of personalities, quirks, oddities, and dispositions I have seen. In addition, I discovered these men and women are the salt of the earth. But I can honestly say of all the interesting people I have met, a fellow I encountered back in 1975, during my college years, was one of the most memorable.

I was trying to doze, but the dust, bumpy ride, and the roar from the Jeep's engine were making that impossible. Fred was at the wheel of our 1950-something Jeep, and it was obvious he was in a hurry. It was late Friday afternoon, and he did not want to miss the last log train leaving camp. Last week, through letters, he had made arrangements to meet his future bride in town for the weekend. "Town," which was some ninety miles away by train, was where he had met her a year earlier.

Courtship had grown into a promise to marry, which had resulted in Fred riding the train every Friday down to Lewiston
and returning Sunday evening … except for last Friday, when
I was at the wheel, and I was inspired to take a shortcut back
to camp. That shortcut resulted in a tour of the north fork of
the Clearwater River and me with a less-than-amiable partner
to share the lonely weekend.

This time, Fred was driving. The whine of the engine
prompted me to open one eye and then to quickly shut it. Fred
was passing a log truck on a narrow stretch of trail, which in
my opinion was way too narrow and twisting to even think
about attempting.

"You must be in love," I grumbled, wishing the Jeep had
come with seatbelts.

As we passed the tail end of the truck, the dust billowed
through the open sides of the Jeep, making what precious
visibility we had almost non-existent. At this point, Fred's sole
goal was not to miss the train again. "Full steam ahead and
man the torpedoes!" was etched on his face. The train ride itself
was a three-hour affair that meandered through the northern
Idaho mountains. There were two engines, fifty carloads of logs,
and a caboose. The caboose held all the men traveling back to
town for the weekend. Tobacco smoke, sweat, diesel, and chainsaw fumes filled the small compartment. On this winding trip,
more than one hitchhiker usually held his head out the window,
gasping for fresh air.

We skidded into the railroad siding, and Fred sprinted toward the train, which was just starting its first "chug-chug-chug"
to get the big wheels moving. Over his shoulder, Fred yelled,
"See you on Monday! Have a good weekend." *Sure,* I thought,
easy for you to say.

I was one of only four foresters stationed at this remote

logging camp, and I was the only one who did not have a reason to leave. My girl was back in Michigan. Along with my co-workers, all of the loggers took the long train ride to be near their friends and families. So, I was the only soul left to hold down the fort.

Wheeling the battered Jeep into the makeshift parking space in front of the bunkhouse, I realized I really wasn't all alone. There, leaning against the rail of the raised boardwalk that connected the foresters' and loggers' bunkhouse to the cook shed, was Oscar. His short, compact body was leaning against one of the log pillars. His hands were shoved into the pockets of his ancient canvas logging pants, and tufts of coarse, white hair poked out from underneath an old, crushed, fedora hat. His slightly clouded blue eyes followed the train as it left the log yard on its journey to bring logs to the mill and reunite the men with their families. His body language said lonely, forlorn, despondent, and friendless.

Seeing Oscar brought me out of my personal funk. Sure, I was only one of two people left in camp. But I had friends, family, and a future wife who I would see in a few months. This was not the case with the craggy figure staring at the disappearing train. This and other logging camps had been Oscar's home since he was sixteen. Now seventy-five, he was all alone. He never married—not that living in logging camps his entire life gave him much opportunity to court—and all of his friends were either retired or in that big logging camp in the sky. As much as I hated weekends and being alone, it must have been torture on Oscar. Every Friday, the only family he had jumped aboard a train heading south, leaving him alone with only his thoughts.

I shut the Jeep off, threw the keys on the dash, and leaned on the dusty steering wheel looking through the cracked windshield at Oscar. "Well, no sense both of us being miserable," I said, crawling out of the Jeep. I climbed the three steps leading up the long boardwalk. I never really understood why the bunkhouses were connected to the cook shed by the raised, covered boardwalk. Maybe the cooks wanted the men to be dry and mud-free when they ate their enormous meals. Some days, that would be the only time they were warm and dry. I strolled over to where my new best friend was leaning and gave him a pat on the back.

"How are you today?" I asked, moving next to him on the rail.

On the railing between us was perched two items Oscar was never without on these long weekends: a can of Olympia (barley and hops) and a can of Del Monte green beans. The Olympia was usually empty, but the can of green beans was not. Actually, to be more accurate, the original Del Monte contents had been consumed probably during Prohibition. Since then, the can was a dispenser for the juices of Oscar's favorite vice—Copenhagen snuff. Oscar was never without his snuff and his can. He turned to acknowledge my greeting, and I could tell he was already in his weekend mode. Decades of Copenhagen use left a brown stain, which ran from his lower right lip through his gray stubble to the bottom of his chin. And on the weekends, with the help of his other can, the stain was more or less a constant dribble. It was unsightly at best, but just part of Oscar's persona.

"Lots of logs headed to the mill," he said, gesturing to the departing train.

"Yeah, you fellows had a busy week," I said in acknowledgement.

"Not me! All I did was sweep out the bunkhouses and keep the woodstove going," he said with obvious regret.

"Hey, it all matters. You do what you can do."

A pause ensued, so then I added, "Besides, you probably

filled several of those trains yourself over the years. Now you can relax and take it easy a bit," I said. My words felt shallow.

"Humph," and a stream hit the Del Monte can.

For the next minute, we both fell silent, contemplating the lonely days that lay ahead.

"Hey look, it is obvious I have nothing to do this weekend. What do you have on your plate?" I asked.

He looked at me like I had just prodded him about the meaning of life.

"Really, Oscar, I am free. What would you like to do?"

He looked at me and, in full honesty, said, "I would really like to fish."

"Fishing is good. Let's fish," I said with enthusiasm.

He nodded in agreement, and I actually thought I saw a slight sparkle behind those clouded, blue eyes.

The next day, I was back in the battered old Jeep heading down a dusty, rutted trail. But this time, begrudgingly, I was at the wheel. I've never really liked motorized vehicles, and the feeling seems to be mutual. But being a male and twenty-one, I certainly was not going to admit it. Oscar was in the passenger seat holding his two cans while his dog, Felix, sat in the backseat. Technically, Felix was not Oscar's dog. Felix just showed up one day, and they kind of adopted each other. I was getting glimpses of Felix in the cracked rear-view mirror. He was sitting very straight and proper, as if his pedigree dated back to the Romans. In reality, he was such a mixture of breeds that a geneticist would have won the Nobel Prize if they could have pieced together Felix's true background. Rounding out our ensemble was Oscar's twelve-foot aluminum rowboat strapped to the top of the Jeep.

We were heading to one of Oscar's secret lakes. (Pretty much all the lakes are secret in this remote portion of northern Idaho.)

"Here, turn here!" Oscar yelled.

"Where?" I said in confusion. All I saw was a steep drop-off to our right and a sheer mountain wall to my left.

"Down there," he pointed with his Del Monte can.

I slammed on the brakes temporarily, which placed Felix on my lap. Putting it in reverse, I backed up a few meters to where Oscar wanted me to turn. Once the cloud of dust settled, I peered over a precipice in disbelief.

"Come on! I have driven down there many times. You can do it, lad," he said with challenge in his voice.

So, with my young brain saying "road trip," I drove into the abyss.

To my surprise, I was still alive when we reached the bottom of the valley. After a few more minutes of bone-jarring travel, I was told to stop.

"This is it," Oscar said with obvious pride.

I was a bit confused, because all I saw were trees, rocks, and mountains and absolutely nothing to suggest that the fishing would be good. Felix jumped over the seat and onto my lap. I grunted as he sprang out the open door. Oscar was busily untying the boat when I asked, "So, where's the lake?"

"Oh, not too far. Here, grab the other end of the boat."

"Not too far" means different things to different people, as my family would find out many years later. We lugged, pushed, pulled, and cursed that bloody rowboat for almost an hour through the bush. At one point, I asked Oscar if we had lost the trail.

"Trail? What trail?" he grunted as we pushed the boat up and over a large rock.

"I thought so," I grumbled to myself.

We stopped to catch our breath, and I could hear Felix splashing and frolicking in a body of water. One more good shove on the boat, and we were there. I slumped against a large western white cedar and got my first glance of Oscar's secret lake.

"Oh my," I heard myself say.

Before me spread a small lake surrounded by very large, white cliffs. The only entrance was the small crack through which we had just coerced the boat. On top of the steep cliffs stood large western white pines that looked like sentries guarding some ancient ruins. The lake, which was turquoise in color, positively sparkled in the clear, sunny, mountain sky. All of this combined with the scent of the fresh, cool, mountain air made me think I had just stepped into Shangri-La.

"This is absolutely beautiful," I said in amazement.

"Yeah, and the fishin' is good, too," he said with new-found glee in his voice.

Funny, I thought. Oscar sure looked a lot more sprightly than he did standing on the porch watching the train depart.

With the boat afloat, which was good considering the age and condition of the water craft, we started loading our little bit of gear. Oscar threw in two poles, one tattered boat cushion, two mismatched oars, a piece of old bulldozer track (which I assumed was our anchor since it was attached to a long rope), a fresh can of Olympia, the Del Monte can, and an old battered Spam can. My lone contribution to our big day of fishin' was a can of pork and beans and a can of peaches. These were the only food items I could find in the foresters' bunkhouse. It really did not matter to Oscar that I had packed a pathetic lunch, because on the weekends, he only lived on snuff and Olympia. Luckily, neither Oscar nor I were giants among men, because I am not sure the little craft would have stayed afloat if we had been heavier. Oscar was in the stern, I was in the middle acting as oarsman, and Felix was in the prow looking very proud and important.

My orders were to row the boat very slowly, which was not a problem since the boat could have easily been mistaken for an oversized laundry tub. As I struggled to propel the lumbering craft forward, I watched with interest as Oscar set to work preparing the poles. It was obvious he had a set pattern, because everything was done with precise and exaggerated movements. He placed his Oly and Del Monte cans on the seat to his right and on his left sat the old Spam can. He pried the Spam can open, placing the battered top on his lap. Then he took out a can of Copenhagen, opened it, and placed it next to the Spam can. Surprisingly, the contents of the two looked similar. I watched in awe as Oscar dug in the Spam can and pulled out two gigantic worms. After he had expertly threaded them on to the hooks, he carefully pulled a faded bandana from his well-worn green flannel shirt and wiped his hands as if he were a surgeon preparing for an important operation. Then he took a pinch of snuff, placing it between cheek and gums, followed by another pinch, which he placed in the Spam can. Placing the lid back on the Spam can, he looked up, winked, and said, "My secret ingredient." I deduced that the pinch was why the worms were so lively.

Since I was a guest in the state of Idaho and did not have a valid license to extract trout from her waters, I was prepared to spend the day enjoying the scenery, getting an upper body workout, and listening to an old woodsman chaw. I wasn't disappointed.

Rowing with the mismatched oars was a bit of a challenge. Since one was shorter than the other, I had to pull harder on my right than left, leaving me a sore right shoulder. I withdrew the oars from the water, placing them on the gunnels. I could see one raised eyebrow as the oars made a thump as I hit the gunnels.

"Sorry," I said, then asked earnestly, "So, when did you start working in the woods?"

Oscar looked a bit puzzled as he scratched the white stubble on his chin.

"I suppose it was around 1916," came his reply. "My Pa died in fall of 1915, and that winter I started working for my uncle. He had a logging crew out on the forks, and I started as a swamper."

"What is a swamper?" I asked.

"Why, they're the lads that cut all the branches off the tree once it has been felled," he said, reeling in his first trout.

Oscar then proceeded to tell me, in logging lingo, of all of the jobs he had done over the past sixty years. He had been a "feller," who were the gents who cut the trees down. For a while he was involved in twitching the long trees out of the woods to a staging area. The lads doing this task were called "twitchers." In his early days, it was done with animals, then it progressed to bulldozers. He had been employed as a "jammer operator." A jammer is a big crane that pulls large logs up out of a valley to a road or landing. For several years, he had been a "whistle punk." These fellows would hook the cables around the logs that were hauled up by the jammer. Once the cable was around the log, they would blow a whistle and scamper to safety as the logs were pulled up the mountain.

The jobs Oscar had done were impressive, but not nearly as impressive as the nicknames they'd been given. When Oscar explained his current job, his voice lacked enthusiasm, and you could see his shoulders drop. He knew this was the last job he would have in his long, colorful career. Basically, he was the camp janitor. This can be an honorable profession. However, in the world of logging, it is also the last rung on the career ladder. At least when you are put out to pasture in the logging profession, you are given a cool name. Oscar's current position held the title of "bullcook."

A trout struck at Oscar's "super worm," which quickly brought him out of his gloom. From the tension on the pole and the glee in Oscar's eyes, I had a hint this was a keeper. It was a large trout, which Oscar expertly landed and placed on the stringer with several others. A worm came out of the Spam can and a little more snuff went in.

As the lazy summer afternoon lingered and the sun began to fall behind the large cliffs, interesting shadows began to form across the lake. I was admiring them when all of a sudden, the boat lurched to the right, and I was thrown to the left. Felix had decided he needed some attention, so he had leaped from his perch in the bow and was curling himself around Oscar's feet. I could hear Oscar gently muttering to the beast as I regained my position. Felix was trying to stretch out on the bottom of the boat to take full advantage of Oscar's strong hands, which resulted in me getting his hind quarters thrust between my legs. With balance regained, and the canine spread out between us, I did the only thing I could in the situation: I joined in. Felix was getting a full-body massage from stem to stern, and from the silly grin he had, it was obvious he was enjoying every minute of it.

I have always contended that you can tell a lot about a person by the way they interact with animals. For various reasons, we humans sometimes don't interact well with other people. We may be shy, short tempered, intimidated, intimidating, loners, insecure, or have a litany of other quirks when dealing with other members of our species. But when a bundle of sweet-smelling puppy fur comes and places his or her head in close proximity to our hand, we will go out of our way to scratch, rub, and inquire how the beast is doing. We have learned it takes nine lives to work your way into a cat's heart. But we can earn their devotion, via their stomachs, with one can of Meow Mix.

There was a tug on Oscar's line, which resulted in a quick jerk of his right hand to set the hook. As any good physicist knows, every action is countered by a reaction. In response to the quick setting of the hook, the startled Felix leaped into my lap. This action caused me to let go of the oars, which resulted in them slipping out of the well-worn oar locks and into the waters of the clear lake. All of this resulted in Oscar letting loose a sizeable laugh that I didn't know a man of seventy-five could muster.

With our limit for the day filled, Oscar suggested we just row around the lake. I think he suggested this for several reasons—the obvious one being that the lake was absolutely beautiful in the fading sunlight. Moreover, being on the lake and away from camp, Oscar seemed more alive. Employed as the camp's bullcook had a sobering effect on Oscar's normal zest for life. During the next hour, we poked the prow of the boat into the many nooks and crannies that surrounded this cliff-shrouded lake.

Oscar was very relaxed, and while rubbing Felix's ear, he became very chatty. I just sat and slowly rowed as he told me story after story about his life's experiences and adventures. Being a young man and having no life experiences to call my own, I was spellbound. Not only were his stories interesting and full of color, they usually had a small moral lesson attached to make one think. It also dawned on me that his generation may have witnessed the most changes of any other before them.

When he was young, life was without the combustible engine. Man and animal power were the norm. He witnessed the advent of the Model A and the Apollo spacecraft. He was involved in World War I, made it through the Depression, witnessed the horrors of World War II, Korea, and Vietnam, was dumbstruck by the power of the nuclear bomb, and saw the buildup and later decline of several empires. Oscar, like my grandfather, experienced all of this while at the same time keeping his humility, sense of humor, and fondness for the simple pleasures of life. As I rowed, I could only hope I would do as well.

With darkness almost upon us and a long, arduous retreat from this piece of heaven ahead of us, I suggested we head for the barn. Oscar reluctantly agreed. As I rowed toward the crack in the cliffs where our "portage" trail lay, Felix again left his position in the bow and took up a new one on the seat with Oscar. I think Felix could sense Oscar's mood changing, and he placed his head on Oscar's lap. Dogs can tell when a person needs some comfort, probably better than we humans. And what better way to tell someone they are important than to nuzzle them with a cold, wet nose?

Oscar immediately started rubbing behind Felix's right ear, which resulted in Felix trying to snuggle closer and letting out a very relaxed sigh in the process. Oscar chuckled and said, "My grandfather always said a dog has a way of making you think you are comforting them when in fact it is the other way around. Look at this bugger; he thinks I don't know he is trying to cheer me up."

I rowed in silence for a while, then Oscar said, "My grandfather also told me never pass up an opportunity to stop and pet a dog. They deserve it." I nodded in agreement.

Much later that evening, we three sat in the bunkhouse listening to the sounds of fish frying and the crackle of the fire in the big potbellied stove. Oscar sat very close to the stove on a long bench, which normally would hold a half dozen cold, wet, tired loggers. On the bench next to him were the old Del Monte can and a fresh Oly can. Felix lay curled at his feet, enjoying the heat from the stove and the comfort of Oscar's nearness. I was considerably farther away, because the bloody stove was way too hot for this slightly cool, summer-mountain evening. I was, however, transfixed by the smells, sights, and sounds of the fish and fire. Oscar began rubbing Felix's head with a well-worn, red-wool sock.

"I have had a wonderful life," he blurted out.

Brought out of my trance, I replied, "Far better than most, I am sure."

"I have shared a kinship with these mountains and everything that lives and grows in them. And the men that worked in 'em," he said with pride. "A rewarding life, that's what I've had."

I watched with an ache in my heart as Oscar slowly drifted back into his melancholy mood. Felix nudged Oscar's foot as if to say, "Hey! You got me, mate." Even Felix's cold nose and warm heart were of no use. On seeing Oscar's despair, I promised myself I would try to get Oscar back on the lake next weekend. As I watched, Oscar stood, opened his Copenhagen can, and placed a large pinch between cheek and gum. With a chuckle, he offered me some knowing full well I would rather eat dirt. Then he forked out some fried trout from the pan and placed it on a chipped blue-enamel plate. This he placed on the bench between his two cans. He nodded to the heap of trout and said, "Dig in, lad."

In normal circumstances, I would have. But seeing the trout lying between the new and used snuff and the thought of the "special food" that Oscar feeds his worms kind of dampened my appetite.

"I think I will let them cool a bit. How about you telling me about when you worked the river drives?" I said.

Eyeing the trout, I was hoping either the length of the story or another Oly might allow me time to slip man's best friend a few fish bites for his loyalty to Oscar. Looking at Felix, I realized he had the same idea; his whiskers twitched and his nostrils flared. And with Oscar reminiscing, Felix enjoying the catch of the day, and me enjoying the company, I realized it had not been a lonely weekend after all.

After that first fishing trip, Oscar, Felix, and I spent almost every remaining weekend in that small aluminum rowboat. Then in the fall, it was time for me to return to friends, college, and my loved ones. Over the years, I had come to realize I had learned a lot from that old fellow and his adopted dog. I never saw either of them again. But to this day, over thirty years later, I still never pass up an opportunity to bend down and scratch a dog behind its ears. Life should never be too busy to miss a moment to show someone or something you care.

Thanks, Oscar.

Disney and Fire

Idaho, 1975

The door sprang open and a loud voice shouted, "All right, girls. We're finally going to see you work." I knew exactly who it was. It was Ben, the camp foreman. For some reason, Ben never thought we foresters worked very hard, so he called us "girls." I could never figure it out, because I walked up and down mountains all day marking timber, and at the end of the day, I sure felt like I had worked. And I knew plenty of real girls who worked extremely hard. But I supposed Ben felt walking was a piece of cake compared to the hard, dangerous work of logging in these mountains of northern Idaho. And he was probably right.

"Okay, ladies. While you were getting your beauty rest, Mother Nature did her work last night. Our towers have reported lightning strikes all over the region," he said solemnly. "And as soon as it gets light enough, we will have our planes in the air to confirm the number."

I was the rookie on this forestry team, and I was excited to get out there and fight my first fire. But I could tell this was a serious situation by Ben's matter-of-fact tone. Ben normally liked to joke around. However, as he talked, he became very serious.

"The rough count is forty-five lightning strikes. If we can jump on them early, we might be able to keep them from spreading. Last year, we had one get away from us, and it turned into a huge fire. Unfortunately, we lost a man on that fire. So be careful. Pack your gear and keep it light. You lads are going to see some bloody rough country.

"Be ready to go in half an hour," he said, then flew out the door.

I was so excited, I was having a hard time packing. For me, this was the reason I came to northern Idaho in the summer of 1975. It was between my junior and senior years of college, and I was working as a summer forestry intern. My other classmates were stuck back in Michigan working at normal summer jobs, mowing lawns and flipping burgers. But I was having the greatest adventure of my life and being paid for it to boot. Thanks to a contact my future mother-in-law had, I was living in one of the few remaining logging camps in the country. The only fear my future mother-in-law had was that I would love it so much that I would bring her daughter back the next year to live. As I quickly packed my hardhat, flashlight, and several bandanas, the phrase, "we lost a man," did slightly dampen my enthusiasm.

Up to this point, all I had been doing during the summer was marking trees, running survey lines, and taking sample plots. But I was only twenty-one and I wanted some "real action!" As a kid, I use to sit in the den on Sunday nights with my family, eating Campbell's tomato soup and grilled cheese sandwiches while we watched The Walt Disney Show. My favorite episodes were the ones with forest rangers, smoke jumpers, and firefighters. I was so excited on those occasions that I would have a hard time falling asleep. Now here I was finally about to be in a Disney movie, and man, was I jazzed. So jazzed, in fact, some of the veterans were giving looks that definitely said, "Dumb newbie."

Checking my watch, I noticed it was 5:30 a.m. and we were already loaded in our trucks and ready to go. The veteran foresters were not as giddy about the fires as I was, but they were still visibly charged. They knew first-hand how dangerous fires could be, but they also knew their next paycheck would be considerably larger. Fires meant many hours of overtime and a higher pay scale.

Ben had divided us into pairs, which allowed us to cover more country since the strikes were so widespread. The company I was working for had vast holdings in northern Idaho. Consequently, we had our own fire watch and suppression system, which was not linked to the U.S. Forest Service. Each truck was loaded with shovels, axes, water bags, chainsaws, first aid kits, old World War II sleeping bags, two radios, and a Pulaski. The Pulaski is a tool with an ax on one side of the head and a flat digging tool on the other. Ranger Ed Pulaski, who won fame in the 1910 fires in northern Idaho, first developed this tool.

As we were leaving, the cooks ran out with our food for breakfast and lunch. They threw ours through the window and mine landed on my lap. My partner, Frank, and I looked at each other and smiled. We knew what the lunch would be, but we were curious what breakfast held in store for us.

I peeked inside and groaned, "You've got to be kidding." Every lunch since June had contained one fried donut, one can of beanie weenies, one piece of pie, and one very large Spam sandwich. "Yuck," I gagged, peering into the bag marked breakfast. Obviously, the cooks were pressured for time, because lying in a pool of grease at the bottom of the paper sack was a fried egg and Spam sandwich.

Frank and I headed out to our assigned area, which was located about twenty miles up a mountain valley. We were in constant radio contact with a fire tower and spotter plane. Trying to find a very small fire in these vast mountains was the proverbial "needle in the haystack," and the spotters were invaluable. We traveled as far as we could by truck, and then we took off on foot. Loaded down with gear and water, we headed up the draw toward (we hoped) a burning tree several miles away. I had been running a lot the last several years, and I figured I was in great shape, but that unnamed mountain was a giant reality check. Exhausted, we finally reached the summit and could see smoke just on the other side.

Several minutes later, I arrived at my first forest fire. To say I was disappointed would be an understatement. One lone tree was smoldering at the top like a candle on a birthday cake. There was no wall of fire to battle, no clouds of smoke to keep us from breathing. Just this one candle smoking seventy-five feet in the air. But, if I thought the work coming up the mountain was hard, I was in for a tremendous surprise. We had to cut the burning tree down and then dig a fire line around it. Okay, even at twenty I realized cutting a tree was dangerous no matter what you did. But cutting a burning tree really raised the ante. Frank was equally aware of the danger, so we proceeded with extreme caution. Once the tree was safely on the ground, we had to smother any smoldering spots with dirt until it was cool to the touch. We did all of this in ninety-plus-degree heat. This task took us almost twelve hours of grueling labor.

Upon completion, we headed down the mountain to our truck thinking we would be heading back to camp where a shower awaited us. On the seat of our truck sat two disappointments: the map to our next hot spot and our dinner. To me, the map was the lesser of two evils. I recognized the grease stain coming through the brown paper bags. Spam! And this Spam had been sitting in the hot truck for who knows how long? I did my part for the bear population and left mine along the side of the road. Frank, to my surprise, ate his.

Our next destination was located up the opposite side of the mountain. We could not contact the fire tower for guidance, because by now our batteries were dead. However, with our second radio set to a different frequency, we were able to contact the plane. For nearly an hour, the pilot kept circling trying to guide us to the fire. It was obvious this tactic was not going to work. So, before our second radio was done in, the pilot decided to try a new strategy. He had flown many spotter missions over Europe during World War II and had been flying fire patrol ever since. Consequently, he had many tricks, and he was not about to let two young foresters stumble though the mountains aimlessly. But I had to admit I was astonished when I saw a fluttering line of toilet paper trailing out of the plane window. He was flying so low we could see his arm stuck out the window with the TP roll on the end of a brown stick. Obviously, he came prepared. The pilot just flew straight to the source, and we followed the toilet paper to the fire. This was something I had never learned about in school but would surely remember! It is customary that each individual fire be registered and named. You can use your imagination as to what we christened this hot spot.

Arriving at the fire, we quickly noticed this lightning strike had done much more damage than the first. The tree had fallen when the lightning hit it, which created many small fires on the ground. Even though I was dead tired, this was more like the fires I remembered from Disney. We worked on that fire all through the night and into the next day.

Several times during the second day, we had to rest due to fatigue. With our food and water gone, we decided I would go down to the truck and grab more supplies. After all, I was the rookie. So, around 8 in the evening, I headed down the mountain. By 10, I was heading back loaded down with water, a filthy sleeping bag, gas and oil for the saw, and Spam sandwiches. I thought I had experienced fatigue before. What did I know? I have never experienced anything like the trip up that mountain before or since. Darkness had descended, but I was able to use the glow from the fire as if it were a lighthouse. Reaching the fire, I saw Frank leaning on his shovel to keep from falling over. Finding a secure area, I stowed the gear and headed over to him. During my hours of trekking, Frank had successfully dug a fire line around the fire, and we both felt the fire was well on its way to being secure. We desperately needed some sleep, so we both retreated to the secure area. In fire school, we had been taught that creating and maintaining an area that was free of fuel (trees, limbs, and brush) and out of range from any falling fuel was essential to one's safety.

Arriving at our secure area, we sat down among the supplies and tried to eat. I managed to choke down beanie weenies and the pie, but I could not face the Spam. Frank, on the other hand, was devouring his as if it were prime rib. My body was telling me I really needed to eat. So, I put my sandwich on a stick and headed to the fire line to roast it. I stepped around the fallen Pulaski, wondering if there would ever be a tool named the "Stormzand." Maybe an ax with a special Spam holder on the other side? Sitting next to the smoldering tree, while trying to heat all of the grease out of my Spam sandwich,

I suddenly had a craving for Campbell's tomato soup. At the same time, I had a feeling that Mr. Disney had lead me astray. I didn't remember any of his characters looking like or feeling like I did. I was sure they all smelled better.

Maybe something in the Campbell's tomato soup had made things seem more romantic, I thought as my Spam sizzled.

For the next five days, Frank and I fought fire after fire with little sleep, food, or water. At one point, we were so exhausted we took turns crawling into the aged, smoked, sleeping bag. Under normal circumstance, we never would have fallen fast asleep so near a forest fire in such a foul bag. But it was a much sought-after haven for both of us. After the third day, numbness and fatigue were really starting to affect our judgment. How we eluded felling a tree on each other or falling into the fire, I will never know. But gratefully, we did not. We knew we were not alone in our weariness. All of the fire teams were experiencing the same conditions. It was not a lack of organization or incompetence of our leaders or organization that stretched us so thin. It was the sheer magnitude of the situation. Fifty small fires spread out over hundreds of square miles just overwhelmed the available manpower.

Finally, after six days, the fires were out and all of us were allowed to return to camp. Once we had all straggled back to camp, we had to be debriefed by Ben. This meant, to the best of our ability, we had to pinpoint on the topo maps where the fires had occurred. The maps were spread out on the tables in the cookhouse, and as I sat there waiting my turn to pinpoint our fires, I got a real good look at the other pairs. They did not look so good, and if I were a betting man, I would guess I looked no better. This was confirmed when I saw my distorted face in the stainless-steel coffee mug, and the contrast of my hands to the elderly lady who had handed it to me. Moreover, the color of my forearms matched the color of the very strong coffee.

When the debriefing was completed, Ben cleared his throat and said, "Boys, you did well." With that, he left us. The cooks brought out platters loaded with sandwiches and gallons of coffee. Frank got up and said, "I'll grab you a few sandwiches." Returning, he placed a blue enameled plate in front of me with two huge sandwiches. Before he even sat, Frank was taking a chomp out of his. A familiar streak of grease dribbled down his cheek, and I let out a pitiful moan. With a nod, Frank suggested I check my sandwiches out. Lifting the large piece of homemade bread, I was overwhelmed with joy when I saw what was inside. There, sitting on my plate, was a ham—not Spam—sandwich. Frank chuckled, and I took another large bite out of the most delicious sandwich I had ever tasted.

View from the Top

Idaho, 1975

*W*hizzzzz!

"Hey watch it, Tom. You about clipped my ear on that one," I shouted.

Tom turned and said something, but the roar of the river was too great to understand. I squatted back down on my haunches and continued my task. On the ground next to me lay a mass of trout, which I had the unpleasant chore of cleaning. Flies had discovered this mother lode of guts and yuck and were doing their best to clean the fish for me. I heard the whiz of Tom's fly over my head as he expertly worked his fly rod. The sun started to fall below the rim of the valley, casting a slight purple tint to the rushing river. The sun also withdrew its summer warmth, which was replaced by hints of autumn.

Once more, I heard the slight whirl of Tom's fly as it swung over my head. Looking up, I saw Tom on a large boulder working his fly rod as if it were a Stradivarius. His silhouette was enhanced by a backdrop of Douglas Fir, bare cliffs, and far-off mountains. Normally, Tom would not be described as a graceful lad. But at this moment on this river, he was poetry in motion. His long, lanky arms were gracefully working in unison, placing his fly exactly where he wanted it, whether it was behind a large boulder, on the edge of a swirling eddy, or underneath a fallen log. It did not matter. He was in the zone.

A fly trying to crawl up my nostril brought me back to my place and duties on the river. Trout and lots of them needed to be cleaned. To my chagrin, Tom's mastery of the fly rod was making me an expert on fish anatomy. But I was not about to complain. Tom was catching enough for us to enjoy a wonderful evening meal. I just wished I had paid a little more attention when I was a lad. I could remember the smell of my grandfather's pipe, and the way his hat tilted back on his head, and the way he bobbed his head when he chuckled, but not much of his fishing advice. If I had, maybe I would be the figure silhouetted on the large boulder rather than the kid with fish guts under his fingernails.

Dusk was rapidly approaching, and both Tom and I knew we had a bit of a hike before darkness set in. I slung the branch upon which I had strung the fifteen trout over my shoulder; Tom tucked his fly rod under his left arm, grabbed his small tin box, which held his precious flies, in his right. We started our ascent up Elk Mountain. On top of the mountain stood a fire tower, which played a key role in our dinner plans. We more or less trotted the two miles up the mountain to the tower . . . not so much because we were on a fitness craze. We were just concerned about navigating up the mountain in the dark lugging ten pounds of pungent fish. Twilight was the witching hour for bears, and we had no desire to be involved in a game of tag with us being "it."

Dark descended before we reached the top. But the light from the large windows that circled the fire tower was like a beacon on a far-off shore. We could see our destination, but not the roots or boulders beneath our feet. Consequently, by the time we reached the top, my stringer of trout had scraped the turf several times, as had my knees. A shout of welcome came from the tower as we approached its base. Tom, with his long legs, bounded up the metal stairs two and three at a time. I, with considerably shorter legs and balancing ten pounds of dinner on my shoulder, ascended more cautiously. I could hear a hardy, "Hello, good to see ya!" and "What took you so long?" long before I reached the top.

When I reached the platform, directly below the tower's perch, I placed my branch of fish in a large tub that I assumed acted as some sort of sink. Located on this level were several large containers that I guessed held water and supplies. A clothesline was strung between two tower legs where a worn flannel shirt and a pair of frayed trousers hung limply. *I guess we won't be dressing for dinner*, I thought. I climbed the steep ladder through the large trap door and up into the crow's nest. Jack, exploding with enthusiasm, grabbed my arm and yanked me up the final two steps.

"By garsh, it is good to see ya," he said, pumping my hand violently. Jack was from Minnesota and had a wonderful accent, which was enhanced when he got excited.

"Good to see you, too," I said, rubbing my shoulder.

Jack then turned around and grabbed his rucksack and flashlight off his small cot.

"Right, then, I will see you Sunday night," he said, slinging the pack over his shoulder.

"You're leaving already? But I don't know what to do," I said, a bit surprised. Tom, who was going to leave with Jack, also questioned Jack's speedy departure, stating that we had yet to eat the mass of trout he had caught.

Pointing to a stack of notes lying on a small shelf next to

the cot, Jack said, "It's all there. Everything you need to do and when." He headed for the trap door.

I looked at Tom, who just shrugged and stared after the fleeing forester.

Just then Jack popped his head through the trap door and shouted, "What ever you do, don't forget to radio in at the correct times or you will be drawn and quartered."

With that bit of advice and the stack of notes in the corner, I became the official fire ranger on Elk Mountain . . . at least, for the next forty-eight hours.

I stepped out onto the catwalk that surrounded the tower and peered down into the growing darkness. I could see two bobbing lights as Jack squired down the mountain with Tom in quick pursuit. I wondered why Jack was in such a hurry. It was so peaceful and tranquil up here. For several minutes, I watched the two erratic lights until they disappeared into the valley. For a long time, I leaned against the rail of the catwalk gazing up at the stars as they became more numerous and the night sky grew darker. I had always enjoyed looking up into the heavens, but this was a completely different experience. The sky seemed so much larger, and the stars were so bright and clear. Maybe it was the higher elevation, or the lack of any artificial light, or maybe I was just closer. It did not matter. I was entranced, and for several more minutes, I lingered.

Turning, I discovered I was in complete darkness. The only light was the reflection of the stars in the windows of the tower. Groping my way around the catwalk, I finally found the door to the tower. Once inside, I realized the only flashlight I had seen was the one Jack fled with. I bumped into the cot and sat, trying to adjust my eyes to the complete darkness. After several minutes it was obvious my sight was not improving, so I tried the Helen Keller method of navigation.

After knocking most everything over including, I would shortly find out, an open bottle of Dr. Pepper, I finally discovered a book of matches. Striking a match, I was pleased to find a gas lantern. As the gentle hissing of the lantern filled the quiet night, I said, "Let there be light," realizing I had been alone on the mountain for about fifteen minutes and I was already talking to myself. This was not a good sign.

The room seemed a lot smaller than it had in the twilight. I figured it to be about fourteen-by-fourteen feet with a large, chest-high table located square in the middle. I found a hook to hang the lantern on, and I sat back on Jack's cot to access my humble abode. The long shadows cast by the lantern gave the room an eerie feel. The lantern's reflection was also in every window pane, which had the effect of a house of mirrors. Everything was below the level of the windows, which made sense since this was an observation tower. On the far wall were shelves that contained personal effects like clothes, bedding, cooking supplies, and a mason jar with a well-used toothbrush. To the right of the cot were shelves that contained books, journals, cards, and a very old turntable with equally old records stacked against it. Left of the cot was a long, low table, which was littered with maps, aerial photos, charts, a compass, and other instruments. Next to the cot was the shelf with Jack's written instructions, which were weighted down with some sort of large skull. After more examination, all I could tell was the skull was not human.

Removing the skull from the stack, I placed the notes next to me and started reading Jack's instructions. They included use of the radio, various pieces of equipment, observation hints, likely hot spots, water gathering, and how to take a shower. That bit of advice talked about a creek and a pail with holes in it. In addition, instructions for the gas stove and refrigerator were included. The hissing in the lantern was getting quieter, so I gave it a few pumps resulting in much more light. I caught myself before I repeated the "let there be light" thing. Included in the stack of information was a forestry manual entitled "Fire Detection and Reporting," dated 1931. Laying back on the cot with my head propped on several less-than-clean wool blankets, I started perusing the manual. I skimmed through the parts about Morse Code, since we were a tad more advanced than that, and was deep into the description of various types of smoke when I heard a large bang just below me.

I leaped off the cot, striking my head on the hissing lantern, which made it swing violently. Sounds and lots of them were coming from the storage level just below my feet. I quickly searched for some type of weapon, finally settling on a pan that had some telltale signs of an ancient meal. With pan in hand, I cautiously approached the trap door.

"Hey, get out of there!" I shouted.

The light from my lantern revealed a family of raccoons down below, devouring the mass of trout that I had left in the tub. As they scurried away, two of them with trout tails still hanging from their lips, I realized all of Tom's artful fishing had just fed a furry family of four.

I climbed down the ladder to see what was left in the tub. I saw two trout that were kind of salvageable, so I climbed back up, opened the gas refrigerator, and tossed them in. Returning to the cot, I resumed my studies. The rest of the night passed uneventfully, with me falling asleep with the fire detection manual and a half package of saltine crackers on my chest.

I awoke to one of the most amazing sights I had ever seen. The sunrise scanned the whole eastern horizon from north to south with purples, reds, and a mixture of orange and yellows. On the eastern slopes of the mountains behind me, the tops lit up like candles on a cake as the sun grew higher. Valleys were cast in dark-green shadows, and any body of water sparkled like it was covered with diamonds. And the vista was constantly changing as the sun rose in the morning sky. For close to an hour, I roamed the catwalk outside taking in all the beauty. Leaning against the railing, I realized I had really never witnessed anything like it, and I was completely awed.

My serenity came to a screeching halt as the radio crackled out, "WST923 DO YOU COPY? WST923 DO YOU COPY? THIS IS BASE." Jolted out of my bliss, I looked at my watch and realized, per Jack's warnings, I had missed my morning radio check. As I dashed through the door, the radio squelched again, this time a little more urgently.

Reaching for the handset, I saw the radio call letters taped to the radio. I clicked the mic with my thumb and somewhat hurriedly replied, "Base, this is WST954, I copy."

"Ah, that is fine, but I am calling WST923," the radio chattered back.

Somewhat confused, I studied the fading call letters taped to the radio, realizing I was not being paged.

"Base, this is WST923, sorry I was getting water," the radio crackled.

"Butte Mountain, please let me remind you of the importance of checking in at the proper times," the radio replied rather sternly.

"Roger that, WST923 clear," came a response.

"Elk Mountain, I assume you're still in contact," the voice at base said, somewhat irritated.

"Roger base, all present and accounted for," I said cheerfully.

"Elk Mountain, please identify yourself," the radio commanded.

I gave him my name and told him I was relieving Jack until Sunday night. The voice did not seem overly pleased to have a rookie up on Elk Mountain and grilled me on my duties as if he were a drill instructor. I was fully expecting him to tell me to hit the deck and give him fifty pushups when I was saved by another tower checking in. I listened for several minutes as more towers checked in, then it was quiet.

I brewed a cup of tea and strolled back out on the catwalk. I could not get enough of the view. I could see for countless miles in all directions, which was just intoxicating. I hopped up on the railing that circled the platform with my legs resting on an interior bench, and I balanced the mug of tea on my knee. I could see hawks below playing in wind currents, which were created by the land slowly heating up. The warm air rose up through the valleys, creating a rollercoaster ride for all types of raptors.

In a meadow below, I noticed a small herd of elk grazing on the fresh summer grasses. Turning to get a better view to the north, I jostled my tea. Moving quickly to keep it from spilling, I momentarily lost my balance on the narrow railing. As soon as I caught my balance, I leaped off the railing onto the platform, sending tea flying everywhere and my heart beating like I had just sprinted up the mountain. A horrible thought had gone through my mind. I remembered a story I had heard earlier that summer while attending fire school. Several years ago, a young college student had been stationed up on Butte Mountain, and one afternoon she had missed her radio check. A group of foresters working in the area were radioed and directed to ascend Butte.

What they found was very disturbing. The young coed's body lay at the base of the tower and not far away lay a journal, which she had been keeping. The assumption was she had been sitting on the rail writing in her journal when the tragedy occurred. I also remember hearing that all of the towers had been fitted with safety nets, which was the case as I peered over the edge. With my calm somewhat shaken, I headed into the tower for my morning observations.

In the middle of the crow's nest—the room at the top of the tower—lay the meat and potatoes of the fire tower system, the Osborne fire finder. This device was on top of a flat desk about four feet high that looked out upon a panoramic photograph of the surrounding area. Placed on top of that was a sighting device that, when adjusted, could pinpoint a fire's exact location. The Osborne's real advantage was that a new observer could identify peaks, ridges, valleys, and streams at a glance. If one could read an aerial photo, make a few adjustments to the sight, one could radio in the exact location of smoke with complete confidence . . . I hoped.

I also noticed that the wooden desk had some very interesting handiwork. Along the edge where the large photo did not cover the wooden top, past-tower occupants had carved their initials and dates of service. Obviously, the tower rats, which was what they were called by us foresters, had a lot of time on their hands, because there were some very elaborate carvings. The occupant from 1932 had turned his initials and date into a wall of fire and smoke. 1942 had his initials and date shaped like a battleship. And the tower rat from 1968 had intertwined the letters and date to form a peace symbol. I realized that these carvings were like looking at ancient drawings found in caves and on cliffs. They told a story about their time and place.

My admiration for the carvings was cut short by the growling in my stomach and the realization that the last real meal

I'd had was breakfast the day before. I started taking stock of the food stores and was not impressed. It quickly became obvious that Jack had not been resupplied in a while. Either that or he ate a lot in his free time, of which there was a lot up here on top of the world. In fact, my culinary choices came down to a few cans of beanie weenies, half a box of Bisquick, a few saltines in a tin box, one can of creamed corn, and a large half-gallon tub of lard. A bit frantically, I descended the stairs to where the gas refrigerator and storage bins were located. Inside the frig, I found the two half-eaten trout, one can of tomato juice, and a lot of stuff growing green mold. The storage bins revealed shovels and other firefighting equipment along with one old army surplus sleeping bag. From the condition and smell, I think I would have taken my chances with the elements rather than crawl into that bag. A few minutes later, the smell of trout rolled in Bisquick and frying in lard was mixing with the fresh mountain air.

I brought a stool out on the catwalk so that I wouldn't be tempted to sit on the railing again. Leaning back on the stool with my feet propped up on the rail, I enjoyed the view and a grand meal along with a glass of fine red tomato juice, vintage unknown. After several minutes of complete solitude, I was again yanked out of my wilderness daydream by the crackle of the radio. But this time I did not rush to the radio, because I did not hear my call letters. After a few seconds of chatter, I strolled to the radio to listen anyway. Smoke had been detected by a tower north of me and a lot of information was being bantered back and forth between tower and base.

I glanced down at my large photo and topo map trying to pinpoint the location. Like a captain of a submarine lining up a destroyer, I swung the sight over to the right peering at the correct bearings. After a few seconds of squinting, I stood up in complete astonishment and blurted out, like Captain Ahab, "There she blows!" I grabbed the large binoculars that hung on a nail next to the door to get a better look. It definitely was smoke. Not a lot of smoke, but certainly smoke. More bantering was coming through the radio as arrangements were being made to check out the source of the smoke. I took the binoculars out on the catwalk and set them next to my stool, then returned to my trout fried in lard. The fish, surprisingly, was quite good. From my perch, I watched the morning shadows turn into midday heat. More birds seemed to be taking advantage of the updrafts, and they were putting on quite an aerial circus. Glancing at my watch, I realized I had about thirty seconds to make my next scheduled radio check. No worries, mate, I thought to myself as I strolled to the radio. I am almost a professional at this. I spotted my first fire.

Reaching for the handset, I was yet again startled when the radio blurted my call letters with some annoyance. About to answer, I remembered that my watch had been running a quarter of an hour late all summer. I had never bothered to fix it, because correct time was not a real issue when walking in the woods all day.

After the expected bawling out from base and my assurances to be more prompt, I was assigned the task of keeping a vigil on the smoke and reporting any changes.

"Aye, aye, sir," I said, staying in character as Ahab.

"Elk Mountain, when is Jack returning?" the radio questioned.

"That would be Sunday night, sir," was my sheepish reply.

"Good," my talking box barked.

Geez, I thought, *no sense of humor*, as I began my vigil.

For the next several hours, I watched, reported, and gazed into the western horizon. All this came to an abrupt end when my radio reported some hysterical news. It seemed that for the past several hours, I had been keeping a close eye on a sheep-herder's Saturday ritual of washing his clothes. The crew sent to investigate the fire came upon a lone gentleman, somewhat under dressed, manning a fire with a large kettle filled with his smelly shirt and jeans. It was also reported that his flock, which was in a nearby meadow, had the appropriate papers and per-mits to free-range in this part of the state. Upon hearing this news over the radio, I had a good chuckle, and I was pretty sure that the men and women sitting in their towers up and down this mountain range were laughing with me.

The rest of that day and into the next, things were pretty uneventful. I spent time picking berries to supplement my meager food stores. I rigged up the pail with the holes in it for a less-than-perfect shower. In between radio checks, I took a run to the bottom of Elk Mountain and back for a little exercise. And in the evening, I worked on my carving. All and all, I was very content but getting slightly bored.

The final radio check of the night reminded me of the TV show, The Waltons, saying goodnight to each other. Goodnight Jim-Bob on Green Mountain. Goodnight Mary-Bob on Fisher Mountain, and on and on. They really weren't saying that, but the tone of their voices was melancholy and lonesome. I, too, was feeling a bit alone in the world. When I came to this part of the Northwest, I had left behind a dorm full of buddies and a wife-to-be. Now it was just me and a million stars.

I turned on the gas lantern to help ward off this forlorn feeling and continued to work on my carving. Since I was to play a very minor role in the tower's history, I chose to keep my initials very small and plain. For some reason, the hissing from the gas lantern was making me even lonelier. In fact, I was starting to feel like I did when I was young and my folks would drop me off at my grandparents' cottage … homesick. So, I left the carving and turned on Jack's prize possession, his personal battery-powered radio. I tuned in a station from somewhere in British Columbia and listened while a talk show host and his callers bantered back and forth about some new crown tax. It was riveting stuff. But at least I did not feel quite so alone. And an extra bonus: The droning of their voices made me very drowsy. I turned off the gas and radio and fell instantly asleep.

BAM! BOOM! CRACK! was my wakeup call.

I leaped off of Jack's cot into a world of flashing light and horrendous noise. Lightning and lots of it had descended upon me. I had been mystified by the view, stars, and panoramas, of the previous days, but I was blown away by the spectacle before me. Now from my vantage point, it seemed like all of northern Idaho was being struck by lightning. In every direction I was seeing lightning strikes followed by almost a constant barrage of thunder. The first thing that came to my mind was Mr. Tufton. He was my high school shop teacher and was involved in the Battle of the Bulge during World War II. When he was in a certain mood, usually on a gray, winter day, he told us stories of the nightmares the GIs witnessed during the shelling of Bastogne. They were pinned down by the Germans, and the world around them was nothing but flashing lights, unimaginable noise, and exploding trees.

I was not getting shelled, but the conditions around me sure got my attention. Then I had my second thought. Are fire towers grounded? More specifically, was this one? I was still watching the light show as dawn approached. The lightning was still all around me, but with the coming of daylight, the flashes were less dramatic. However, the noise from the thunder was still earsplitting. For several hours I sat pinned down in my fourteen-by-fourteen cubicle. Then the inevitable happened, the tower was hit. But just before I became a lightning rod, the weirdest thing happened. I was leaning against the Osborne fire finder with my right arm lying across the big aerial photo, and a nanosecond before the strike, the hair on my arm stood straight up. This was followed by a great flash and crack that left me sprawled on the tower's floor.

I laid there a bit, taking stock of the situation. The tower was not on fire, I was not blown to bits, and I did not see blue bolts of electricity bouncing around the room. I guessed that the question of the tower being grounded was answered. While lying on the floor, I noticed a wooden box tucked underneath Jack's cot. I yanked it out and sat on it for a few seconds while my nerves settled down. All around me the world was still nothing but flashes, cracks, and booms, but I felt a little less excited about it. I had made it through my first direct hit, and all I had to show for it was the knowledge that no one saw me hit the deck when it happened.

Curious, I stood up and lifted the lid off the box.

"Well, I'll be," I said in surprise. I had just found Jack's food source. The box was filled with potatoes, onions, canned meats, tins of crackers, peanut butter, candy bars, cookies, and little cupcakes wrapped in plastic. I had no idea why Jack had this stash under his bed, but now I was kind of glad I dropped when the tower was hit.

Several hours later, the storm subsided, replaced by very low clouds and constant drizzle. The tower was filled with the smell of fried potatoes and onions and some kind of canned mystery meat. I had made all of my radio checks on time, finished my carving, filled up the water container from the nearby creek, and finished the fire detection journal. Glancing at my watch, I realized I had eight more hours before Jack returned. I could not spend my time gazing at the beauty which surrounded me because I could barely see the edge of the catwalk through the fog. So, I started doing what most tower rats do ... absolutely nothing. As the hours dragged on, I made a mental note to stop by more often to see Jack. Also, in the future, I would try to call him more on the radio. Maybe I could talk to all of the foresters in the area and suggest they visit their tower rats more often. Man, was I bored and lonely. Rainy days up here were the pits.

As dusk approached, I heard the thump of someone ascending the tower stairs. I leaped to my feet, darted through the trap door, and yelled, "Hello! How are you? What took you so long?"

Jack was wearing a large, green pack, which seemed to be bulging with stuff.

"So, how was your weekend?" I asked.

"Oh, kind of boring, not much to do down there," he replied, gesturing downhill. "How about you? Any excitement?" He dropped his pack on the cot.

"Well, the tower was hit by lightning," I said excitedly.

"That makes twenty-one times this summer," he said, kind of nonchalantly.

"Really?" I said, deflated.

"Yeah, happens all the time. No big deal. Did you find everything?"

"All but the bloody food. Why do you keep it under the bed?" I was somewhat irritated.

"Coons. The only door or lock they can't open is the trap door," he said. "Thanks for covering for me. If you ever want to do it again, just radio me."

He tossed me the flashlight. I nodded, thanked him for the

offer, and turned to go. Before I was three steps down, I heard Jack radioing in. Basically, from the response I was hearing from base, they were very pleased to hear his smooth, steady voice across the airwaves. Well, what did I expect? He was a professional, after all. I was just a weekend warrior, and very glad of it.

I stopped and checked on Jack at least once a week the rest of the summer. And I always enjoyed the view, although not as much as the descent afterward.

Memories of a Tree

New Hampshire, 1977

As usual, my Golden Retriever, Cedar, was letting her presence be known. She had just tripped me, again. It is her habit to carry a stick at all times just in case I have the urge to toss something. And if I do, she is prepared. It certainly helps that her master (I am not sure who is master and who is pet) is a forester and works in the land of sticks. But if the timing is right, and when I least expect it, the stick she is carrying gets lodged between my legs. And I go down quicker than Enron stock. And I am always surprised. It happens several times a week. I shouldn't be.

As I lay there with my face buried in about a foot of snow, I had a déjà-vu moment. This seemed odd, because I was not in a real comfortable position. Usually when I have a flashback, it is about a pleasant experience. The first whiff of woodstove smoke in the fall always reminds me of Vermont. My wife making bread is another good example, as is the first snowfall of the winter. But lying in a drift with my face beginning to freeze wasn't pleasant. Slowly, I got back to an upright position.

Cedar was pleased with herself, since she had just scored another coup. She was flitting here and there, her swirling tail kicking up clouds of freshly fallen snow. As I brushed myself off, it dawned on me what the feeling was: different dog, different state.

Northern New Hampshire, December 1977: Lying in the snow with both snowshoes tangled up, I had to laugh. Kipper, my one-year-old Golden Retriever, had just tripped me for the third time that day. She kept stepping on the tails of my snowshoes, and that always had the same result: me face first, in a nonprofessional manner, into the deep snow. But I could not get angry, because it was purely unintentional. For the past several hours, we had been scouting for two perfect Christmas trees. We were in the foothills of the White Mountains, on a parcel of land that was about to be harvested. I had located two large balsam firs that were marked to be taken, and I cut them down. Then I lopped off the very top, which made a perfect Christmas tree.

Leaving the rest of the tree to be used by the loggers, I started the laborious task of dragging the tops to my truck. And that's when this latest trip occurred. Once untangled from my snowshoes, I tucked the base of each tree under my arms and continued the plodding process. It became apparent, relatively quickly, that I needed to drop half of my load. The terrain and thickness of the bush made it impossible to maneuver with two trees. Leaving one, I headed up the steep hill to where my truck was parked. On my return trip, I managed to catch the tip of my snowshoe on a hidden stump, and this time I went head over heels.

This was just way too much excitement for Kipper. So, she

jumped on my back just to make sure I got a good face washing. After retrieving the second tree, I stood them both up next to my pickup. I was impressed. Both trees were almost perfect, the quintessential Christmas trees. My wife would be pleased, but I was really excited with the opportunity to present the second "perfect tree" to the Baker sisters. When my wife and I had first moved to this rural portion of New Hampshire, the sisters had befriended us with their hospitality and kindness. We lived in a small cabin within a stone's throw of their big New England farmhouse. Our house once served as the ice-house for a large hotel, which had been located on the lake the Baker family farm surrounded. The sisters never married, and they had been living alone on the farm ever since their parents passed away in 1950. We were two lonely newlyweds, far from our families, and the sisters were two elderly ladies just waiting for the chance to tuck someone like us under their wings.

The sisters were both in their seventies but as spry as a couple of spring chickens. They no longer worked the farm. But it had not been that long ago that they did all of the labor, including splitting firewood, baling hay, and taking care of twenty milk cows. They were still doing tasks like stacking firewood, making maple syrup, and maintaining a massive garden. To my eye, this garden could have fed half of New Hampshire. In addition, they still kept chickens, two pigs named Ham and Sausage (really), and one Jersey cow named Buttercup. They certainly knew where their food came from.

When my wife and I had first arrived in this little corner of New Hampshire, we were full of excitement. This was our first great adventure as a couple. We found a perfect little house to rent. Little might be a bit of a stretch. Actually, it was a very large closet with a stone fireplace and no insulation. But it was our first home, and we were elated. We were in a very beautiful part of the country, and we had our first "real" jobs upon graduation from college. Life was good, but it got better. Into our lives dropped Emma and Ellie Baker. Before we had half of our small stash of worldly goods unloaded from our rented U-Haul, they appeared to help. As I protested, they started carrying really heavy things into our house. Later, I learned the two of them probably could have figured out how to move the truck inside if given enough time.

As time progressed, I learned a lot about each of the Baker sisters. Emma was the brains of the duo. She had attended college and had a short career in law before she decided her life was more fulfilling back in the hills of New Hampshire. Ellie, who had stayed home to help on the farm, was the clown. Everything this spry lady said was laced with humor. Sometimes it was on the surface and sometimes it was buried very deep. But, as I found out, it was always there. Once, the sisters asked me to shovel off the snow that had accumulated on their roof. I was more than willing, because I wanted to repay them for all of the kindnesses they had shown us. It was a daunting job. The roof was steep, and the snow had been covered with a thick layer of ice. But, being young and dumb, I was willing to tackle anything.

I had been working for several hours when I had the misfortune of sticking my shovel through one of their upstairs windows. As if that was not bad enough, Ellie was in the room that hosted the window. I was so upset I about fell off the bloody roof. Ellie popped her head through the window and said, "Well, it was getting a bit stuffy in here. I sure am glad we have a young man around the place to take care of our needs. I was about to suffocate in here. Thank you."

As winter turned into spring, I had many opportunities to witness Ellie's humor. And a lot of the time, I was the perfect catalyst for her wit. Like the time I brought her some early lettuce from our garden only to find out I had picked very young broccoli leaves. She assured me that with enough salt and butter, you could eat just about anything.

Soon after our arrival to the icehouse, the sisters started inviting us over on Saturday evening. At first, my wife and I were somewhat reluctant. We were both twenty-three and we felt spending our Saturday nights with a couple of seventy-year-olds would be a bit boring. But were we wrong . . . for several reasons. One, their life had been full of adventure and excitement. And two, they liked a bit of the "amber." To this day, I have not found a more enjoyable Saturday night than the ones we spent with the Baker sisters sitting in their big kitchen, warmed by the woodstove, eating wonderful food they had grown, listening to their stories, while they stirred their memories with small, delicate glasses filled with Scotch.

I was brought out of my daydreaming by a loud bark. Kipper had sent a red squirrel up a tree, and the two of them were making enough racket to wake Rumpelstiltskin.

I loaded both trees into the back of the truck and started the long, downhill drive home. As soon as Kipper and I were in the truck, she did her circle routine. She would go around in a circle about ten times, then flop down as close to me as possible. If allowed, half of her body weight would be on my lap. This got old really quick. If she was wet, we started the shoving game. She would snuggle, trying to dry her wet fur on my wool pants, and I would respond with a shove across the vinyl seat. She loved the game, but I got more irritable the longer it went on. Eventually, I would place my hard hat between us, which meant "game over."

My wife was still at work, so I figured I would drop off the sisters' tree first. As I pulled into their dooryard, I saw the two of them struggling with a very tall ladder. "Now, there is a surprise," I blurted out with a small touch of sarcasm. Kipper looked up, wondering if my outburst needed her attention. It seemed whenever I showed up, they were doing some feat that a young man should be doing. Consequently, I spent a lot of time doing chores for the Bakers.

As I tried to get out of my truck, Kipper played another one of her favorite games, which was leaping over me, trying to be the first one out of the truck. On this occasion, I could understand her hurry. She loved the sisters, and they adored her.

"Hello, ladies! What are you doing?" I asked.

"We are about to put the star on the weather vane," they said in unison.

This topped it all. They were going to crawl up on the barn roof and put a star on the weather vane. I just shook my head and told them that I would take care of it later.

"Well, ladies, I have a surprise for you," I said with excitement. "I got you a Christmas tree."

I pulled it out of the truck. As I struggled to get it upright, I was surprised not to hear any chatter from the sisters. Smiling, I stood holding the tree. The big smile quickly faded when I glanced at the sisters. They were standing with their arms around each other, and tears were streaming down their faces.

"What's wrong?" I pleaded. The last thing I wanted to do was to make these ladies cry.

Emma said with a sad grin, "Nothing is wrong. It's just memories. We have so many memories of this farm and our family. But Christmas time always brought the best memories.

"Each year, our older brother would bring home a Christmas tree to present to the family. He would start scouting for it in the summer. And he was always so proud when he brought it home. Well, you standing there proud as a peacock with your tree just brought back a wave of memories.

"No, don't be sorry," she added. "You and your tree are the best Christmas present we have had in a long time. Oh, the memories of those many trees."

She then grabbed my arm and said, "Come on, are you going to put the star up, or am I?"

Later that evening, when my wife and I were trying to make a very large tree fit into a small room, she asked, "Do you think these are the kind of memories the sisters were talking about?"

"Not exactly!" I shouted as I once again tripped over Kipper and ended up sprawled on top of our little tree.

Lying there, I looked up and said, "Maybe."

Bouncing Bears

Idaho, 1975

I started my forestry career in 1975. Of all the wonderful, exciting, and fascinating experiences I've had, my meetings with bears have always created the most vivid memories. And as you get older and more mature, you become wiser and more respectful of the experience. In short, I was lucky to make it past my first several encounters with the big, furry guys.

Those events don't include my meetings with other beasts— like the times I chased moose, leaped over badgers, or inadvertently walked into a circle of hormone-crazed elk. Ignorance, as they say, is bliss. But with bears, I had a double whammy. Not only did I not have a clue concerning the danger, I was young and male. Wives, mothers, and girlfriends all know what I mean. Young men (and, my wife would add, certain older men) just do stupid things. They do it to impress others, test their courage, test themselves, or just 'cuz.

My family always jokes that my tombstone will feature two inscriptions. The first will read, "IT SEEMED LIKE A GOOD IDEA AT THE TIME," and the second will say,

"HEY GUYS! WATCH THIS."

I usually point out that if it weren't for us GUYS, there would not have been conquests like walking to the North and South Poles, climbing of Mount Everest, flying across the Atlantic, or walking on the moon. I am reminded by the females in my family that most wars, if not all, have been started by the young males of our species.

I don't have a comeback for that.

But as I have grown older, my respect for bears has manifested into such a state that my canoeing and backpacking cronies think I am too cautious. No longer are the days when we just tuck our food under a big rock not far from our tents. Now, I have ropes and small pulleys that suspend our provisions high into the trees. My friends call it our bear piñata, and anything with a smell goes into the suspended food pack. This includes gum, toothpaste, deodorant, soap, bug dope, and anything else that might give off a scent.

The reason for my caution is very simple. I work where bears live. I have seen four-inch-diameter branches broken in two by a bear as it tried to reach a few juneberries. I have seen cabin doors pulverized because a bear could smell a half-empty bottle of mustard inside. I have also witnessed a bear running so fast—thankfully, away from me—that the speed turned his normally black, shiny coat purple. I have experienced how upset a momma can get when you are between her and her cubs. I have been stalked, charged, hissed at, and stared down. On several occasions, I have had bears stand on their hind legs and gnash their teeth at me. That gets one's attention! So, I shrug off my fellow backpackers' ridicule and keep filling up that piñata.

With all of the encounters I have had, there is one that was so utterly bizarre that I can remember it like it happened yesterday. But it happened a long time ago, when I was young and somewhat foolish.

Idaho, Clearwater National Forest, July 1975: It was a grand July day in the mountains of northern Idaho. The sky was very blue, which was enhanced by the higher elevation. The air had a hint of autumn, even though it was mid-summer. There was a slight breeze, which made the large Douglas and Grand firs sway slightly. This movement filled the mountain gorge with a light rustling sound.

John and I drove our old truck many miles up a rutted mountain road until we reached our destination. John stopped, and I scurried out of the truck to help direct. It took him several minutes to turn the truck around and face it back downhill. It was drilled into our heads that we should always have our truck pointed in the correct direction and free of obstacles before we started our workday. The reason, we were told, was if you were injured, you wanted to be able to get into the truck and quickly head for help. If one had a broken leg, it would be nearly impossible to maneuver the clutch, gas, and brake necessary to turn around. This made sense to us so, we dutifully made a habit of it.

We grabbed our gear and headed down a steep slope following some pink ribbon. As we walked through the ferns, shadowed by large Douglas firs, we commented on "what a cake job" we had today. Both John and I were summer interns, which meant several things. First, we were not yet graduate foresters, both having our senior year left. And second, interns got the less desirable jobs. Or as our boss liked to say, we got the "special jobs." Up to this point, we had been doing a lot of grunt work in high elevations where young legs could walk all day. We had also been involved in several forest fires. The week before, we had seven days with little sleep, hardly any food, and even less water. So, when our boss gave us today's task, we were mildly pleased, surprised, and, quite frankly, a little cautious.

Big Ben, our boss, was a very large man with hands the size of catcher's mitts. He was a very jovial guy with an infectious laugh. He could be assigning you the worst job in the world, but if he smiled and let loose his famous chuckle, you felt honored that he had blessed you with the task. It wasn't until hours later, when you were up to your armpits in muck, that you realized his chuckle was on you. Hence our concern over today's task: there had been a big grin and a loud laugh.

The ribbons we had been following stopped at a large Grand fir with several paint marks on it. John put down his heavy chainsaw and said, "Well, this must be it." I walked around the large tree several times, noticing a big blue splash of paint. "Yup," I said, "this is the one."

Ben had explained that we were to cut down a tree that was slated to be harvested. The reason we were to cut it down before the logging crews got there was because we were to collect the cones. Ben informed us that this tree, which was very old and half dead, had been designated as a "superior" tree a decade ago. The idea was to collect the cones, send them to the research station where they would extract the seeds, and pass them along to the nursery where they would grow into young seedlings. These seedlings would then find their way to harvested sites throughout Idaho, Washington, and Oregon. You might have called it early genetic engineering. It was a cake job all the way.

After many tries, the big, heavy chainsaw finally started. John was running the saw, and I stood behind him with my hand on his shoulder. My job was to look straight up, and if something was wrong, like a branch was hurtling towards earth and about to flatten us, I was to remove my hand from his shoulder, and we would both run. This is what they had taught us at fire school.

I could see some obvious flaws to the technique. The most obvious, of course, was which way to run. But I was an intern. What did I know?

John made a huge notch on one side of the tree, and then wrestled the saw to the other side, where he made a slight downward cut intersecting his notch. The tree slowly started making its plunge toward earth, and we both ran back a few yards to watch it fall.

I was just about to yell "TIMBERRR" (I always wanted to do this) when John smacked me so hard I about fell over. I looked at him, his mouth wide open, and he was pointing at the tree. I glanced back at the falling tree and was stunned by what I saw. There, riding the tree down as if it were a surfboard, was a momma bear and her two cubs.

Now, being mature males, we thought this was a hilarious sight and started laughing hysterically. At this point, danger was not even on the radar. Luckily for the family of bruins, they were on the upside of the tree as it hit the ground. The top of the tree was very lush, which cushioned their fall. In fact, they bounced.

John decided that while this was still a grand lark, it could get dicey quickly. So, he bolted for the truck. Seeing John sprinting away from me—and momma thinking about heading toward me—I realized that the last man to the truck would not just be a rotten egg but toast, too.

As I ran toward the truck like a Heisman Trophy winner, I looked over my shoulder and realized that momma's mothering instinct had bought me several seconds. She was nuzzling each cub to make sure they were alright. But once assured, she was on a mission—which was us. As John and I leaped over fallen logs, dodged boulders, and scrambled up the hill, we were still giggling. In our dash for the truck, we realized the danger we were in. But it was so bloody hilarious, we could not stop laughing.

I was gaining on John, and momma was rapidly gaining on me. The truck was getting closer, but the question in my mind was, "would we make it in time?" Maybe it was the lack of oxygen, or the noise the bear was making behind me, or maybe I was rapidly maturing, but the severity of the situation finally hit home. This made the adrenaline kick in, and I bolted by John, but only briefly. I tried hurdling a large, downed tree and caught my trailing foot on a branch, which caused a face plant in the fertile Idaho soil. John cleared the log with feet to spare, and again I was first in line to take momma's wrath.

I jumped up, gasping for air, and started running faster than I dreamed possible. The ground leveled off a bit, and the traveling became easier. John reached the truck first, and, to his credit, he went to the far side and jumped in. He then flung the other door open. I now had a target to head for: the open door. I was probably ten feet from the door when I dove. Being still young and agile, I could grab the handle on my way in and yank the door behind me.

The second the door slammed shut, the bear rammed into it. The only thing that separated us from an irate mamma bear was some fine Detroit workmanship. Momma walked around the truck several times while we were trying to locate the keys. Then she stood up on her hind legs, placed her sharp paws on the roof, and started rocking our Ford. Looking out the window, we realized how lucky we really were. We were looking at the bear's midsection in our four-by-four pickup with extra-large wheels.

John luckily located the keys, and I started the truck. One would think the roaring of an engine would affect a bear, but she only rocked harder. I put the truck in gear and slowly moved forward. The bear sidestepped with the truck—as if she were doing a waltz. John urged me to get the heck out of there, so I floored it. In the process, we heard an ear-splitting version of nails on a chalkboard. In the rearview mirror, I watched momma chase us a few seconds, then stop and rear up on her hind legs.

After several minutes of reckless driving, I slowed down to negotiate a tricky curve. Then it started . . . both of us: first, slight snickers, then uncontrollable laughter. I had to stop for fear of driving off the mountain road.

Several hours later, we pulled into the forest headquarters. Ben was out front talking with some fellow foresters. As we pulled past him, he quickly glanced our way and then resumed his conversation . . . but only briefly. In the rearview mirror, I was surprised to see Ben scurrying after us. I shut off the truck, and we both meekly extracted ourselves. Ben just stood there, running his eyes back and forth across our truck.

"Did you boys have any trouble today?" Ben asked, a little alarmed.

John replied, rather sheepishly, "A piece of cake."

I turned around to see what Ben was glaring at, and I knew our cover was blown. From the windshield to the tail lights, across the shiny metal, there were claw marks a quarter-inch deep.

The next day, we realized just how "hilarious" our situation really was.

In our haste to leave, we forgot all about the cones, which meant we had to return to the scene of the crime. Talk about two terrified interns! Once we finally got up the nerve to get out of the truck, John confirmed that he no longer thought that this assignment was a piece of cake. And we never giggled once, for fear of momma bear's long memory.

Young and Foolish

New Hampshire, 1977

As I crested the ridge, I could see a small lake several miles off in the distance. I had been walking for several hours, and this seemed like a perfect place to take a break. I wriggled out of my cruiser's vest and hung it on a branch. I always forget the weight of that garment until I take it off. It is a vest with many pockets and a built-in backpack. It carries all of my forestry tools, water, lunch, and if needed, additional clothing. It is functional, not comfortable.

I grabbed my water bottle and sandwich out of one of the pockets and leaned against a large oak. Cedar, my ever-faithful Golden Retriever, watched this whole process with interest. She was not happy we stopped, but she was happy I pulled out the sandwich. As I plopped down, she took up a position directly in front of me so I was sure to see her. She sat staring with her tail wagging. Her tongue was drooling, and her tail was kicking up dry leaves and a bit of dust.

"Cedar! Please, go somewhere else with that tongue," I said, holding my hand over my sandwich.

She got the hint and went off to find a rock to play with, or to dig a hole for me to step in, or to chew up a big stick. With the beast gone, I sat back and enjoyed the view. The sun was making the lake sparkle with thousands of small flashes. It also felt really good on my face after a long, gray winter. The leaves were not out yet, so the woods were very naked. For a forester, this is a great time of year. We can find things on the forest floor, and we can also see farther than a few feet. Also, there are no bugs, which is a big plus.

To my surprise, Cedar was not doing anything destructive but just exploring. When I am walking, she always stays close. But when I take a break, she cuts loose. She uses the same pattern every time, never straying far and always keeping an eye on me. When I get up, she is right under foot. It is very gratifying to have such a trusted friend in the bush. In addition, she thinks all the choices I make in a day are perfect ones. You could not ask for a better work partner. With that thought, I made a mental note to share my sandwich next time.

As I watched her explore, I started thinking of my first forestry companion. She was also a Golden, and her name was Kipper.

New Hampshire, 1977: Early in 1977, my wife and I got our first dog. We were living in Colorado with lodgings that really did not warrant a dog. But we were young, fresh out of college, and we did not think about practical matters. So, we were about to move to New Hampshire in the middle of winter. What was the problem? A puppy would just add to the adventure. It's nice being young and having no experience to jade one's judgment.

Once in New Hampshire, I secured my first fulltime forestry

job. For the first month, Kipper was too small and the snow was too deep for her to accompany me. We were living in a very rural area, and my wife had not been able to secure employment yet. That was good for the pup. I was gone, we did not know anybody, and if we did, I had the vehicle. Needless to say, they were good company for each other. But the day came when my wife became employed, and I felt Kipper was old enough to go with me on my wilderness travels. So, one spring day we had our first, and almost last, day together.

On the eve of Kipper's first outing, we had a tremendous rainstorm followed by extremely warm temperatures. It was late March, and in a matter of twenty-four hours, we lost about two-and-a-half feet of snow. I about dropped my mug of tea when I opened the door in the morn. The snow was all gone, and I was looking at bare ground. Normally, when I opened the door in the morning, the pup would scoot out. This morning, she came to a screeching halt on the stoop.

"Come on girl, out you go," I said, giving her a little nudge with my foot.

She went off the stoop and sat down on the top step. I was a bit confused with her lack of enthusiasm, and then I realized in her short life she had never seen bare ground. I scooped her up and placed her a few yards out into the yard. She again sat down. I left her and went inside back to my mug of tea. I stood next to the kitchen window enjoying my tea and watched Kipper first take small steps, then larger ones, and finally take off in a full gallop as she enjoyed her first steps on solid ground.

When I emerged a half hour later, she was still flitting here and there, examining every rock, twig, and bush. On one of her laps, I scooped her up and placed her on the seat of the truck. As we drove off on our first day together, I knew we had some issues to work out. First and foremost, I needed to find a way to keep her on the passenger side of the truck. Trying to drive the winding back roads of New Hampshire was going to be a bit dicey with a wiggling dog on my lap. My big, old brown briefcase did the trick.

The first stop of the day was to check out a harvesting project my company was doing for a private landowner. The week before, I had marked the trees that I felt needed to be removed to improve the health of the forest. The property was roughly twenty miles away. In the hour it took to get there, Kipper probably traveled twenty miles inside the truck. She was against the window, leaping against the old brown briefcase, down on the floor peering through the holes in the floorboards (the truck ran but it was not pretty), and back up on the seat putting nose prints against the back window. As we arrived at the site I muttered, "Tomorrow you get decaf."

I removed the barrier between us and picked Kipper up under one arm. She started to squirm, and it took both arms to contain her. I was stunned at how fast the conditions had changed. The day before, I had been on snowshoes marking timber, and now I was sinking in mud up to my ankles. So, the squirming puppy stayed under my arms.

This whole job had been a lot of fun for me. My boss had given me the reins on the entire project, and I had taken a lot of pride in it. I was finally able to put four years of college to the test. However, there was one hitch to the project I had not learned in college. The property I was to manage was on the other side of a small river. I had to figure out a way to get the forest products across the river. Basically, I had to build a bridge. My ever-knowing boss knew this would be a bit tricky for a young forester to figure out, so he dealt me an ace. His name was John, and he was a big, strapping logger from Vermont who now worked for our company. His main job was to run the bulldozer fixing roads, putting in culverts, and any other task we thought he could handle. In my opinion, he could have built Interstate 75 by himself under budget and ahead of schedule. So, for several days, John and I cut some of the big hemlocks I had marked and dragged them down to an old gristmill site.

This site was used back in the eighteen-hundreds to grind the local farmers' wheat into flour. The river had steep banks here, and huge, granite slabs had been placed to force the water through a channel about thirty feet wide. This water was then sent into a confined trough, where it turned a large wheel, which in turn moved a bunch of wooden gears, which turned a large stone, which ground the wheat. It had long ago been abandoned, and the upriver side where the granite slabs had been placed made a perfect abutment for our bridge. The entire time we worked on this bridge, I was in seventh heaven. It was a bloody ball. This was a man's job.

Walking down to the river, I was now amazed at the tremendous noise. When we had built the bridge, all was frozen and quiet. Now, however, it sounded like Niagara Falls. As I came in view of the river, I stopped in my muddy tracks. When we had built the bridge, it was at least six feet above the ice. Now I could not even see the granite slabs, the water was so high. I tried to see how far below the water the bridge sat, when I realized there was no bridge. Gone, vanished, and completely washed away . . . not a trace. Nothing was there to give the slightest hint that there had been twenty large hemlock trees cabled together. The sheer force of the river had turned my bridge into a Huck Finn raft.

For the same reason people are drawn to the edge of Niagara Falls, I started walking closer to the river, in complete awe. But I was brought out of my reverence by the sight of Kipper taking her first steps into a small pool created by the backwash. I had forgotten I had finally put her down, and the trance of the river had also attracted her. I bolted toward the pool, but the current of the river beat me to it. Before I could grab her, she was drifting toward the whitewater. I made a feeble attempt to grab her from shore and fell far short.

Without much thought, I jumped in after her. Since the water was snow and ice just twenty-four hours earlier, the temperature was hardly balmy. Kipper was near the point of no return, so I dove in, took a few quick strokes, and made a final lunge. In one motion, I grabbed her tail and flung her to shore. Now *I* was drifting toward the point of no return. I frantically swam and kicked myself off the river bottom until I, too, was out of harm's way. Upon reaching shore, I was greeted by the wet pup. I could tell from her antics that in her short life, this was the most fun she had ever had! And could we please do it again? I, on the other hand, was extremely cold and miserable. I scooped her up under my arms and headed toward the truck, with Kipper washing my face the whole way.

The rest of the day was incredibly dismal. I was unable to get dry because I had broken one of the cardinal rules of forestry: always have backup clothes. In addition, the heater in my truck was less than perfect, and our warm spell was on its way out. Kipper was pleased, though. To conserve or to create some heat, I took down the barrier. The old brown briefcase was on the floor and the pup was on my lap. I also had the comforting thought that I did not have to come home and tell my wife that I had last seen our puppy going down a class-five rapids heading toward the Atlantic Ocean.

That evening, while Kipper and I huddled by the woodstove, my wife was curious how our first day went. Since I really hate lying, especially to my wife, I had been working on my story all day.

"Well," I said cautiously, "It was interesting. We got a tad wet, but one could expect that this time of year."

As I spoke, I noticed Kipper, who was almost under the woodstove, look at me and give several thumps with her tail.

🐾

I was unceremoniously awakened from my daydreaming by an object that dropped in my lap. Cedar was done exploring, and she felt it was time to do something constructive, like throw a rock.

As I tossed it, I had a slight grin on my face. It dawned on me that Kipper knew something I did not know that night she lay under the woodstove. She knew that for the next fourteen years, I would have to edit my evening accounts of our days together, because her first day with me was only a small sample of the many predicaments we would find ourselves in.

Kipper, I am still smiling.

Autumn Days

New Hamphire, 1977

"*A*utumn days" means different things to different people. For some, it means getting out in the woods, marshes, or fields to hunt. For others, it means football and lots of it. And to some, it means watching your spouse watch football and lots of it. I realize I am fortunate, because my forestry profession allows me to enjoy all of what autumn has to offer. But the smell of autumn brings a strong emotional response for me. The smell of wet leaves, wood smoke, and even the fall rains send me into a state of reminiscing. And today, these smells were working overtime. Cedar and I were marking a stand of northern hardwoods in very hilly terrain. With each step, I had a different fall smell. The dry leaves smelled different than the wet ones under foot. The small brook I had just crossed had a clean, fresh scent, which mingled with the smell of rotting vegetation. All of these different scents were enhanced by the crisp fall air.

My mind kept bringing me back to a perfect fall day many years ago. It was one of those days that you never forget. We all have days we wish we could forget, and mostly they are made up of bad experiences. But for some reason, my mind likes to store pleasant days, and it doesn't take much to transport me back to that time. So, why fight it?

"Cedar," I called, "time to take five."

We sat on an old humpback, a mound of earth that was once a tree stump and all of its roots. When mature, a large tree will finally succumb to wind and gravity and blow over. The roots are torn from the ground, leaving in its place a large hole. When the roots rot and turn into soil, you end up with a large mound and behind it a hole where the roots used to be. This is what we foresters call a humpback. I'm not sure of the scientific name. Sometimes a windstorm or insect infestation will attack a forest, and you will have many of these humpbacks. What is really interesting is that many forms of wildlife burrow underneath these humpbacks to form a perfect condo. I have been startled many times by rabbit, coyote, grouse, fox, and even a badger as they bolted out of their burrow just as I walked by. I also realize that domestic canines like the humpbacks. While I sat on the humpback, Cedar started to dig for a rock in the base of it. *She will be entertained for at least fifteen minutes*, I thought as I sat back to marvel at the blueness of the autumn sky.

With this small event, I was off, thinking of a good day some time ago.

New Hampshire, 1977: I don't know what causes the sky to seem so clear in the fall. It may be the angle of the sun, lack of moisture, or the brilliant fall colors of a northern forest. Whatever the cause, the sky today was about as blue and clear as a new marble. Of course, my vantage point was quite good.

I was up on top of a two-story cabin, which was located on top of a ridge. Stretched out before me was Mount Kersage to the north and Mount Sunapee to the southwest. Scattered in between were many lakes and ponds.

Along the lakes, there was a mixture of green and yellows, which represented the conifers. Tamarack is the only conifer to lose its needles in the fall. When mixed with spruce, balsam, cedar, and pine, the yellow provides quite a contrast. The maples, birches, basswood, and aspen represented the reds, oranges, golds, and yellows. Oak and beech were showing several shades of brown. In among all this brilliant color, there stood several large, majestic, white pines with their green tops.

A bark brought me out of my color tour. Peering over the edge of the roof, I saw my dog, Kipper, looking up at me. She was very annoyed with the current situation. Not having thumbs or the ability to climb a ladder, she was left on the ground while I scurried up the old rickety ladder to my present location.

"Hold on girl. I will be down in a bit," I reassured her.

I picked up the broom I had carried up the ladder and started sweeping. The green shingled roof was covered with needles, cones, and branches from the pines that loomed overhead. I needed to keep this and about thirty-five other roofs free of the fall debris and winter's snow. In fact, when applying for my current job, that was one of the first questions: "Are you comfortable with heights?" I had no clue what the uniformed lady was implying. But like most people who really want a job, I said "no problem" and would worry about the details later. A few years after, I would use the same approach when asked if I had ever been a waiter. I really needed an extra summer job, so we could get a new wood stove to help keep the new baby warm in the old house. I felt my years of experience clearing the table filled the bill. One problem arose, however: I never had to balance a tray the size of a car hood loaded with the "Lobster Special" for a family of six. I quickly used a new tactic on the management: pity. I explained the need for the new stove for the new baby and the old house. I also pointed out that I was a college graduate and "had to be a quick learner." Come fall, the baby was warm, and my efficiency rating for clearing the table went way up at home.

I started sweeping at the top of the roof and worked my way down. It was not the height of buildings that bothered me but rather the slippery surfaces, sagging boards, and steep angles. They kept me on my toes and sometimes on my knees. This roof was the worst. The sign in front of the building said, "WELCOME TO CAMP OSSABAW," and in smaller letters underneath, "Greater Boston Girl Scout Council."

When I found out that the camp was looking for caretakers, I thought my wife and I were the perfect candidates. She had been a Girl Scout, and I was a forester. What more experience could they ask for? Besides, like most young newlyweds, we were broke, and free rent sounded very appealing. We could work our normal jobs during the day and take care of old Ossabaw at night and on weekends. My wife was a bit skeptical, but I won her over with my charm, or the economics of the situation. Anyway, we became the caretakers of thirty-five buildings, twenty canoes, five sailboats, ten rowboats, three shower houses, and several stray cats, all spread over one hundred and twenty acres. We also inherited several large families of raccoons. These masked bandits, whom the Algonquin Indians called arakunem—"he who scratches with his hands"— would increase my camp workload tenfold.

Kipper was very happy to see me descend the ladder. This meant I could proceed with my real role in life—throwing her a stick. Actually, she had been very content because branches had been falling from the roof for the past hour, and she had retrieved quite a pile of them. I picked one up and gave it a toss toward the shower house. It bounced off the sheet metal roof, and five raccoons came scurrying out. Kipper had learned long ago to stay clear of these camp mascots. Raccoons have paws or "hands" nearly as flexible as those of a monkey and as quick as Muhammad Ali. These paws are so adept that there is not a trash can, trash bin, or camp door that they can't open. We had four families of coons that called Camp Ossabaw their home. Minus the damage and mess they made, I had become quite fond of these families and even found myself saying "hello" as we passed.

I slung the broom over my shoulder and headed down the lane to the infirmary. This is where my wife and I lived during the winter months while the camp was not in session. It was a rather old, dark cabin with lots of nooks and crannies where creepy crawlies and, on occasion, a few bats could hide. But it was our creepy-crawly cabin, and we loved it.

The lane I was walking on was lined with stone walls on either side. The property the camp sat on was originally a farmstead. Most of the old fields had reverted back to a forest, but all of the stone walls remained. The soil in New England is very rocky, or as the locals called it, "boney." As the area was settled, the trees were harvested to make way for farmland. Then the land had to be freed of rocks before tilling could take place. So, the rocks were stacked to make stone walls. These walls were used for boundaries between neighbors, fences for livestock, walls around family cemeteries, and for anything else that needed an enclosure. The lane I was walking down was used as a cow path between the pasture and the lake. It was lined with large sugar maples, which were all different shades of colors. Some had leaves the color of oranges. Others were a slight translucent red, and a few maples were dropping leaves that were a brilliant yellow. I knew scientifically these leaves were different colors due to the amount of nutrients, moisture, and the genetic makeup of each tree. But I could not help thinking that "Mother Nature" was just a very good artist.

As I rounded a slight bend, I had a picture-postcard moment. There ahead of me was my Golden Retriever strutting down the lane with the perfect stick in her mouth. She was flanked by stone walls and large maple trees, and in the brilliant-blue October sky, a few leaves were floating down to join their friends already covering the path. In the background was the old, white barn. I actually had to stop to take it all in. The barn was sided with cedar shakes. These shakes or shingles were about eighteen inches long and six inches wide. The shake is made by taking blocks of cedar and splitting them into very thin pieces of wood. When this barn was built, that task was done by hand, which had to be a long, arduous project. The way the sun was hitting the side of the barn, each shake had its own individual shadow, giving the whole barn a unique look.

Kipper again brought me out of my trance. This time, she and a red squirrel were playing tag along the stone wall. Actually, the squirrel was dodging in and out between the stones chattering. Kipper would run to that crack, and the chatter would come from a different hole down the wall. After a few minutes of this game, the squirrel got bored and bounded off. I continued down the lane with Kipper behind me looking over her shoulder for her playmate.

Again, I rounded a bend, but this time I was not rewarded with a perfect view. Instead I saw one raccoon head and three raccoon rear ends sticking out of the garbage cans.

"Hey, get out of there!" I shouted as I ran toward the cans.

Reaching the cans and the mess, I was cursing and shouting, trying to get the raccoons to move on. There had been a troop up for the weekend, and I had not yet had time to remove the trash from the cans. This particular family of critters had hit the motherload of trash and was not going to leave just because I wanted them to. I was banging lids, kicking cans, and shouting with zero results. In fact, if I had not known better, one of the raccoons had just given the sign to "buzz off" with one of his agile hands.

In the midst of this chaos, my wife had come out to see what all of the commotion was about. She surprised me when she said, "Having some problems?"

"Of course I am. Can't you see all of this mess?" I said, banging another lid.

She turned to go and said, "Why don't you just use your charm? It always works so well on me."

Later, I came to learn that in Algonquin, Ossabaw means, "RACCONS RULE AND CARETAKERS DROOL!"

So, It Wasn't a Perfect Day
New Hampshire, 1978

*R*ecently, I overheard two gentlemen talking, and one of them mentioned that he was having a real bad day. He mentioned things like lost car keys, spilled coffee, burnt toast, misplaced toothpaste caps, and so on. In my opinion, it seemed like a pretty normal day, and I was humored by what he felt would qualify for a bad day. Now, some people truly have bad days. Like finding out that your son just witnessed the family car go through the ice and sink to great depths while he safely sat in his fish shanty. Or then getting a call from your insurance agent that your son, who had just gotten his license, is not yet covered. And, "Oh yes, there is also a clause about great depths." That, in my opinion, would warrant saying, "I am having a bad day."

Time also plays a factor in *having a bad day*. At the time, you may feel you are having a bad day. But as decades pass and you remember that bad day, it may turn into a great story. That is how one of my worst days turned out.

New Hampshire, April 1977: The morning was typical of many mornings before and since. I awoke to a dog jumping on the bed and the faint smell of wood smoke. During the winter months, the air is colder and the wood smoke moves freely from the chimney. During the early spring months, an inversion layer of warmer air may develop, trapping the wood smoke closer to the ground. Consequently, there is a faint, smoky smell in the morning. I arose, stoked the stove, started the teakettle, and was pretty pleased with myself. The reason for my high spirits? It was my birthday. And being only twenty-three, I still enjoyed getting older. I would later learn to curb my enthusiasm a bit.

Just as I sat down to enjoy the fire and a mug of hot tea, the phone rang.

"Well, hello Ed," I said, sounding overly chipper. Ed was my boss, and I wanted him to know I was a "morning person."

"Yes, ah ha, okay. I did? How could I have done that? There is a stone wall around the property! Well, okay. I will meet you around eight," I said, hanging up the phone.

I wasn't so chipper anymore. My wife, hearing the exchange, looked concerned.

"It seems I marked some trees over a property line, and they have been cut," I said rather sheepishly.

"Oh!" my wife said and shot me a knowing look of dread.

As most foresters know (especially a newly employed forester), cutting a neighbor's trees is frowned upon.

I no longer had a taste for my tea. I threw on my wool pants and sweater and headed out the door with Kipper, our year-old Golden Retriever. My wife gave me a hug as I flew by and wished me a happy birthday.

Arriving at the property in question, I saw Ed and two other fellows. The older gentleman in the red-checked coat, with a pipe, and unruly white hair, I recognized as Red. I was certain the big mop had been red at one time, giving him his nickname. The other gentleman I did not know and I presumed he was the neighbor on whom I recently trespassed. *Well, he looks like a nice man. Maybe he will only sue for a million*, I thought as I got out of my beaten-up International Scout.

After the insincere pleasantries of shaking hands, we walked to the scene of the crime. I kept wondering how on earth I could have gone over the three-foot stone wall. It became obvious once we got to the trees. When choosing which trees should be harvested, one is always looking up. As I was looking up trying to determine which trees to mark, I had walked through the only hole in the stone wall. This gap was about twenty feet wide and was, presumably, a gate to let the livestock wander from pasture to pasture. This was obviously many years ago, because very large white pines now stood in the pastures. Fortunately, the landowner knew it was an honest mistake, and he conceded that the pine should have been harvested years ago. All he wanted was the actual payment for the trees harvested. This was the best birthday present I could have hoped for. I really wanted to hug the guy, but it did not seem like the appropriate thing to do.

Then my day got better. About an hour later, I was in the town of Center Tuftonboro. We were about to do a harvesting project in this town, and I had to fill out the appropriate forms. Towns in New Hampshire are tracts of land varying in size, with very irregular boundaries. They can be the size of a small town or a small county. But when logging takes place, a form is filled out estimating the value of the timber to be removed. To do this, I had to go to the selectman's office. A selectman is like a county commissioner or township supervisor. In Center

Tuftonboro, the selectman's office was located on the only street in town. This street, which was on a very steep hill, held the selectman's office, and also the post office, gas station, and general store.

I parked my Scout in front of the post office, set the parking brake, and went across the street to fill out the forms. After doing my civic duty, I came out and walked to where my Scout should have been. But the Scout was nowhere in sight. My first thought was somebody stole it. Then reality set in. Who would steal a 1968 Scout in the middle of nowhere (Center Tuftonboro) in the middle of the day? The answer was nobody.

Looking up and down the street, I saw nothing. So, I started walking downhill. After a few steps, I saw my runaway vehicle down the hill turned sideways into the general store's parking lot. I ran the two hundred feet wondering the whole time who drove it there. I flung open the door, and there was Kipper sitting in the driver's seat with a very worried look on her face. After a few minutes of reflection, I could only guess that the hill was too much for the parking brake. As it was my birthday, luck seemed to be on my side. Not only did my dog and first company vehicle go for a joy ride together, they had turned just in time to slide between two parked vehicles and stopped just short of becoming the window display at Center Tuftonboro General Store.

After the trespass interview, Ed and I had made arrangements to meet later in the day across the river in Reading, Vermont. We were going to show Red some really nice white birch that he could use back at his mill in Maine. Red's mill made doweling, and they preferred white birch. Red, being close to eighty, was content to have us show him the over-mature white birch in Reading by the drive-by method. Ed happily volunteered to drive Red in his brand-new orange Scout, while

I followed in the '68 Scout. The day before, Ed had been driving my '68. He had certainly upgraded!

The drive-by method worked like this: Ed would slow down every few minutes, point out the window, and he and Red would look at some birch trees as we drove by. Like a well-trained dog, I, too, would glance to where Ed was pointing and look at the birch, or the mountain, or the moose, or whatever he was pointing at. This went on for about an hour, becoming very monotonous. We crossed a small brook, Ed pointed, Red looked, and I looked. Then, BANG! For the first time that afternoon, Ed stopped when he pointed. While he was stopping, I was looking, and my '68 Scout ran into the back of his new '77 Scout, which, I was now sure, would never be my old '77. As if rehearsed, Ed and Red slowly turned their heads around, and their eyes bore giant holes into me. This was becoming a very, very bad day.

I leaped out of the Scout to see what horrible damage I had caused and what I could salvage of my career hopes. Ed, on the other hand, slowly removed his six-foot frame one bone at a time. I could tell he was trying really hard to refrain himself. Red leaped from the passenger side as if he was eighteen and was giggling like he was fifteen. This was obviously the funniest thing he had seen in a very long time. He had probably been driving with Ed for the past nine years in the old Scout, and he knew Ed was excited to have his new one. He could not wait to see what the outcome might be. But since it was my birthday, I was saved again. I had hit the protruding trailer hitch on the new Scout, and it dented the bumper of the old Scout.

Ed, in a very calm voice, said, "I will meet you in Newport around four. Pick up the map of the Perkins property. If I am a little late, stay. I am picking up my daughter from school."

That was pretty straightforward. So, I slinked back to my Scout and drove away. How much longer would this day and my luck last?

A little after four, Ed arrived with his six-year-old daughter, Katie. He did not look like the happiest man in the world. In fact, he looked like Scrooge. Grabbing the Perkins map, I strolled over to the hood of his new Scout. I was about to lay the map on the hood, as all foresters do, when I caught Ed's eye. It said, "Don't even think about it."

I held the map up so we both could see. As I was holding the map and Ed was explaining where we should lay out the logging roads, we heard a blood-curdling scream followed by a long wail. Katie came running from my Scout, holding her hand and crying like only a six-year-old can. Looking back at my Scout, I noticed Kipper had her head hanging out the window. Dread filled me. Then I heard the words that confirmed my fears. "Sheee bit me."

I knew it was true. Kipper was very protective of her domain. And this '68 Scout was now hers to defend. Young Katie had stuck her hand in to pet the cute puppy, and the worst had happened. I stood there helpless as Ed mopped up the tears and examined the hand. Unbelievably, I was saved again. The bite had not broken the skin. But at this point, it wasn't much of an issue. Ed mumbled something about seeing me in the morning, put Katie in the new 1977 Scout, and drove away.

While I was driving home, I kept kicking myself for leaving the window of the Scout open. I had now cranked them closed. Everything else that had happened that day could be overlooked. But don't be responsible for hurting the boss's daughter! I was starting to get a real bad headache when I realized the Scout smelled of exhaust. With the windows open earlier, and all the sight-seeing, I hadn't much noticed.

Then I remembered Ed telling me about the holes in the floorboards, and how we should get them fixed. I was being asphyxiated by the exhaust of my '68 Scout! Down went the windows, and both Kipper and I had our heads hanging out. My wife had just arrived home from work as we rolled into the yard.

"So, how was your day, birthday boy?" she asked earnestly.

"Well, it was not perfect. But hey! It could have been worse," I said, breathing in large gulps of fresh New Hampshire air. "Despite all that happened, I'm still employed!"

The Three Sisters

Michigan, 1980

The voice on the other end of the phone sounded rather distraught, almost panicky.

"Mr. Stormzand? Is that you?" the voiced asked.

I always look for my father or grandfather when people call me Mr. Stormzand. I wondered if I would ever break that habit. After all, I was almost fifty.

"Yes, this is Mark, er, Mr. Stormzand," I cautiously replied.

"I want to know why you are cutting all of the trees down in northern Michigan! I have been coming up here since 1938 to see the trees and breathe the air, and you are ruining that!" she fumed.

Oh boy, I thought, *what a way to start a New Year.*

"Ma'am, could you be a bit more specific? Where exactly are the trees being cut?" I asked.

"My father bought forty acres out here on the Sutton road back in 1922, and the property next to it has been logged since I was last here. The neighbors out here say you are to blame," she said.

I knew where the property was now. It was the Stamford parcel.

"Well, ma'am, I don't think 'blame' is the appropriate word. I did recommend to the landowners that twenty acres of their land be harvested. The trees in that area were over-mature, and once harvested, a new, healthy forest will start to grow," I said.

There was a very long bit of silence, then I heard, "Yes, but all of those lovely trees are gone and it looks so ugly!"

She had me. I could tell that over the last sixty years she had grown fond of her northern Michigan forest. There was only one thing I could do.

"May I ask your name?" I said.

"Certainly, young man. My name is Mrs. Bear," she said in a slightly calmer voice.

"Mrs. Bear, may I come out and visit with you and explain why we harvested the property next to yours? I think it would help clear up a lot of questions for you," I said.

"You most certainly may. My sisters and I are truly upset, and we want some answers!" she proclaimed.

"Right. Then I can be there in about an hour, if that's all right?" I asked.

"Fine. WE will be waiting," she said testily.

I placed the receiver down with a heavy groan. Prairie, hearing my sigh, got up from her corner of the office and strolled over. She kept nudging my hand to pet her. She can read me like a book. After several minutes of rubbing the top of her head, behind the ears, and under the chin, I felt calmer. Dogs sure can sense the moment, I thought to myself.

As I drove, I had visions of three elderly women wearing shawls and sitting in rockers by the fire. I could not have been more mistaken. As I pulled into the dooryard, three very energetic ladies wearing red-plaid wool coats greeted me in wool pants, caps of various colors, and old L.L. Bean swamper boots.

The shortest of the three came up to me and asked, "Mr. Stormzand?"

"Yes," I replied, "But please call me Mark."

"I think I will stick with Mr. Stormzand," she said.

The tension went up a notch, so I felt that this would be a good time to let the cute, furry dog out of the truck. The small woman continued, "My name is Carrie and these are my sisters, Maria and Jackie."

I shook their hands, and before I could let go of Jackie's, she was pulling me down the road toward the harvested area.

We stood for a minute looking out over the area that had been harvested. Then the silence was broken as one of the sisters let loose a deep howl … like a moose in distress. This was followed by her saying, "It's such a pity, such a pity. The forest is ruined. Why, I can remember when we first started coming up here almost sixty years ago. It was right after the fire, and the trees were just starting to grow, and now they are all gone."

She sighed again. "Such a pity!"

"Ladies, may I explain why we harvested this area?" I asked. Their various colored caps all bobbed up and down. I took that as a yes.

"The trees that were in this area were all mature and ready to be harvested. They had lived out their life span and were beginning to die. As a forester, I determined it was time to harvest these trees and let a new forest grow. Do any of you ladies have a garden?"

Again, the slight bobbing of the caps.

"Well, it is the same concept you use in your garden. In the spring you plant, and in the fall, you harvest the mature vegetables. Granted, gardens only take a few months to mature, as compared to the fifty years that this aspen stand took, but the process is the same."

"Yes, but with a garden you replant each spring," Maria retorted.

"That's true, but here in northern Michigan, Mother Nature takes care of that for us. Especially, in an aspen-mixed hardwood stand such as this one. Look closely at the ground; even with the snow you can see new young aspen and white birch shoots sticking through the snow. Look," I said, pointing out the shoots.

With that, all three sisters were wandering through the harvested area in search of new trees sticking through the snow. This proved to be too much stimulation for Prairie, who had been uncommonly calm up to this point. She leaped from one sister to the next, hopeful that sticks would be tossed for the cute dog. I had to intervene, as I was afraid Prairie was going to tackle Jackie. I was already on shaky ground; I did not need Jackie to do a face-plant in the snow because of my dog.

The searching sisters slowly started their quest. Then it became a contest—who could find the most? Then it grew into who could find different trees. I was called upon to act as referees several times to determine the difference between species. It dawned on me that these three probably have had these types of competitions throughout their lives. I was hearing, in very rapid succession, "Here's an aspen," "I have a balsam!" and "Red maple over here!"

This continued for about a quarter of an hour.

Eventually, they returned to where I was standing looking very pleased with themselves. Prairie was also pleased, because she had found a very large stick to chew on. Jackie spoke first.

"I guess we can look at it two different ways. We lost our old forest, but we gained a new one."

"Don't get me wrong, ladies," I said. "We are not just out here cutting trees helter-skelter. This forest was over-mature. If we had not made the harvest, it might have succumbed to disease, wind, or fire just like it did prior to your first visit. This forest will keep going through these life cycles indefinitely. The new forest grows old and mature, dies, and a new forest begins. Since these trees are renewable, and no other natural resource is, we can harvest these trees before they die and use them for our needs. If you take iron out of the ground to make steel, it does not grow back. Trees will return."

"Do all forest have to be managed for man's use?" Carrie challenged.

"No, and they are not. Many lands are set aside as wilderness areas, wildlife areas, parks, and wetlands. Also, let's look at this area we just harvested. If you look way off near that tree line, you can see an area we stayed away from. That was a wet area, and we did not want to disturb the fragile environment. While you were looking for the young trees, you probably saw many different sets of animal tracks. If we came back in the spring, we would probably hear the songs of a dozen different birds. So, as you can see, this area is being used for all sorts of things. Yours was a good question and sometimes we *need* to do a balancing act between man's needs and the environment around us.

"Sorry for the lecture," I concluded.

It was quiet for a while, except for the gnawing from Prairie and a woodpecker working on one of the dead trees we left standing (for that purpose). Then, in a soft voice, Maria said, "You know, while we were growing up, the forest grew with us. We are now mature as the forest was. Mind you, I am not ready for the chainsaw yet! But I see a new forest emerging, and at the same time, we all have grandchildren growing. As they mature, so will this new forest. It is all rather cyclical, don't you think?"

Then Carrie said something that made me think I might have changed her mind about the harvest.

"You know, girls, individuals and families are like trees and the forest. Individual trees don't last forever, but the forest can. Right, Mark?"

I was sure I had successfully made my point. She had called me Mark.

Little Man and the Beast

New Hampshire, 1982

*I*sn't it odd how small things can jog your memory and send your mind reeling on a nostalgic journey? Not too long ago, I was sitting in the waiting room of a car dealership while my truck was being repaired. I noticed a gentleman leaning against the coffee machine. With just one glance, I was reminded of an old farmer I met in New Hampshire almost a quarter century ago. The memories of that farmer and the day we met were starting to fill my head. I knew I had a long wait ahead of me, so I leaned back in my chair and let my memories take me back.

I had arranged to meet Mr. Perkins early one morning at his small farm in Cornish Flats. Cornish Flats is a small farming village located on the New Hampshire side of the Connecticut River. Since I lived in Vermont, I had to cross the river on one of the longest covered bridges in New England. I had used the bridge many times, but I will always remember this particular crossing.

Luck was with me, because as I approached the bridge, I could see that the ice in the river had just started to break up. This is a big event up and down the Connecticut River Valley, and many a wager is made each year on when the ice will go out. I felt very fortunate to have witnessed the beginning. Even though I had picked a date two weeks earlier in our break-up-pool, the sight of the beginning was worth the loss. I lingered on the Vermont side of the bridge for as long as I could, but I knew that being late for a meeting with a New England farmer was very much taboo. So, I headed across the bridge, trying to catch glances of the ice between the cracks in the bridge.

As I pulled into the dooryard (a Yankee driveway), I could see Mr. Perkins trotting toward my truck. I had to chuckle at the sight because a Hollywood wardrobe expert could not have gotten the quintessential Yankee farmer look any better. He was wearing knee-high black rubber boots, an old red sweater, faded green, wool pants, and a red and black plaid wool cap on his head. The cap looked like it had been put on in a hurry, because it was quite askew, with tuffs of coarse, white hair popping out.

Mr. Perkins was holding something in his hand that bounced in time with his trotting. It was some type of black box with a brown strap, but I was clueless as to what it was. As I started to get out of the truck, he waved me back in. He opened the passenger door, flung himself in, and yelled, "The river!"

We had never met in person and only talked once on the phone, but I was pretty certain he knew who I was, because I could not imagine this little fellow jumping into a truck with just anybody.

As we traveled the short distance to the river, I introduced myself, and Mr. Perkins told me to call him Guy. Traveling the road next to the river, we could see mountains of ice piling up against the old covered bridge I had just crossed. Upon arriving at the bridge and before we came to a complete stop, Guy leaped from the truck and ran for a big boulder next to the river. Poised on the boulder, he held the black box with the brown strap at his waist and looked down as if he were aiming it at the bridge.

"Of course," I said to myself. It was a camera—a very old camera.

I parked the truck and walked down to where Guy was perched next to the boulder. We both stood there watching the ice and all of its chaos. Guy held up the camera and proclaimed, "I have been getting a picture of 'ice out' for almost forty years, only missing '42 and '43 due to the fact Uncle Sam had me in the Pacific."

The roar of the river and the cracking of the ice made talking almost impossible, so we just both stood there watching in awe. After a bit, Guy elbowed me in the ribs and motioned for us to leave. I was hesitant, but I followed this wiry fellow as he jumped from boulder to boulder.

When we arrived at Guy's farm, he bounded from the truck toward his woodlot. Hurrying to catch up, I realized Guy was not your average over-the-hill kind of guy (no pun intended). In short order, we were walking through a northern hardwood stand that was very impressive.

The species in such a tree stand—sugar maple, beech, white ash, basswood, and yellow birch—are shade tolerant. This means they can grow and prosper with limited sunlight, which allows you to selectively harvest them. When properly done, you have an uneven aged stand that consists of large trees, medium size trees, saplings, and very young seedlings covering the forest floor. Guy's woods had it all.

Stopping near an old stump, I said, "This woodlot is amazing, Guy."

He took a seat on the old stump, smiled, adjusted his cap, and said, "You know, my grandfather bought this farm in 1890, and we Perkins boys have been working these woodlots ever since. We have been cutting firewood and sawlogs out of these woods for almost ninety years. We used the lumber off our property for barns, outbuildings, furniture, houses, sleighs, firewood, and even buckets."

While filling his pipe, he continued. "In fact, back in 1932, when the covered bridge was damaged by ice, our woods supplied some of the lumber for repairs."

"That's amazing, because you have the most heavily stocked forest I have seen in a long time," I said. "Looks like you Perkinses have been practicing sustainable forestry for a long time."

"What's that son, sustainable what?" Guy questioned.

"Sustainable forestry is a term describing management practices that ensure that future generations will have the same abundant forest that we enjoy today. And it is obvious that many generations of the Perkinses have been doing that," I said.

Guy frowned a bit, shifted on the stump, and said, "It seems to me that not only my family but all the families up and down this river valley have been practicing that sustainable thing."

"That's right. In fact, not only in this valley, but in the whole state and across the country, people and companies have been practicing sustainable forestry," I said. "Did you know that in the United States, the net annual growth of trees exceeds the removal through harvesting by an impressive thirty-seven percent? And we have seventy percent of the forest land that we had when the Europeans landed."

"With a population of over 260 million, all using forest products, that is an impressive figure," I added.

Guy nodded as he stood up.

"Now," Guy said as he started walking, "let me show you how we have logged these forests since my granddad's day."

We headed down an old tote road that wound through a valley of sugar maple, hemlock, and large white pine, where it ended in a pasture.

Across the pasture, I could see a beautiful, old New England barn that was attached to the old, white farmhouse. Smoke was rising from two chimneys, one in the center of the house and the second in the low building that connected the house to the barn. I assumed the second was the kitchen cookstove, and Guy confirmed that when he said, "Mother has the cookstove going for noon meal."

Entering the barn, I was immediately struck by the smell of livestock and hay. After a long winter, the nose longs for earthy smells, so the smells from this barn were pleasant to me. Guy walked me over to a group of stalls where two enormous beasts stood. Guy wedged himself between the two oxen, reached up, and patted both of them on the shoulder. He had to reach up because the backs of these giants were taller than he.

"Holy wah!" I said. I had never been this close to oxen before, and they were huge. I am five-foot four-inches, and the oxen's' backs were level with my head.

Guy backed them out of the stall by gently leaning on each of them and speaking a few soft words. The sight was amazing. This little elderly man was standing between the oxen, leaning on one, then the other. If either of them had shifted his weight, Guy would have been squashed like a bug.

Out in the pasture, Guy hooked the yoke to the pair and showed off their skills. With small taps from a willow branch, these two huge animals maneuvered around the pasture like two figure skaters. With a whole lot of pride, Guy said, "This is how the Perkins men have been getting the logs out of their forest for generations."

After the oxen were put back in their stalls, Guy invited me up to the house to share lunch. I had a lot to do yet that day, but I accepted. The kitchen was warm from the cookstove, and the cooking smells were wonderful. Guy's wife, Martha, was as pleasant as Guy. The kitchen, the animals, and these folks were something out of the past. As we were about to enjoy the noon meal, Martha informed me that since it was Guy's eightieth birthday, she had made something special. I could not believe that this wiry little man who shoved huge beasts around like they were nothing was eighty.

The meal was fantastic, and the stories they told me about their life on the farm were equally wonderful. I thanked them sincerely as I got up to leave.

Reaching for my coat on the rack, I noticed a whole wall of pictures that I had not noticed earlier. There was the covered bridge with ice piled up around the piers and the little dates in the right-hand corner of each picture. I looked at Guy, and he smiled.

"I told you I have been doing this for a few years" he said.

We shook hands, and I headed outdoors to my truck. Halfway there, Guy called out, "Son, that sustainable forestry thing sure makes a lot of sense. But I still say it ain't nuthin' new."

"You are absolutely right, Guy. But as a forester, my job is to see that we keep practicing sustainable forestry."

As I drove past the bridge and saw the ice, I was not sure what impressed me more: the power of the river or the zest of Mr. Perkins.

Prairie, A Good Friend Is Hard to Come By

Michigan, 2001

*H*ow is it that we can become so attached to a dog, so attached that when the dog is gone, we have a giant hole in our heart? All animals may have this effect on humans, but dogs in particular seem to crawl into our lives and latch on to any hope of acceptance. Dogs that are chained to a doghouse all of their lives will, if let free, travel to the Yukon and back if asked. Dogs whose main desire in life is to find a scent and chase it will come back to us when called. A dog's other desire is to please us. There is absolutely no doubt in my mind that whomever coined the phrase "man's best friend" had a dog like I did.

For ten years I had the pleasure of the company of one of God's sweetest creatures. Her name was Prairie, and she was a Golden Retriever. In theory she was the family dog. But in reality, she was my dog. She was so attached to me because we were always together. My job as a forester allowed us to spend all day together. If she was not by my side walking all day, she was lying next to my desk in the office or sleeping behind me in the truck.

Our incredible bond began in January 1992. We got Prairie in September as company for our aging golden, Kipper. Kipper passed away in November, and in January, I had a back operation, which left me in a cast and bed-bound for three months. The family was off to work and school, so this left one gangly puppy and an invalid to pass the time together. We were each grateful for the other's company. There were some disadvantages to the situation, though. I, with a cast from hip to breast, was unable to bend at the waist. This meant Prairie went without food or the tossing of toys during the day. She got back at me by insisting on sharing my convalescent bed. We had moved a bed downstairs to the living room. To say I was a bit tender after this operation is an understatement. I would be in bed watching the ceiling fan go around when I would hear a thunderous noise. It was that gangly pup getting up enough steam to jump onto the bed. Prairie was never noted for her athletic ability, so most of the time her leap would land her half on and half off the bed. I would let out a groan, and she would back up and try again. Luckily, as the weeks progressed, her leaps improved and my back healed.

As the winter turned to spring, I was finally able to "walk." We would shuffle down to the mailbox around noon and then around four to meet the school bus. These walks taught Prairie to stay close and not wander. This inadvertent training paid off when I was finally able to return to work. There is nothing worse for a forester than to have his dog take off while working. I have known foresters who have had to stop taking their dogs to work because they would spend half the day looking for the wanderer. Or worse, the dog would come back with the leg of a deer in its mouth. This really did not sit well when talking with a landowner about proper wildlife management.

But not Prairie; she never wandered. In fact, I used to play a game with her. Every once in a great while, Prairie would get slightly ahead of me. I, thinking it would be funny, would duck behind a fallen tree and watch her. She would walk a couple of feet, turn, and look for me. When I was not there, she would bound back trying to pick up my scent. As with her athletic ability, Prairie also had no sense of smell. She could hear the icebox open and know when someone was having ice cream. But she was absolutely horrible at finding animal or human scents. Not finding my scent, she would head back the way we came. When her master was not found, she would frantically race back to where she had last seen me. She always looked so lost that I could not stand it, and I came out of hiding. She was so happy to see me. I only did this a few times, because I realized I was really scaring her. She was like a child lost in a crowd.

I know I am a bit prejudiced, but I have never met a dog as amiable as Prairie. Over the years, Prairie and I had the opportunity to be around hundreds of landowners, loggers, and school children. I can only remember one person who did not care for my work companion. Actually, I am not sure it was a real flaw in this gentleman's character. We had just gotten into my truck on a hot August afternoon. I had an extended cab, which provided a perfect spot for Prairie to travel. She would sit or lie behind me as we traveled the highways, byways, and two-tracks of northern Michigan. I could tell this fellow was not a dog person, but that never stopped Prairie from turning on the charm. In fact, she took it as a personal challenge to convert this man into a dog lover.

She might have succeeded if it weren't for the fact that she reeked. Her coat and breath would have taken the varnish off a canoe paddle. Earlier in the morning, Prairie had found something very ripe to eat and roll in. The dead animal was so decomposed, I really was not sure what it used to be. I, being a veteran of over twenty-four years of having a dog accompany me to work, was prepared. At the next source of water, I gave her a bath with the organic shampoo I always carried with me. But it did not cut it. She was quite offensive to the nose. As the gentlemen entered the truck, Prairie stuck her head over the seat for a greeting. To make matters worse, it was over 90 degrees, and the smell was overpowering. To the man's credit, he did ride with me for a while as we toured his property. Prairie kept putting her muzzle on his shoulder, which normally did the trick. But the man was quick to take his leave, and I never heard from him again.

Prairie was a dog of many faces. She had a very large, square head with two very animated eyebrows. As I spoke, she would move her eyebrows up and down. It was very comical to try to read those expressions. We had many cats during Prairie's tenure. Some would curl up next to her or even lie on top of her. We had one very young cat that thought Prairie's elbow was its mother and was constantly trying to suck on it. One of our cats is very small and has only one working eye. She would come up to Prairie and rub herself on Prairie's nose, back and forth and back and forth. Prairie would raise one patient eyebrow, then the other. She was the canine combination of Mother Teresa and Mahatma Gandhi.

There is no question that Prairie loved children the best. I have talked to countless school groups about forestry. I would always have Prairie with me as I tried to educate these children. I quickly discovered that Prairie got all of the attention. So, being somewhat smarter than the average elementary student,

I would leave Prairie in the truck as I gave my speech. Out of the corner of my eye, I could see her patiently watching us. Her vibes were telling me to get on with it, that the kids were bored, and she would take care of that. When I was finished, I would let Prairie out of the truck. The scene reminded me of the old newsreel film of when Lindbergh, after completing his trans-Atlantic flight and landing his aircraft, was mobbed by the Parisians. Every child would try to pet Prairie. All I could see was this large, blonde dog with her tongue hanging out trying to accept each individual hand.

When I was young, my grandfather tried to teach me how to fish. As we sat in his old wooden boat, I can still remember him saying, "patience is a virtue." I did not really know what he meant at the time. Maybe he was trying to tell me to keep my line in the water? But as I grew older, I understood. Prairie had enough patience for ten dogs and as many humans. I never saw her snarl or growl at any living creature. Cats would rub, children would pet, and feet would step on her nose. She never raised an eyebrow. Since Prairie slept next to our bed (always on my side), she had the misfortune of being stepped upon most nights. When I got up and clumsily stepped on her nose, she would lie there and assume it was her lot in life to have her nose stepped on. Other dogs would have clamped their canines around my ankle. Not Prairie. She was tolerant. In fact, even during her last few days as she battled illness, she was like that. Vets probed, poked, and palpated, and she just stood there wagging her tail.

In the end, the illness won, but Prairie was given the chance to face it in her favorite spot. When it was time to relieve her pain and agony, our vet was kind enough to put Prairie down as she lay behind my seat of the truck with me holding her head. It was the place she had loved most. All the way home,

I kept putting my hand behind my seat to say goodbye. The ride home was a long one for my wife and me.

But life has to go on. Now, I put my hand behind my seat and a little fur ball nibbles on my fingers. This little nipper is a female Golden Retriever named Cedar. On the day we picked her up, I commented to my wife that this was the first time we had smiled in weeks. She is now just eight weeks old, and patient she is not! She may not know it, but she has some major paws to fill. I still look at her and think of Prairie. And it does not help when I mistakenly call her by her predecessor's name. In fact, she probably thinks her name is Prai . . . Cedar. She is already showing her own personality, though. We affectionately call her "Wild Thing." She barks. She chews. She runs and runs. She will keep us hopping, I am sure.

But I know there's a Golden "up there" having a good laugh at our expense.

"You didn't think you'd get another one like me, did you?"

No, Prairie, Cedar will have her own spot in our hearts soon. I just hope you left her enough space.

See ya, my friend.

In Benedict Arnold's Boots

Maine, 1984

*I*n the winter of 1983, I was working as a forester in northern Maine along the Quebec border. I love this area of Maine, because it is immensely beautiful, isolated, and wild. Few places in our ever-expanding world are considered wild anymore. But this stretch of Maine certainly is. In fact, the stretch of the Appalachian Trail that runs through this part of Maine is one of the most remote sections, and hikers are warned to be prepared for anything. The terrain is rugged, the people are few, and the snow is plentiful. The particular area of Maine I was responsible for was in a township called Carrying Place. Of all the places in which I have had the fortune to practice forestry, this little corner of Maine is one of my favorites. The township of Carrying Place received its name from an historic event, which took place during the Revolutionary War.

Most people think of Benedict Arnold as a traitor, the man who unsuccessfully tried to surrender the fort at West Point on the Hudson to the British. However, early in the war, before he became disillusioned with the army and its politics, he was one of most cunning and brave commanders the Continental Army had.

In 1775, Arnold's and Ethan Allen's troops captured Fort Ticonderoga on Lake Champlain from the British. This was important, because it cut off communications between the northern and southern British forces. Additionally, on hearing of the capture of Ticonderoga, General Washington sent Colonel Henry Knox to Lake Champlain to retrieve fifty-nine captured cannon and bring them back to a poorly defended Boston. Knox completed the three hundred mile journey in fifty days. Ticonderoga's cannons were placed on the Heights of Dorchester within range of Boston Harbor. Realizing that their fleet anchored in Boston Harbor was in peril, the British retreated and sailed back to Halifax, Canada.

In 1777, Arnold also played a key role in the battle of Saratoga, which stopped the British General Burgoyne's attempt to split the New England forces from the southern colonies. But by far his most daring and dangerous campaign was in the fall of 1775, when he convinced Washington that if the rebels could capture Quebec City—the key to British Canada—the war would be shortened. So, in September of that year, Col. Arnold and eleven-hundred brave souls loaded up their gear in clumsy boats called bateaux and headed up the Kennebec River towards Quebec City, a mere three-hundred-fifty miles away.

The trip was up river all the way and exceedingly dangerous. The men battled rapids, freezing temperatures, leaky bateaux, and spoiled provisions. The portages were long, back breaking, treacherous, and exhausting. There were very many unforgettable portages, but Carrying Place was one of the most wicked. Carrying Place is a series of ponds that connects the Kennebec and the Dead rivers. The bateaux had to be manhandled a distance of twelve miles on an elevation rise of one thousand feet. In addition, there was no portage trail. It had to be hacked out of the bush, forest, and swamps. In fact, the Appalachian Trail between West Carry and Middle Carry Pond follows part of the trail that Arnold and his men hacked out of the wilderness.

At this stage of the expedition, Arnold's men were already on half rations, and the rain and snow were adding to their misery. All of the adversity of the journey started to take its toll. At the end of Carrying Place, five hundred men were either dead or had turned back for home.

In the end, only six hundred weak and feeble men climbed the Plains of Abraham to attack Quebec City. Arnold realized there was no hope of taking Quebec, so he retreated to await reinforcements from General Montgomery. In December, the attack finally took place, but the American forces were defeated.

Benedict was involved in many other campaigns throughout the war. But, as with many strong-willed leaders, his ego got the better of him. He became very disheartened with the army, and as they say, "The rest is history." Nevertheless, his trip up the Kennebec and Dead rivers remains one of the greatest—and least-known—adventures in American history.

More than two hundred years later, I had the opportunity to understand some of Arnie's misery. One cold December day, I was doing some timber-stand mapping around Carrying Place. I had been following the edge of a stream for about two miles through a small valley. The snow was only about a foot deep, so there was no need for snowshoes. Time came for me to cross the stream and head up a small spur to the north. I found a place along the stream where I felt I could jump safely. Planting my right foot, I sprang for the opposite bank hoping for a solid landing. However, just as I leaped, my right foot slipped, which threw my body horizontally. I landed in the middle of the stream and was entirely submerged—a real belly flop.

As soon as I felt my foot slip, I knew I was in deep trouble. The temperature was around ten degrees, the snow was falling, and the wind was blowing up the valley. I knew hypothermia was a real threat, and I did not hesitate for a moment. As soon as I righted myself in the stream, I crawled up the slippery bank and started trotting the two miles back to my truck. The weight of my wool coat and pants was tremendous, and you might have thought that by trotting with all the extra weight, I would have warmed up. That wasn't the case; I started shaking several minutes into my run.

Normally, I would have had Kipper, the Golden Retriever, with me. But her paws had been damaged the day before when we spent a good portion of the day climbing up ridges with very ragged rocks. Consequently, she was home by the fire. I certainly could have used some warm canine company at this point. Also, it was deer season in Maine. An obvious perk of being a forester wandering the wilds of Maine is the chance to get off a good shot or two. So, my deer rifle was slung across my back and shoulder when I took the unexpected dip. Now, I could feel the leather strap freezing to my wool coat, which made swinging my arms difficult.

Because of the underbrush and trying to maneuver with frozen gear on my back, the two-mile trip back to my truck took a ridiculous amount of time. Reaching the truck, I was faced with a whole set of new problems. First, I was shaking so hard, I was not sure how I was going to get the keys out from under the bumper (which is the sacred place where foresters store keys). Second, how could I possibly hold still long enough to turn the lock? Then there was the problem of the frozen, loaded rifle stuck to my jacket. And, as cold as I was, could I really take off my mittens to hold the keys?

First things first. I had to warm my hands enough to loose the rifle and retrieve the keys. It was also very clear I had to keep moving. So, while I jogged around the truck, I worked at pulling my frozen mitts off with my teeth—no easy task. Finally, free of the mitts, I worked my hands underneath the frozen wool coat and several layers of sodden clothing and up into my armpits. Gross as that sounds, I had learned from my wilderness-survival class in college that warmth resided there.

After an eternity, I finally started to get some feeling back into my fingers. Keeping one hand inside, I took the other and pried the frozen rifle strap away from my chest, freeing the rifle. Before I lost all feeling in my hand again, I ejected the shells. With hands back under my coat, I took a few more turns around the truck. The key under the bumper had me worried, because if I fumbled it and it fell into the foot-deep snow, the game could well be over. When I felt both hands were ready, I went for the keys. It took one hand to grab the keys and one hand to be backup. I did bobble the keys, but my second hand made the save. It also took one hand to keep the other hand from shaking as I unlocked the door and started the ignition.

With the heater on full blast but very slow to warm up, I had to make some important decisions. I needed to get somewhere really warm to prevent hypothermia. So, my first thought was to drive the hour back home. But I knew there was no way to warm up quickly enough if I continued to remain in soaked clothing. Against all instinct, I stripped my frozen clothes and boots off. Then, without a stitch of clothing on, I drove down into the valley toward some heat. The trip to our house consisted of about forty-five minutes on a logging road and roughly fifteen minutes on a county road. The majority of the travelers on the logging road were loggers, log trucks, an occasional hunter, or some lost traveler. Luckily for me it was mid-week and a miserable day, so most of the vehicles I passed were loggers I knew.

Back then I had somewhat of an odd reputation among these loggers. They had seen my dog and I run down this road in the dead of winter and the heat of summer. Where the road was tar, they had seen me on my roller skis practicing for cross-country ski racing. They had passed me biking miles away from home "just for exercise." They all had dangerous, hard, labor-intensive jobs, and for the life of them, they could not figure out why I would do such things. So, the thought of them seeing me driving my truck in the middle of winter with nothing on made me laugh. And I knew I was just adding to my reputation. As I passed each truck, I gave a hardy wave as was the custom, and the looks were almost worth the soaking.

Pulling into the dooryard, I started blowing my horn. Parking the truck rather hurriedly, I saw my wife looking out through the curtains with a curious expression on her face. This was a bit odd, me coming home mid-morning and honking the horn. She must have thought I was either hurt or we had just won the Maine Sweepstakes.

Rolling down the window, I shouted, "Turn on the shower! It's freezing out here." A few minutes later, she was back confirming that the shower was on. I turned off the truck, opened the door, and sprinted for the house. My wife, seeing me in my unclothed state, seemed less startled than the loggers. I guessed she was getting used to my antics.

Later that afternoon, after a long shower and a long explanation to my wife, I sat in a rocker by the woodstove. I was holding my son on my lap, and I was finally feeling warm again.

Sitting there with the glow of the stove and the warmth that a sleeping baby radiates, I could not help but think of Arnold and his men. For over two months, they battled the elements and the hardships of the expedition, and in the end, they had to face the British to boot. It had to have taken an almost superhuman effort to accomplish the feat. Arnold must have been one heck of a leader to have gotten even half of his men to Quebec alive.

During the next year, I spent much of my time working in the township of Carrying Place, traversing the area where Arnold and his men endured unimaginable hardships. I have spent a good portion of my life outside, either at work or at play, and nothing is more of a deal breaker than the elements. When you are warm and dry, life is good. If you are wet, you are close to miserable. Wet and cold bring out the worst in most all of us. Throw in hungry and no chance of improving your situation, and you have the makings of a palace revolt. Arnold had to have been a much better leader than I; I have a hard time keeping a family of four happy on canoe trips in the dead of summer.

In 1780, a disillusioned Arnold conspired to turn West Point, an important fort on the Hudson River, over to the British. For this treachery, Benedict was promised the rank of brigadier general in the British army along with a monetary award. The plot was uncovered when a message was intercepted between Arnold and the British. When he knew he'd been discovered, Arnold narrowly escaped on a sloop down the Hudson. After the war, Arnold fled to England, where he resided until his death in 1801.

Gazing down at my sleeping son on my lap, it dawned on me that fate plays a huge role in one's life. If I had been a few more miles away from my truck, I was not sure I would have been sitting in front of this fire. As I started to doze off, I also realized that if Arnold's fate had been slightly different, the whole history of North America might have been altered.

And if my foot had not slipped, I might never have appreciated how much frozen wool chafes.

A Skunk's Life

Michigan, 2002

*S*itting down next to the woodstove, I began to read.

Striped skunk (Mephitis mephitis) *This striking skunk has a notorious reputation for its vile smell.*

"No kidding," I told myself.

The lingering odor is often the best sign of its presence.

"Or just seeing the bloody thing," I grumbled.

Widespread throughout all but the extreme northern latitudes...

"I would take a herd of Lemmings any day," I grumped.

...the striped skunk enjoys a diverse range of habitats, especially open woodlands and brushy area.

"Great. We have a virtual skunk Disneyland out there," I said as I pointed the book toward the window.

It dens up in the winter, coming out in the warmer days of the spring.

"Not true!" I snorted.

Skunks mostly walk—with such a potent smell for their defense, and those memorable back and white stripes, they rarely need to run.

"Now, *there* is something I agree with," I said.

101

I threw the book down on the chair as I got up to pace.

"There is not one thing in that book on how to get rid of the stinking skunk," I complained.

My wife, who had been very patient during my readings and rantings, pointed out that probably *Animal Tracks of Ontario* was not the best source of information on how to get rid of a skunk.

"Good point," I admitted. "All right. First thing in the morning, I am going to contact my source. He will know."

To say I was miffed with my *Mephitis mephitis* was a gross understatement. The little bugger had nailed our Golden Retriever, Cedar, twice in as many weeks. Even now, as I paced back and forth in front of the woodstove, I could smell the effects of her latest encounter. For her part, I don't think she was enjoying it, either. She lay as close as possible to the woodstove without bursting into flames. She just had endured another de-skunking bath and was trying to warm up.

In the morning, I met my skunk expert. He gave me a large, metal live-trap along with some confidential advice. I listened intently as he explained in great detail how I should take a dog biscuit smeared with peanut butter.

"Creamy or crunchy?" I asked.

"No matter. Just lots, and place it at the back of the trap. This is fool-proof," he said.

"Okay, now that I have him, how do I let him go?" I asked.

"Let him go?!" he snorted, incredulous.

"Why yes, after I catch him, I would like to transport him out in the bush somewhere and let him go," I said.

"That won't work," he huffed. He leaned closer and said in a hushed tone, "You have to dispose of him."

"Dispose of him? What do you mean, dispose?" I asked cautiously.

"You know, end him," he whispered.

"You mean, kill him? I can't release him after I catch him?"

"Nope," he said. "The only way is to do him in. You have two choices. You either throw a blanket over the trap and throw the trap in the water. Or you throw a blanket over the trap and run a hose from your truck and gas him.

"Since everything is frozen, except for your hot tub," he said, chuckling, "it looks like you have to use the second method."

As I drove away, I could see "my source" giving me the thumbs-up in the rearview mirror. I, on the other hand, had very mixed emotions. As I have aged, the thought of killing is less and less desirable. My job as a forester allows me to see many living things on a daily basis. And except for the blackfly, I enjoy watching all of nature's creatures.

During the next several weeks, the score was "Skunk, 3, Would-Be-Trapper, 0." Twice I came home in the evening only to find the skunk strolling across the front yard by the garden. I ran in the house, grabbed the shotgun and flashlight, and returned only to find the yard empty. I would take off in the direction I saw him last waddle, hoping to catch up with the striped beast. It is probably lucky I did not locate him, because the shotgun blast might have made things worse. The last time I was hunting a wild beast (weasel) like this, I ended up blowing a huge hole in the chicken fence and prematurely slaughtering a few chickens. And as the feathers drifted slowly back to earth, the weasel scurried away.

Then there was the matter of supplies. I had gone through lots of dog biscuits and several jars of peanut butter with nothing to show for it. "Fool proof?" Yeah, right.

Finally, one morning while brushing my teeth, I glanced out the window and noticed something different about the trap.

"Ah ha, I got him!" I yelled, toothpaste splattering the mirror.

Rushing to put my boots on, I nearly tripped over both cats and the dog, who were excited by my yells. Even in my excitement, though, I had enough sense to approach the trap cautiously. I stopped about ten feet from the trap to examine my nemesis. For the past month, we had been doing battle. Finally, I had the upper hand.

But for some reason, all of my pent-up anger for this animal disappeared. There in the trap was a creature with a beautiful coat (albeit with a fragrance) of black and a very large white band down its back. He was larger than I expected, and his feet sported five very long claws. He stared back at me with small eyes on either side of a long, narrow nose. He was probably thinking, "He is smaller than I thought, but he does have blond hair. No wonder he botched it."

After several minutes of staring at each other, I realized I now had to do the act I had been dreading. I threw a blanket over the trap, backed my truck up, and ran a hose from my muffler to the trap. I started the engine. Retreating to the house, I felt miserable. For over an hour, I sat in my office, busying myself with paperwork.

Finally, I summoned up enough courage to go take care of my enemy.

I shut off the truck and removed the hose. I lifted the trap to put it in the back of my truck. When the trap was about eye level, the blanket slid off. And there I was, staring at my very-much-still-alive striped friend, eyeball-to-eyeball, with nothing but a few thin strands of wire between us.

My eyes widened with the fear that I was about to get sprayed. The skunk's eyes were glazed over; he had one heck of a hangover. But he was still standing up, albeit swaying a bit. As if handling a live grenade, I gingerly placed the trap into the truck. Equally as gingerly, I took several steps backward. I then grabbed the blanket and threw it over the trap.

"Now what?!" I shouted to no one. My source said nothing about skunks holding their breath. I really only had one choice. I had to figure out a way to release the trap without getting sprayed. One thing was certain: at least I could take this fellow to a new neighborhood.

I dashed back into the house to finish dressing and say goodbye to my wife. She reminded me that if I was unsuccessful in my release, this might be the last hug I would get for a while. I understood. "I really don't want to get sprayed, either," I said, rushing out the door.

I took the little fellow to a remote location about ten miles away. Cautiously, I lowered the tailgate, gently picked up my cage of nitroglycerin, and placed it several yards away from the truck. I was counting on him still being stoned

Now for the tricky part.

This live-trap had a latch system that was released only on the right side of the cage. To release it, you had to be very close, which at this point I considered a major design flaw. I removed the blanket on the opposite side and rattled the trap with a stick as a diversion while I frantically tried to release the latch. This would only work if, as I unlatched the door, I could also insert a long pole to prop the door open.

Finally, I succeeded in opening the door and placing the pole. But now I had to find a heavy object to keep the pole in place. Luckily, I found a suitable rock several feet away. But, as I leaned to grab it, the pole moved, jarring the latch, which in turn closed the trap door. I had to go through the whole process again, knowing that my odds of getting sprayed were multiplying by the second.

After several minutes of white-knuckle work, I got the door open. I flung back the blanket, revealing those small eyes and pointed nose staring right back at me. He would not move. He just stood there. I was saying really encouraging things like, "Shoo. Skidaddle. Hit the road, Jack! Please shoo." But nothing happened. Just that stare.

I ran into the bush and grabbed a long, pointed stick. On the way back, I noticed that my friend had, at least, turned around and was looking at the open door. I stuck the stick through the mesh and was poking him in his rear. I figured when the tail lifted, I would scramble. But while the tail was down, I would continue my coaxing.

This went on for several tortuous minutes until my prisoner at last left his cell. Overjoyed, I bent down and picked up the blanket. Turning to place it in the truck, I almost stepped on my newly free friend. Leaping over him, I nearly landed on his tail.

That seemed to wake him up at last. He started chasing me around the truck. Who knew that skunks would chase you? During all of this, Cedar had been in the driver's seat, watching with interest. One time around, I tried to open the truck door, but it was locked. Cedar has a lovely habit of leaning against the automatic door locks. On the third revolution, I leapt into the bed of the truck. To my amazement, the skunk made two more laps. Mercifully, he finally got bored and moved out about twenty feet from the truck, turned, and stared at me.

Cautiously, I crawled out of the back of the truck, grabbing the spare key in the process. As soon as I hit the ground, he again started toward me. I quickly unlocked the door, shoved Cedar over, and jumped in. Sir Skunk took another quick lap around the truck. Satisfied that I had disappeared, he slowly started wandering toward the bush. I was not taking any chances this time. I waited until there was no sign of him. No way did I want my little Mephitis following me home.

Driving back, I had a nagging feeling that I should contact the authors of *Animal Tracks of Ontario* and have them add a few items to the chapter on Mephitis mephitis:

Caution, will chase. Very hearty. Interesting if cornered.

And one I proved and was proud of:

May be released successfully from live-trap.

As luck would have it, while working in this same location several weeks later, I saw my friend again.

How do I know? I'd know those beady eyes anywhere.

Stone Wall

Michigan, 2000

*J*ust as the last few rays of the weak December sun faded, I placed the final stone. Taking a step back, I looked at my creation. Something on the end just did not look right. I adjusted the headlamp and scanned the surface of the wall. The light bounced off the lighter stones and was absorbed by the darker ones. I picked up a flat, white stone, flipped it over, and moved it closer to the corner of the wall. I stepped back and scrutinized the wall again. A sense of pleasure and gratification filled me.

"That's it, girl, we're done," I said to my dog, Cedar, lying next to one end of the wall. She glanced up at me and gave out a sigh. She was not pleased.

The reason for her displeasure was the concept of "double standards." I had spent the last four hours digging, moving, hauling, and placing stones, but every time she would dig for or grab a stone, she was scolded. My dog's favorite objects in the world are stones. She loves to dig for them, chew them, roll on them, and present them to you as a gift from Heaven.

So, after a day of being scolded for being underfoot while I worked with the stones, she opted to lie as close to the stone wall as possible and pout.

As a goodwill gesture, I picked up a small stone and threw it into the woods. Cedar bounded after it, and I knew I had restored our good master-dog relationship.

Some people like to paint. I have always enjoyed building stone walls. In fact, I just enjoy looking at a stone wall. My wife and I moved to northern New England in 1977, and the moment I laid eyes on the stone walls that dot the landscape, I grew fascinated. Probably one of the reasons I am transfixed by stone walls is historical. I really enjoy history, and each and every stone wall has a story. The stone walls of New England played a very important role. They were mainly used as boundary lines. But in reality, any place where something or someone needed to be kept out or kept in, stone walls were used. In fact, in the 1800s, once a stone wall was completed it had to be inspected by a "fence viewer." This governmental employee would determine if the wall was sound and straight. If approved, the owner of the stone wall was not held liable for crop damage done to other farmers' crops by his animals. Because there were so many stones in New England, they used them to build fences instead of wood or wire.

Cedar proudly returned carrying the stone I had tossed. Placing it at my feet, she waited "patiently" for another toss. That's when our second series of "double standards" began. Since she was a pup and started this infatuation with rocks, I have tried not to encourage her. But, to my chagrin, I am the only member of our family that even remotely tries to discourage her from her stone habit. It is not from weakness of character that they cave in and give the stone a pitch. It is Cedar's doggedness, single-mindedness, and those big brown eyes that wear my family down. In addition, sometimes we just forget and pick up and fling whatever she has dropped at our feet. My wife gave up long ago and now pays the price every time she is outside. A stone or rock will instantly appear, followed by a series of barks. When our daughter is home, she does not even hesitate, pitching the stone before the official bark. And, when our son visits, he has the audacity to bring out his old baseball bat from grade school and knock the presented stones into the field.

Usually after a day with Cedar, I admit defeat and pitch the stones, too. However, when she brings me a rock, we often go through a script that's something like this: Rock is placed at foot, I ignore it, Cedar pulls back on her haunches and growls, I ignore it, Cedar lies on stomach and barks three times, I say, "I don't do rocks. Find me a stick."

Three more barks.

"Stick, stick," I say.

Then there is a pause as she determines how serious I am about this stick thing.

"Stick, stick," I say again.

After a slight hesitation, she bounds off to find a stick. Upon returning with anything from a twig to a two-by-four, I say "Good girl" and heave the stick.

This pattern is played out with such regularity and consistency that a ballet could be written to its score.

She returned the stick, which I heaved over the wall. To my surprise, she leaped the wall to retrieve it. While she hunted for the stick, I leaned up against a large maple and gazed at my stone wall creation. I learned to build stone walls from the masters. Granted, I had never met them. I came on the scene several hundred years too late. But they still influenced me. The years my family spent living in New Hampshire, Vermont, and

Maine were my tutelage years. Like an art student gawking in a big-city museum, I studied the "great stone walls" of rural New England.

The way I studied them was a bit out of the norm. Most of the stone walls I came in contact with were "wild walls" (that is an official term). "Wild Walls" are stone walls that once fenced in pasture and farmland but now enclose towering pines, hemlocks, and hardwoods.

The golden age of stone wall building was from 1775 until about 1825, and it is estimated that there are approximately 250,000 miles of stone walls in New England. But in 1825, the Erie Canal was completed, and New England farmers found that their hold on the market in the East was threatened by farmers to the west. In addition, these same New England farmers started heading west themselves, taking advantage of better soil, a larger land base, and a landscape with fewer rocks. Consequently, the farms of northern New England started to be abandoned.

Couple this with the fact that many farmer-soldiers did not return after the Civil War, and the rural demographics changed drastically. Since military companies were made of the local men, the male populations of many small farming villages were decimated, if not completely wiped out altogether. The result was that much of the land that had been cleared for farming and pasture reverted to a forest setting. The farms were gone, but the stone walls that identified fields, house sites, and graveyards all remained. A hundred-plus years later, I showed up on the scene, and the mature forest in which I was working was lousy with stone walls of various shapes, sizes, and importance.

During the course of a day, I probably leaped over, walked through, sat on, or leaned against several miles of stone wall.

They were everywhere, but I never grew bored with them. On occasion, I even found myself replacing a rock or two that had become dislodged. I only remember one time when I felt uncomfortable with stone walls. Nearly a quarter of a century later, that day still stands out in my mind.

It was a gray, drizzly, November day, and I was about two miles from anything that even resembled a trail. There among the white pines and mist was a small plot of land enclosed by taller-than-normal stone walls. The enclosed area was about the size of a small garden plot.

When my dog and I stumbled upon it, we both froze in our tracks. Our first Golden, Kipper, was rarely afraid of anything. But this eerie sight had her squirming between my legs. I did not know why this structure gave me the hebe-jeebies, but it did. I saw there was a small opening in one of the walls, so with my dog hiding behind my legs, we waddled through it. Inside we found seven old gravestones. A white pine had sprouted up in the small graveyard, pushing several of the gravestones slightly aside at awkward angles. With a little courage and a lot of curiosity, I attempted to read the headstones. After rubbing the headstones with my sleeve, I was able to determine that it was a one-family cemetery. Four of the headstones told me of a tragic time in this farm-family's life. They all had died within several weeks, which I concluded was contagious illness. Two had died as young infants, and the final headstone told me of a man who died in the early days of the Civil War.

I don't know if the chill that ran down my neck was from the cold rain or the eerie setting, but Kipper and I quickly took our leave.

I learned to build stone walls by being in the right place at the right time. I happened to be working in a woodlot one day when I heard a lot of loud thuds in the distance. Curious, I wandered over to see what the racket was. To my horror, a backhoe was removing part of a stone wall, and the loud thuds I heard were the stones falling into the metal bed of a dump truck. After some inquiries, a lot of pleading, and promises given, I became the owner of about fifty feet of stone wall ... disassembled, of course. An addition was being added to a barn by its owners. The hired contractor needed to move the section of stone wall before the work could begin, and I became the subcontractor tasked with taking the rock.

My payment? Fifty feet of stones, and they needed to be moved pronto. My pregnant wife was far less excited than I about the arrangement, which became abundantly clear when we were still hauling stones at two in the morning. I pointed out it was Friday night, we were broke, and wasn't this a cheap form of entertainment? I have used this ploy before and since and always with the same dismal results.

My newly acquired stone wall now sat in a heap in our yard. Over the course of the weekend, I reassembled it. In the process of dismantling the stone wall, I had been able to grasp the rudimentary skills of wall building. Large stones on the bottom, small stones in the middle, and flat stones on top. In addition, each stone needed to be snug, no wiggling. This meant that a lot of little flat stones were used as shims. Thanks to the lessons I learned from the folks who had originally built my stone wall, my reassembled wall still stands thirty years later. A visit to the old homestead a few years ago confirmed this.

Until recently, I have not been able to indulge in stone wall building. But with both kids grown and gone, I seem to find myself dabbling in my art form more frequently. When bored, I can always lift and heave. My most recent wall can be seen from our kitchen window, and I find myself staring at the wall more times than I care to divulge.

Cedar had returned with a rock, not a stick, and placed it on my boot. But before I had to endure the same old routine, Cedar's attention was diverted. A red squirrel, which had taken up residence in the wall months ago, had scurried along its top. Cedar darted after it, but the small, agile, squirrel was in no real danger. I was about bent over with laughter as Cedar poked her nose into one crack and the squirrel poked its head out another. This went on and on, and I finally left the two of them to sort it out.

Inside, I threw off my wet coat and placed my gloves next to the woodstove. I took the kettle off the woodstove and made myself a mug of tea. Like a moth attracted to a light, I strolled over to the kitchen window to gaze at my wall. The moon had appeared, and I saw that the hide-and-seek game was still in progress. Framed by the window and with the shadows cast by the moon, it was almost as if I were a kid watching a cartoon on Saturday morning.

I called to my wife to see the spectacle outside, and for several minutes, we gazed and laughed.

"See," I said, pointing to the stone wall with my mug, "stone walls are a cheap form of entertainment."

Sweet Smells of Spring

Michigan, 2002

One thing nice about taking a hot sauna after working all day in the cold drizzle is that you finally relax. You can let go and let your mind wander. Usually in my case, I like to reminisce. And tonight was no exception. Earlier in the day, I had passed my neighbor's young children checking the sap buckets on their large maple trees. This image really took me back to when our kids were young. Now sitting in the sauna relaxing, I could see a particular Saturday long ago as clear as if it were last Saturday.

Michigan, 1990, an early spring day: I was sitting with my back against an old maple tree, my eyes closed from the bright, warm sun, listening to one of the most beautiful sounds of spring. I could hear "drip, drip, drip" coming from a maple tree not far away. It was the sound of sap dripping from the spout into a metal bucket. For some reason, this sound has always been pleasing to me. Maybe it reminds me of the years I spent in Vermont, where everybody made syrup. It seemed along every country lane, main street, and woodlot, maples were tapped. Maybe it was all the good times my family and I had making maple syrup.

A chickadee called in the distance, which stirred me out of my trance. I supposed if I was going to make syrup this year, I had better get to it and quit the daydreaming. I glanced up to see my young son coming toward me carrying two empty sap buckets.

"Which trees do you want me to put these buckets on?" he asked.

"Follow me, mate. I know where there are some perfect maples for tapping," I answered.

I grabbed the sled, which contained all of the tools we needed for gathering syrup, and headed across the field to four old sugar maples that also marked our property line. Prairie, our dog, bounded ahead of us in the knee-deep snow. As I struggled with the sled, my son started a litany of questions.

"Why do we only make syrup in the spring?" he asked, trying to keep up.

"Because that's when the sap starts to flow. When the warm, sunny weather arrives in the spring, the sap begins to flow through the tree. This sap contains all kinds of nutrients, minerals, and water, which in turn help the leaves open and grow. All trees do this, but sugar maples have a higher concentration of sugars in their sap. So, we tap them in the spring to make syrup."

Reaching the first maple, I grabbed my grandfather's old hand drill out of the sled. I bored a three-eighths-inch hole into the maple about an inch-and-a-half deep, approximately four feet above the ground. My son handed me a spout, hook, and a wooden mallet. I placed the hook over the spout and gently tapped it into the hole. I then placed a sixteen-quart bucket onto the hook, and immediately the sap began to flow. My helper placed a lid on the bucket to keep any rain, dirt, and some of the bugs out of the sap.

Heading to the next tree, I was asked how many taps we could put on one tree. I explained that I had learned a great rule of thumb while living in Vermont. Trees twelve inches in diameter, put on one bucket. Sixteen, you could hang two, and anything over twenty-two inches, you could hang three.

My son started laughing as only a seven-year-old could. I was curious at his sudden outbreak, and he pointed to the tree we had just tapped.

"It looks like we have a leak," I said with a chuckle. There was Prairie standing under the bucket, trying to lick the drops as they dripped from the bottom.

After we finished tapping the maples down by the fence line, we made our way up the hill to some maples we had tapped earlier. It had only been about six hours since we had tapped these trees, but already the buckets were full. We emptied the buckets into a large holding container down by the road, which we would fetch later.

My accomplice sang out, "We have enough sap to make a swimming pool of syrup!"

"Well, not quite, son. It takes about thirty to forty gallons of sap to make one gallon of syrup. And as the season progresses, it may take even more. The first run in the spring usually has the highest concentration of sugar."

This went right over his head, as do a lot of things dads say. I tried another bit of fact, or lore, depending on your point of view.

"It's really kind of funny. Some trees run better in the early part of the season and some later. Taps that are on the southwest side give sap earlier in the day than those on the northeast. Later in the day, the taps on the northeast side may run better. Through the years, you learn all of the different habits of the trees you tap. Just like I know you like getting up early, and your sister is not known as Ms. Happy in the morning," I said.

Another question popped up.

"Dad, does the hole you put in the tree hurt it?"

"Actually, no, it heals rather nicely. If you cut your finger, a scab forms, and under that, new skin grows. Same holds true for the trees. In fact, some groves of sugar maple that have been tapped for over a century are doing fine," I said.

We finished pouring some of the sap into the container on the sled and cautiously headed to our rather primitive sugar shed. Someday I would have a proper sugarhouse within which to boil down the sap. But for the present I had to make due with a cinder-block stove and a large pan on it. My daughter was sitting next to the stove on a pile of firewood, reading.

"How is the boiling going, young lady?" I inquired, peering into the pan.

She had been placed in charge of keeping the fire going and adding sap to the pan. As the sap boils, the water evaporates, leaving a liquid high in sugar. My daughter, being only nine, was very proud of the responsibility thrust upon her. At least that was how I liked to see it. She probably was more than happy to sit by the fire reading and occasionally adding some wood or sap, while her younger brother struggled with the buckets.

She looked up from her reading and said, "Pretty well. But I will tell you one thing. I am not sure I want any maple syrup for a while. This smell is awful sweet."

She was right. The fragrance of maple syrup just kind of

hung in the air, and smelling it all day can get to you.

"How can we tell when it is ready?" she asked.

"When we are boiling it outside, I taste-test it. If it starts to taste strong, I pour it off into a smaller pot. In fact, this batch is ready for the next step," I said, tasting the drips off of a small twig I had dipped into the pan. Both kids protested at my choice of utensil.

The three of us carefully drained the boiling pan into a smaller pot, which had a felt filter over it. This filtering process was one of three I would use to strain out any dirt and debris, which darkened the syrup. The clearer and lighter the syrup, the more desirable it is.

We carried the syrup into the house and placed it on the stove. My wife was standing in the kitchen waiting for us. She enjoyed the syrup-making process up to this point. But now that the finishing process was inside, she knew disaster could strike at any time—especially with me behind the wheel.

"I know I don't have to say this, but please be careful," she pleaded. Two years earlier, I had let the syrup boil over on the stove, and she just couldn't seem to get past that.

Carefully, we brought the syrup to a boil, trying to reduce the water content even further . . . all the while feeling a strange sensation that someone was watching me. Looking over my shoulder, I gave my wife a sheepish grin. Soon, the candy thermometer told us the syrup was ready. I drained the syrup through two sets of filters into sterilized canning jars. With this done, my wife sighed in relief, given my spotty history of flooding the kitchen floor with syrup.

My son looked at the fruits of our labor and exclaimed, "That's it? All that sap fit into three jars!"

"That's right, son. But I bet when you taste it, you will agree it was all worth it," I said.

With that, everybody agreed to wait till morning. The sweet smell was still too overpowering.

The next morning, we were all treated to a great pancake breakfast with all of the syrup we wanted. Even my daughter had her share. As we ate, I knew this was my chance to start quoting my favorite sayings I learned from an old sugar maker in Vermont. I started:

"Warm days and freezing nights are a sugar maker's delight.

"Sap runs better by day than by night.

"Trees differ as much for sugar as cows do for butter.

"Trees by a brook run well into the spring."

The kids begged me to stop, "Please! No more! We can't stand it."

"Okay, just one more," I promised.

I kind of sang this one.

"The darker the evening, the sooner the sap will stop, doo-da, doo-da."

I ducked as the kids and wife all threw their napkins.

"You forgot my favorite," my wife added. "Good syrup is made by a big sap."

The kids liked that one.

The Smell of Success

Michigan, 2002

$\mathcal{S}$tepping to the cool barn, I was struck by the strong smell of earth. The warm weather had thawed the dirt floor of our barn, and the smell was a welcome one. This was the true sign of spring in our family. I stood motionless for a while, letting my eyes adjust to the darkness. *Funny,* I thought, *I would have sworn that I had just seen both cats sleeping on the couch a moment ago. What was making all of the noise in the corner?*

Bending down, I took a couple of steps closer to examine the noise. Then I realized I was staring a skunk right in the eyes. I leapt for the door. Thankfully, the skunk was just as surprised, so I escaped, un-skunked.

My wife witnessed this event from the kitchen window. From the look on her face, it was obvious she was having great difficulty opening the window. When she finally did, she burst out laughing.

"I had never seen you exit a building so fast," she said between spurts of laughter. "Trouble, Mark?"

I explained that I was just trying to locate the planting

bar—a tool for planting trees—when I met the skunk. She said it was safe now because, last seen, the skunk was heading toward the bush.

Gingerly, I entered the cool barn again, and this time I successfully found the bar. On my way out, I grabbed the big canvas bag with the shoulder strap. Once outside, I cautiously looked inside the bag to see if I had any winter lodgers still inside. They were gone, and only small pieces of leaves and paper remained. Hefting the planting bar over one shoulder and slinging the canvas bag over the other, I headed for my truck just as my wife let out our dog. In a straight line, my truck was only thirty yards away. But with a five-month-old pup weaving between my legs, the distance was easily doubled.

I threw the bag and bar in the back of the truck to be used later. Reaching down to grab the bundles of red-pine seedlings, I was met with a big, wet, sloppy kiss across my face. This was my dog's way of saying, "Good morning!"

"Ah, Cedar. Do you have to do that?" I grumbled, lifting the seedlings into the truck. She wagged her tail as if to say, "Yes, it's my bloody job, mate."

Cedar and I arrived at the elementary school just as the kids were coming out for recess. A huge crowd of them swarmed my truck to say hello and to get a look at Cedar. It was obvious Cedar was the main attraction. She had the edge over me, because she was cute and furry. The kids were asking me to let her out so they could pet her. I told them that maybe when they came out with their classes to plant trees, it could be arranged.

For the past ten years, I have been coming to this school to plant trees. The kids at this school are very lucky, because they have a school forest, which consists of over one hundred acres.

Each year I show up with roughly three hundred seedlings, one for each student, and we plant them together. This is one of the highlights of my year, because I get to work with kids and talk about forestry.

As I awaited the first class, I sat on the tailgate of my truck sorting through the wet bundles of seedlings. The red-pine seedlings were packed in a wet moss and paper mixture with fifty seedlings per bundle. I sorted through the bundles, pulling out any bad seedlings. At the same time, I cut back the root systems to a more manageable length. Then, I repacked the seedlings in the wet mixture so the roots would not dry out. Filling my canvas bag with the seedlings, I noticed Cedar was staring mournfully at me through the back window.

"Not yet, girl. We need to plant some trees first," I said.

The year before, I made the mistake of letting my old dog, Prairie, out first. After the kids chased her all over the school-yard, planting trees was kind of anticlimactic.

The first class appeared across the field walking in single file behind the teacher. From their size, I could tell it was my favorite group: the kindergartners. Standing huddled around their teacher, I could feel their big eyes fixed on my every movement. After our greetings, I started my speech, which I would have to give ten times that afternoon.

"First, I take the planting bar and stick it into the soil and make a hole by moving the bar back and forth. Then, I place a seedling in the hole and work the bar so the seedling is covered with soil. As I pull the planting bar out, I want to pack the earth around the seedling with my heel."

I said this in my best kindergarten-teacher voice. This did not come easily, because I am also a high-school coach. As such, I rarely use my kindergarten voice.

We began to plant. Some of the kids would put the tree in

the hole upside down, or step on the tree as they packed it down. Some tried to completely bury the tree. But in the end, they each planted a tree. Luckily there were a few minutes between classes for me to fix these minor mistakes.

As the classes came and went, I had a chance to talk more about forestry and answer some questions. I explained that the spacing for the trees should be roughly seven feet by seven feet. We plant red pine here at the school, because the soil is very sandy and the red pine is well adapted to poor, sandy soils. As the young seedlings grow, they will provide shelter for some forms of wildlife. Red pine is also a native species to this part of Michigan. After a while, I realized there were as many questions as kids.

The sixth grade showed up, and it was obvious that some of them felt they were way too cool to be planting trees. Well, they weren't and they did. After a while, even the cool ones started asking interesting questions. One young lad asked if we were going to run out of forest. My answer was a very straightforward *NO*. If we practice sound forest management and responsible stewardship, I said, we will have forests in North America forever. In fact, in Michigan alone we are currently harvesting less than forty percent of the annual growth. In addition to thousands of acres we regenerate each year naturally, we plant over thirty million seedlings a year just in our state.

Another student asked that if we recycle, why do we need to cut any trees? I assured him that most foresters and the forest industry are two hundred percent behind recycling. But paper can only be recycled a few times before the cells break down and become useless. This means we always need a fresh source of wood fiber to add to the process. Also, our population is rapidly expanding, and the additional timber resource will be needed to meet the demands for houses, furniture, and other products made from trees.

As the sixth grade sauntered away, the cool ones well in the back, the third graders appeared. I knew a good portion of the kids in this group, and I also knew they were quite spirited. To my surprise, the planting went smoothly. So, after we were done, I asked if anybody would like to see my five-month-old pup. Shrieks of "Yes!" came from the group. I told them to sit down and stay perfectly still as long as they could.

Walking over to my truck, I could see my dog with her nose plastered against the window, drooling. I opened the door, and she headed straight toward the third graders. Watching her, I could certainly see where the saying "the tail that wagged the dog" came from. The kids were able to control themselves for about five seconds before they all jumped up and started chasing Cedar. Cedar was in complete ecstasy. She was whining, the kids where screeching, and the teachers and I were laughing. Cedar flopped on her back trying to maneuver so all thirty pairs of hands could rub her belly. This went on for almost ten minutes when the bell rang announcing recess. As if pre-rehearsed, the kids darted off in unison. Some headed to the slide, swings, the ball field, and some to small groups to talk. Cedar sat there looking very disappointed with a very long tongue hanging out of her mouth.

I herded her back to the truck while she looked over her shoulder toward the playground. I opened the door, and she jumped in the back seat, plopping down with a big sigh.

"Come on, girl, brighten up. Who knows what adventures await us next?" I said in my best kindergarten voice.

I walked over to the planting area to retrieve my gear, and I noticed a group of kids milling about making sure all the trees were planted right. The sight of those kids gave me a feeling of satisfaction that would last a long time.

Just as I was leaving, one young lad ran up to me and asked, "Mr. Forester, why do red pine trees smell like skunks?"

Light My Fire

Michigan, 2001

*I*n my mind, I have always considered myself a romantic. Okay, maybe not a romantic in the classic sense, but a romantic all the same. My idea of what makes a romantic thought, setting, or situation is slightly different than my wife's. That might be a bit of an understatement. Soft music, candlelight, fine conversation, and moonlight are all considered by most females to be romantic. But I say that is too commonplace, lacking in pizzazz, no imagination.

Woodstoves! Now there is a word that conjures up romance. That's something novel, original, and imaginative. Why settle for humdrum when something like a woodstove can bring out the spark in one's life? Like most humans, I have always been entranced and mesmerized by the flicker of the flame. Since the first fire was brought into the cave eons ago, man has sat and stared at a flame. With the soft-yellow glow bouncing off the cave walls, one can imagine Mr. Caveman grunting to Mrs. Cavewoman, "You want to come in and see my etchings on the wall? I have a great drawing of me spearing that woolly beast."

Bookshelves are stuffed with books that tell of men and women sitting around fires. The fire might be a roaring one in the great outdoors, a banked fire in an ancient stone fireplace, or a glowing, potbellied woodstove in some general store. Today, it's an airtight woodstove in someone's living room. The same allure of the flame that attracted Mr. Caveman still charms Twenty-First-Century man.

Since 1978, my wife and I have been heating our homes with a woodstove. We dove into the life of wood heat by necessity. Like many newlyweds, we were flat broke. So, we concluded that one way to make ends meet was to burn wood. In theory, this was a grand idea. But there were some drawbacks. First, as much as I loved physical labor, I did not have the time to cut all the needed firewood by hand. So, we had to buy a chainsaw. Then there was the problem of the woodstove. We didn't have one. So, we had to buy one. Since we could not afford to have wood delivered, we had to find a place to cut it. Being a forester, this was not a problem. But hauling the firewood became an issue. Since my company vehicle was a beat-up jeep, I was only able to bring home a few pieces at a time, all winter. This obviously was not the ideal solution. However, being young (and some might say *foolish*), none of these issues was a big deal. In fact, I could not wait to get into the world of wood heat. To me, the thought of creating our own heat by not using oil, gas, or electricity was and continues to be very gratifying. Our first-ever political bumper sticker that we slapped on our vehicle said, "Split Wood, Not Atoms."

Since our budget did not allow the purchase of the Cadillac of woodstoves, we had to settle for an old cast-iron box stove that I found in the cellar of Ned's hardware store. It was ugly and not very efficient. But it was cheap, and my wife thought it was cute. After some dickering and a promise to buy all of my hardware needs at Ned's, we became woodstove owners.

Just as homes have their own personalities, so do woodstoves. We placed our first woodstove in a blocked-off fireplace. The fireplace was located in an old cabin, which we called home. This home was only temporary, because in the summer it would become the infirmary for the Girl Scout camp that surrounded it. We were the caretakers. Once installed, my wife and I were eager to fire it up and bask in its glow and enjoy our first warm night that fall.

Well, it was not to be. The glow was obscured by a curtain of blue smoke. Cast iron is a very porous material. And this cast-iron stove had been in Ned's cellar for a very, very long time. It became painfully obvious that over the years, our stove had soaked up all sorts of oil, thinners, paints, and who knows what else. Since all the windows were open to let out the smoke, we endured another chilly fall night.

That stove traveled from New Hampshire to Michigan with us, and it tried in vain to heat our next hovel. We were renting a turn-of-the-century, one-room schoolhouse with no insulation and lots of big windows facing northwest. Being the romantic, I would sometimes cook dinner for my young wife. Dressed for dinner in our down coats, we would sit at the table with a candle burning between us. All was well and good, until the wind would blow out the candle and deposit minute particles of snow on our fine cuisine. To its credit, the little box stove was doing its best, turning beet red and roaring like a steam engine. However, no matter how hard it tried, it was the engine that couldn't.

One February evening in 1980, I tried to dance with the little stove with almost disastrous results. I had just watched the USA Hockey team beat the Soviets on our little black-and-white TV and was dancing all over that old schoolhouse.

I tripped on the brick hearth and placed my hand on the stove to stop my fall. *OUCH!* My wife happened to be out of town, so I was sleeping on the floor next to the stove to keep warm. Later that evening, she called. The phone was on my right and stove on my left. The phone rang, I rolled left, stuck out my hand for the phone, and got the hot stove instead. *OUCH AGAIN!!* Perhaps the two beers I had enjoyed earlier were two too many.

In 1981, we moved back to New Hampshire and purchased our first house. We had a trend going, as this house was even older and less insulated than the schoolhouse. I purchased a homemade woodstove thinking, incorrectly, that it would heat our new abode sufficiently. Even experiencing hot flashes and all, my pregnant wife froze. So, the next summer I got an extra job to earn the money to keep mother and young child warm. In the fall, with cash in hand, we purchased a wood furnace for maximum heat. It was hot alright, but it was severely lacking in the charm department. No cuddling up to this baby. She was big, bulky, and in the damp stone cellar. All you could do was stand on a grate to feel its warmth, which was nice but not very romantic.

Several years later, we moved to northern Maine, and you guessed it—the house was even older and less insulated. It had been built in the late 1700s and was fascinating to live in. There was a fireplace in every room, which made it very cozy if there were fires going in each room. If there weren't, it was bloody cold. We purchased yet another woodstove and placed it in the fireplace in the kitchen. The fireplace was huge, and the bricks would heat up and radiate heat for many hours. My wife, two small children, dog, cats, and I would spend hours lying or sitting on the brick hearth to keep warm during those cold Maine days.

In 1985, we again moved back to northern Michigan, bringing that woodstove with us. We decided to build our own home, and in designing it, we were determined to be warm. Consequently, we used lots of insulation, big windows facing south, and positioned our woodstove so it would heat the house evenly. We were successful, and to this day, our friends refer to our house as the hot house. But my family might argue that distinction. When guests arrive, it is usually evening, which means the stove has been burning hot all day. But early in the morn, the scene is slightly different. Or, I should say, the temperature is slightly different. I usually load the stove around nine in the evening, dampening it down so there will still be coals by six in the morning. So, some mornings when the temperature is a bit brisk outside, it is a tad frosty inside, too. Many times, the small hearth in front of the stove would hold two cats, one dog, two kids, my wife, and me, all clamoring for a bit of warmth. Now that the kids are grown and gone, and probably enjoying central heat, there's less competition for the space.

I am not so sure our kids feel the same way I do about woodstoves. I have two memories of them that make me wonder. One is the vision of the two of them sitting at a small child's table placed as close to the woodstove as safety would allow. They both have quilts over them, and they are eating their breakfast to fortify themselves for a long day of school. The second is a picture of my son lying on the hearth in his Ninja Turtle PJs. He is prostrate on the hearth as if he were trying to soak up the heat like a cat.

I am fairly certain the lore of the woodstove evades my children. Woodstoves burn wood. The good news, of course, is that wood does grow on trees. But in my children's eyes, the bad news is that the wood needs to be cut, hauled, split, stacked, and moved again before it becomes heat. I love every aspect of the process. But I have to admit, the thrill of this process probably wore off in the first fifteen minutes for my children. If one did a scientific study to compare the calories burned while preparing a winter's worth of firewood to the BTUs created by the burning of the wood, it would probably be equal. Unfortunately, for my children, I considered the gathering of firewood great sport and family fun to boot. Maybe we will have a discussion of this on Dr. Phil someday.

My job as a forester often has me battling the elements. Consequently, many days my dog and I come home wet and cold and plop down on the warm tile directly in front of the stove. You can't do that with gas, oil, or electric. Of course, there is the occasional smell of scorched wool, skin, and fur. But the risks are well worth it. In addition, this same surface area becomes the perfect clothes dryer. Wet boots, socks, mittens, wool pants, caps, and an occasional pair of long underwear find a place on the warm hearth. After thirty years of marriage, my wife has learned to overlook wet laundry in the parlor. Of course, there is the odd occasion when we have unexpected guests and I have not yet collected my dried attire. Nothing boosts one's standing like having a living room full of wet wool when her college roommate shows up to surprise her. At times like that, I play my green card.

"Hey, it is environmentally friendly, and no global warming from my clothes dryer," I point out.

In addition to our woodstove in the living room, we have an old wood cookstove in the kitchen. On weekends and really cold days, we fire her up as well. Besides the extra heat, we get some added entertainment. During the week, the cats' food bowl is placed on top of the cookstove so we don't have an obese Golden Retriever. Obviously, when the cookstove is in use, the dish goes somewhere else. But each time we light the kitchen stove, we get to witness an aerial expedition that would put the Blue Angels to shame. The cats jump up to eat, encounter heat and flame, somersault in midair, and land on all fours on the floor. It is quite entertaining.

Over the last several years, I have become, in my opinion, master of this cookstove. During the long winter months, weekends are broken up into only a few tasks, which include cross-country skiing, removing snow, keeping the woodstove going, and cross-country skiing. Since the woodstoves are throwing out all of that heat, why not utilize it? So, I have started cooking dinner by throwing a bunch of stuff in a pot and placing it on the woodstove all day. My wife is so kind; she never questions why I thought cucumbers and chicken were a good combo. Or, what might have possessed me to use sweet potatoes as a stock for soup. I guess she is just happy to have a man cook for her. They say a way to a man's heart is through his stomach. That saying goes both ways.

Sometimes there's a miracle, and what I create actually tastes quite good. On these occasions, my wife asks about the ingredients. To me, if it is in the kitchen, pantry, freezer, or frig, it has the potential to be in the dish. The only problem is that when something does taste good, you have no clue how to make it again.

Woodstoves are interesting and add spice to one's life. But mostly they are romantic. This morning, my wife and I shared a small wooden bench placed on the warm tile in front of the stove. The sun had not yet risen, and in silence, we watched the yellow flame dance across the window of the stove. Next to us lay our dog, and curled up behind the stove lay our two cats. We each had a cup of tea, and we leaned against each other for balance and warmth. It is March, and the fire in the stove had been burning since October. A one-match fire, which had lasted six months.

We talked about the kids, discussed the weather, rubbed the dog with our feet, and sipped our tea. It was not a candlelight dinner or a walk on the beach, but it was romantic just the same.

Guys, it's never too late. Take my advice and get a woodstove.

The Coming of Spring

Michigan, 2000

*H*olding my hand up to shade my eyes, I squinted at the torrent before me. Rivers of water were pouring down our driveway, taking away anything in their paths that they could. That included most of the gravel, leaving behind a muddy mess. The source of the water was a five-foot-high snow bank on either side of the drive, which was succumbing to the warm sun. Everywhere else, the snow had melted. But during the course of the winter, these banks grew to resemble the foothills of the Rockies. Consequently, they had become the headwaters for the class-three rapids that normally passed for our driveway.

Such is life in the north, I thought to myself as I slogged down to the mailbox. Parked next to the mailbox were my truck and my wife's Blazer. Even though they were both four-wheel-drives, our muddy driveway would have swallowed them as if they were small sports cars. Our drive is more like a short road. It is almost a quarter-mile in length. In the city, it would probably be lined with dozens of houses and be called "Blissful

Way" or "Lazy Lane." We just call it "The Gauntlet." My wife and I give up washing the vehicles this time of year. If you go slow enough to not dirty up the vehicle, you risk getting stuck.

What a stark contrast it was. Even though winter was going back and forth not knowing if it wanted to leave or stay, the wildflowers were starting to pop their small, delicate heads above the frozen debris of winter. Leaves were lying very flat on the forest floor, having been compressed by the winter snow. Small, green shafts of vegetation were emerging despite the conditions. Winter was losing its grip, and its retreat was welcome by all. Well, by most. Even though the warmth of the sun and the faint smells of spring awoke my senses, I still am a sap for a good old-fashioned snowstorm, which we recently had experienced. After the storm, a clear moonless night followed, revealing stars that jumped out of the sky. The light from the stars made each snowflake glow. But the sight of spring on the offense, shedding winter's overpowering grip, was good, too. Right now, in this woodlot, spring was starting to get the upper hand.

Cedar came out to greet me as I strolled along the path up to the house. She was somewhat confused, because I had asked my wife to keep her in the house for a few minutes while I got the mail. Cedar did not need another bath, and the trip to the mailbox would have surely resulted in the need for one. So, when my wife felt enough time had elapsed, she let the howling beast out. When in doubt, Cedar will greet me as if I had been gone for months. This involves an upper lip curled back, high-pitched whining, and a figure-eight march through my legs. This was cute the first hundred times. But it has become a bit much.

After the greeting, she ran off to find something for me to throw. This was pretty easy, because the snow had uncovered a virtual toy box of things we had tossed for the dog since November and which she had not returned. If, in the greeting process, Cedar happens to be inside, she will grab something and bring it outside. Let me say that in a different way. She is possessed. She absolutely needs to bring something from the inside outside to meet some canine instinct. Consequently, a lot of things go missing. Some examples: slippers, shoes, socks, hundreds of tennis balls, various dog toys, floppy disks, magazines, food wrappers from the trash, firewood stolen from the bin, tops to milk jugs, reading glasses, unopened mail, and even a toothbrush I placed on the counter while I was answering the phone. And now here they were, all uncovered. She was so excited, she kept dropping one item and grabbing another.

One thing was for sure. I knew which spring chore my wife wanted me to do first. We call it Dump Day … spring cleanup. That day was here, and as the day progressed—and the back of the truck filled with debris—it actually started to get warm. Warmth in the spring is a relative term. Where "sunny and forty-two" in the fall would send you inside seeking something hot to drink, the same conditions in the spring will have you looking for the sunblock and thinking about a barbecue.

I walked over to the woodpile to take a break and enjoy the sunshine. Leaning against the pile, I let the warm sun fall on my face. Living above the forty-fifth parallel, one does not experience this for months at a time. So, it felt wonderful. There was not even a hint of a breeze, and every sound was crisp and clear. Circling above were a dozen or more seagulls. Their white bodies were a sharp contrast to the deep blue of the early-spring sky. The squawks and hoots they made were comforting. It was the sound of summer and warm weather. I could almost smell the sand and water. Our house is located on a large hill, from which we can see the eastern end of the Straits of Mackinac, about eight miles away. I could still see ice between the mainland and Bois Blanc Island. But with the arrival of the gulls, I knew the ice would be departing soon.

A hairy woodpecker drummed a steady beat on a dead snag somewhere not too far off. Because of the stillness, it was hard to tell how far away the bird really was. He certainly had rhythm. I was also pleased that it decided to peck on a tree and not our house. Throughout the winter, this woodpecker and I had been at odds over where the best pecking might be. "Woody" felt that the cedar clapboards on the north side of our house were a perfect spot to spend the winter sharpening its pecking skills. I thought any spot besides the clapboards of our house was a better place. Consequently, I spent much of the winter shooing away Woody. This consisted of several tactics, which all failed miserably. I tried throwing snowballs, opening windows, yelling "shoo! away with you," slamming doors, and even using an air horn to scare the living daylights out of anyone or anything within earshot. The bird was not shaken, but my wife had to peel herself off the kitchen floor. (I forgot to warn her about the air horn.) But now, I could picture his red-spotted head slamming into a tree, and all was forgiven. I only slightly hoped it was a very hard tree.

Cedar was becoming bored with me not doing anything constructive. Her hints were pretty obvious. Sticks were hitting me in the back of the head as she wrestled with them, rocks landed in my lap after she spent considerable time digging them up, dirt flew in my face as her backend faced me.

Cedar has one bad trait that really bugs me. She will dig anywhere, anytime. It is not the digging that enthralls her. It is the possibility of finding a rock. She absolutely loves rocks. Period. If you laid a rock and a two-pound steak next to her, I can guarantee she would go for the rock. She constantly has a rock in her mouth. The thought of having to chew my dog's food for her is not very appealing. And I don't know if they make canine dentures.

Then there are the holes she leaves as she satisfies her addiction. Our yard and surrounding acres look like we had been shelled by mortars for a month. Each morning with shovel in hand, I fill in the previous day's artillery barrage. With each hole comes the possibility of a broken leg or ankle. This is just around our house! As a forester's dog, she covers a lot of ground with me in a day. And every spot where we have stopped for more than thirty seconds has a hole to commemorate the occasion. Sir Edmund Hilary could have used her on Everest in 1954.

Picking up a very large stick, I gave it a toss, and Cedar bounded after it. I spent several minutes filling in the holes using my boot as a rake. In the process, I noticed a really strong smell. A musty odor of onions drifted from the forest floor. "Leeks," I said to no one. Digging in the cool soil, I uncovered a group of white leeks about the size of my ring finger. I used to pick them and eat them raw. I don't do that anymore. My stomach and family put a stop to that several years ago. Because they are part of the onion family, leeks have a very strong flavor that stays around for quite a while. Several times in the past, I have filled up my pockets with leeks and presented them to my wife. I would convince her to make leek soup. We found out really quick that it does not take many leeks to make a super-sized portion of leek soup. Strong is a gross understatement.

Cedar returned, hauling her prize. It was not the stick I threw, but a bigger one. She sometimes reminds me of a boat owner—always thinking about getting a bigger one. I hefted this log and heaved it into the field. As soon as I let it go, I was sorry. In my haste to please the beast, I had forgotten about the bluebird boxes, and the stick landed right at the base of one.

Over the past eighteen years, we have tried to coax several pairs of bluebirds to take up residence in our small field. They are a bit on the finicky side, so my stick didn't help convince the birds to stay. They also like their privacy. On the whole, bluebirds are very appreciated by us humans. Unlike some robins, very few bluebirds hang around for the winter. So, their migratory instinct really means it should be spring. But sometimes, as in 1895, a real tragedy occurs when they follow such strong instinct. On their way up north that year, they were caught in a wave of severe weather in the Middle and Gulf States. Thousands of birds perished in the storms and bitter weather, and their frozen bodies were found in outhouses, barns, and along roadsides. Consequently, in those areas, the bluebird was almost exterminated.

But they rebounded . . . as shown by the blue head that peeked out of the box wondering what the big furry thing was doing bumping his house. Cedar recovered the log and placed it at my feet. There she sat, swishing her tail back and forth through last year's matted brown grass, smiling up at me. She had bark hanging out of her mouth, and her chest was covered with dried leaves.

"Cedar," I said. "Since it is spring-cleaning time, what do you think about a bath?"

She suddenly became calm and slinked off into the woods to lie low by the woodpile. Then I said, "You can run, but you cannot hide!"

Then I saw her get up and stroll over to the muddy drive and start digging. She really needed a rock. If you're gonna have to take a bath, you might as well take a rock with you.

Balancing Act

Ontario, 2002

The morning is so quiet that with each stroke, I can hear the water dripping off my paddle. I glance to the right and see a family of Mergansers gliding effortlessly upriver. The mother is in the lead with four or five chicks very close behind. One lone chick is maybe a meter behind the rest and frantically trying to catch the group. Instinctively it knows it needs to be with the group to stay out of harm's way.

The morning mist is gradually lifting its veil to reveal more of the river and countryside. The river changes from steel gray to a gentle green. The mist is moving like a cloud. In some places, it clings to the river. In others, it has lifted, and I can see steep granite cliffs to my left. Perched on the wall of the cliff is one lone spruce tree trying to eke out an existence. A seed probably found its way to a crack in one of the ledges, and there was just enough soil for it to hold on to life. Each time it rains, the crack must fill up, giving the spruce just enough water to maintain life.

At this time in the morning, most of the songbirds are awake and letting the world know it is a wonderful day. I can hear at least six or seven different songs, all different but blending into a morning melody. These birds have migrated from all parts of the hemisphere to this one bend in the river. At this moment, I would not want to be any other place in the world.

Anna, my daughter, is in the bow of the canoe, and she paddles to her left and we slide pass a large boulder. When on a river with lots of current and rapids, the bow person guides the canoe through the perils. The stern paddler keeps the canoe in control and somewhat parallel to the flow of the river. There is a constant balancing act between the two paddlers. Sometimes the bow paddler leans out as far as possible and draws the canoe to a certain position, while the stern paddler is leaning in the opposite direction, bracing. Without this balance of the two paddlers, the canoe will flounder and be in constant danger of flipping. Additionally, if the two paddlers don't communicate and talk about the flow of the river and the best direction to navigate, they end up fighting each other's efforts. And in the end, they end up not communicating at all.

Anna stops paddling and gingerly stands up to get a better view of the river. I brace to stable the canoe as she tries to pick the best line through a set of rapids ahead.

"Dad, this one looks a bit tricky. I think we should scout it," Anna says as she kneels back on her pack.

"Got it," I say as we head to the left bank.

We glide into an eddy next to a line of cedars, and Anna skillfully brings our canoe near the shore. We both get out and secure the bow to one of the trees. I make sure the line is tight. I have had several canoes and kayaks float by as we scouted the river because of poor knots—not a good thing to see when you are deep into the Canadian bush. The rapids turn out to be a bit more than we can handle with a loaded canoe, so we decide to portage our gear and run the rapids empty. We each grab a pack and start up the steep riverbank looking for a portage trail. After a few minutes of struggling through the brush, we come upon it. It is a very worn trail, and it follows the path of least resistance.

"Anna," I say, adjusting the straps of my pack, "Did you know this trail has been used for centuries by people canoeing the river? Many different tribes going and coming to their winter and summer camps have used it, as have the fur traders of the Hudson Bay or the Northwest Companies, and the last hundred years, fishermen and adventurers."

Due to the weight of her pack, Anna replies with a grunt.

After a few minutes of walking on the trail, we come upon an old logging road, which made the walking a lot less dangerous. Portage trails are great, but you are constantly tripping on roots and rocks or slipping in the mud. We follow the old logging road for a quarter of a mile until we are past the rapids. We throw down our packs, and Anna flops down on top of one. We are both tired, and we decide to eat a bit of lunch before we run the rapids.

As Anna eats a lovely meal of prunes and peanuts, she says, "I am sure happy we hit that logging road 'cuz going through the brush was tough."

I nod my head in agreement as I take a swallow of water to wash down the pulp.

We both sit there for a while absorbed in our thoughts. I am thinking how glad I am to be sharing this experience with my daughter. She just completed her first year of college, and it is great to spend time with her.

"What ya thinking?" I probe.

"Well, as I told you before, I really liked my anthropology class, and we spent a lot of time talking about hunters and gatherers. I was just thinking how much the world has changed from the first people who used that portage trail to the latest, which is us. Wow, if those trees along the trail could talk! Just think of all the different languages they have heard and the different cultures they have witnessed," she says, brushing away a mosquito.

"That is amazing," I say. "But it would not be those trees talking; it would be their great grandparents. Just as the voyagers of the past are gone and their ancestors live on, these trees have a life span, too. But I am straying from your point. It is amazing that our world has changed so much," I tell her.

"Yes, dad, your inner forestry self is coming out again," Anna says with a smirk. Having a father as a forester has exposed her to nineteen years of not only seeing the forest through the trees, but also everything large and small in and around those trees.

Gesturing to the vast forest around us, she says, "When do you think this was logged?"

"Well I am sure it has been logged several times, but the last time was maybe ten years ago," I reply.

While tucking the hair back under her bandana, Anna says, "I have so many friends in college who have never experienced anything like this and probably never will. It is a shame, because it is so different from the world they live in."

"Well, we should count ourselves lucky, eh?" I say, removing a fly from my prune.

We both fall silent and ponder our separate thoughts. I lean back against my pack so I can watch the sky. It has turned a most wonderful Canadian blue, with light wisps of high clouds. The rush of the river makes it hard to hear, but I can still hear a woodpecker rapping on a tree looking for some insect to enjoy for lunch. How pleasant this is.

My thoughts start drifting in many different directions but keep coming back to what Anna said. Many people will never experience nature as we get to. In fact, many people really don't have a clue how the natural environment works at all. It is not really their fault. They have grown up in a culture that has drifted from the land to cities, suburbs, and malls. Fewer and fewer people are working on or with the land, and our population is far greater than it was a hundred years ago. What really amazes me is that we can provide millions of North Americans with the forest products they use every day. And yet here we sit surrounded by hundreds of miles of forest. Sustainable forestry seems to be a new term, but foresters have been practicing it for almost a hundred years.

Anna stirs me from my thoughts and says, "Dad, we should probably run the river. We're burning daylight."

"Yes, yes, you're right," I say as I push myself up off the ground. Tired muscles or not, there are more wonders waiting for us around the next bend.

While walking back down the logging trail, I ask, "Anna, I know you have grown up with it, but what would your friends in college think if we told them this area had been harvested in the last ten years?"

Anna glances around at the lush, thick, vegetation and says, "They would not believe it. A lot of them assume the forestry industry is just out to make a buck, and they think harvesting of trees is the work of the devil. Actually, not all of my friends, but many don't understand at all."

"You know, trying to supply the nation with its wood-products needs is a huge balancing act," I say. "Many people feel as your friends do and would like to see harvesting stopped. The main reason is they are misinformed or not informed at all. When I tell people that we are growing nearly forty percent more than we are harvesting each year, they are dumbfounded. And when I tell them the things I do as a forester, they say they hadn't a clue."

Anna spots the portage trail as she ducks under a birch and heads toward the canoe. Close on her heels, I add, "They look surprised when I tell them how we take special care of sensitive areas, strive for good wildlife management, think about the soils and water quality, and try to improve the forest health. We can do all of this while at the same time providing our nation with forest products, healthy forests, clean water, and wilderness areas."

We find the canoe and shove off into the current. Anna hears me grumble, "It's a balancing act, and a darn important one to boot."

Anna looks back over her shoulder and says, "Yes, I know, dad, I will draw to the left and you pry to the right. Geez, this is not the first set of rapids we have run."

"Ah yes, you are right. Sorry."

I don't have the heart to tell her I am not referring to our paddling skills.

Going to Extremes:
"Da Sauna"

Michigan, 2003

I dipped the ladle into the bucket and poured the cold water onto the hot rocks. There was an immediate explosion of steam rising from the stove. I took a second scoop of water and threw it up on the ceiling directly above the stove. This arched stream made a waterfall, creating tiny explosions as the droplets fell onto the stove. Dropping the ladle into the bucket, I climbed up onto the bench and headed to the corner closest to the stove. Feeling the steam's surging heat, I brought my legs to my chest and buried my head between my knees and chest, making it easier to breathe. As the heat rolled past me, I could feel my body relaxing and the sweat starting to pour. The tiny droplets fell from the ceiling at a slower pace, making individual hisses and explosions. These sounds were magnified in this small eight-by-eight room and were mesmerizing.

As the intense heat abated, I lifted my head and leaned back against the cedar-log wall. Directly across from where I sat, I could see the candle flickering through the small window. The frost pattern on the window made the flame dance each time the wind blew. *How pleasant this is*, I thought to myself. The heat soothed the body, the sounds relaxed the mind, and the smell of the wet cedar and wood smoke lodged in your memory forever. This was the magic of our sauna.

Reaching for support against the log wall, I lowered myself off the bench and grabbed the ladle and repeated the process of throwing water on the rocks and ceiling. Again, I crawled back into the corner and was hit with a blast of hot steam. The sauna was particularly hot tonight, and after working outside all day in bitter cold, it felt wonderful. I stretched out on the bench, putting my hands behind my head, and started to drift.

Seeing the candle flicker reminded me of the night many years ago when my family and I were introduced to Sven, the sauna mouse. My young son was sitting in the opposite corner talking to me when suddenly he stopped talking, eyes wide with wonder, and pointed to the wall next to my head. Turning my head, I could see the shadow of a large creature on the log wall. Looking back to the window, I pointed and started laughing. There, on the outside shelf, was a mouse walking back and forth in front of the flame. I instantly named him Sven, and each time we took a sauna, we hoped he would show up. The whole family got into the act. And for several years during our saunas, we would tell "Sven, the sauna mouse" stories, waiting for him to make his grand appearance.

The heat finally got to me, so I climbed off the bench and opened the door. The cold, sub-zero temperature felt just as wonderful as the heat did a few minutes ago. I ran around the corner of the sauna and jumped into the freshly fallen snow. My body sank into about a foot of powder as I rolled down the slight incline. Giving a "whoop," I got to my feet and headed back to the sauna. I crawled back into my corner and felt the rush of the heat. The snow, which had stuck to me, quickly melted into cold streams of water, running down my body. A feeling of a thousand needles pricked my skin as the snow evaporated. My head started to feel light, and a calm feeling came over me. I could sense the stress of the day fade away as the heat started to penetrate. I laid down on the bench, and a complete feeling of relaxation came over me.

According to many ancient cultures of the world, hot and cold help you sort out the body and mind. The idea of using heat and moisture to cleanse and purify the body has been around for thousands of years. Heat bathing was used by the Greeks, Romans, Turks, Russians, Mayans, Japanese, and Native Americans in various forms. Today, when we think of saunas, we think of Finland. In fact, the sauna ritual plays a very important role in the Finnish culture. To the Finns, the sauna is much more than just sitting in a sweatbox. It is a period of physical and mental renewal, a moment for quiet and reflection, and a way of life for an entire culture.

Life was hard in early Scandinavia, and the winters were long. From plentiful woods, the saunas evolved as a way to cleanliness and renewed strength as everyone, young and old, were able to focus on the sauna for periodic escape from the hardships of life. The sauna is so deeply ingrained into the Finnish culture that during World War II, the Finnish army built saunas wherever they were entrenched. Even today, their army uses portable saunas as a normal piece of field equipment.

The heat overcame me again, so I rolled off the bench, opened the door, and waded through the snow to an old hammock, which was stretched between two maples. Most people take their hammocks in when the temperature drops, but we don't. It is a perfect place to relax in the winter. What an odd sight this might have been to a stranger. Me lying in a hammock with snow all around, swaying back and forth, watching the stars as if it were a warm summer's eve. In fact, it was January, and the temperature a minus eight. But the frigid air felt comfortable after the hot sauna. Lying in the hammock, I watched the white smoke rise from the sauna chimney on this windless, starry night. The stars always seem so much bigger and closer on cold nights. The quarter moon and stars were so bright that they cast a shadow of the sauna on the snow. The shadow and the swaying were hypnotic, and I started thinking about the building of the sauna.

In the fall of 1984, we came to Michigan from Maine and purchased forty acres on which to build our home and raise our family. We could not start building until the next spring, so I had some free time on my hands. During the course of the winter, I cut the cedar logs we would need for a sauna. These logs came from an area that had blown down the summer before. I cut each log to the appropriate length, attached a rope, and manhandled them, one log at a time, through the maze of downed trees to a landing area. I would then load them into my pickup truck and transport them home. Once I had all of the logs collected, I had the laborious task of peeling the bark off. This was done with a drawknife. The drawknife is a twelve-inch-long blade with a wooden handle on either end. To remove the bark, you place the knife on the log and draw it toward you. Sounds simple, but believe me, it is not an easy task. Once the logs were free of bark, they were stacked Lincoln-Log style to promote drying.

The first thing I did when the spring thaw came was to build the sauna. I felt an evening of building the sauna would provide some therapy after working all day. Several years later, I did not feel that the metal chimney looked right with the hand-hewed logs, so I built a stone chimney. I selected stones from the stone piles scattered about our forty acres. Early immigrants, who attempted to farm this poor, sandy-yet-rocky soil made these piles. I hoped if I put the stones to good use, the farmers who wrestled them from the earth would not mind.

By now, the cold was too much. So, I dashed back to the sauna. With a splash of water and the hiss of the steam, I was back in my corner. When water is thrown on hot rocks in the sauna, it creates an invisible heat immediately felt as "stinging moisture." This is the essence of the sauna, and the Finns call it "loyly." Sitting in the corner enjoying the "loyly," I started thinking about the early immigrants who had settled our forty acres and who had struggled with those rocks. How ironic that their labors of pulling the rocks from the fields supplied me with materials with which to relax. And as much as they probably worked and cursed getting them out of the way, I was glad to put them to good use these many years later.

Their "folly" became my "loyly."

"Thank you, lads," I mumbled, my head resting comfortably on the cedar bench.

Not a Clear-Cut Issue

Michigan, 2004

*M*r. Colby Drake was not amused when my dog, Cedar, jumped into the truck and put her wet head on his lap. I could tell from his reaction that he was not a dog person. Cedar was not going to hold that against him, however. Nor would I. Of course, even the most ardent canine lover would have a hard time enjoying this wet, somewhat gamey experience.

"Sorry, Mr. Drake. Cedar is a bit on the friendly side. If it gets bothersome, just push her away," I said.

He smiled weakly, tentatively patted her on the head, and said, "Oh, she is fine, I guess."

This is not going well, I thought to myself. First, I almost witnessed a heart attack when I suggested to Mr. Drake that we clear-cut about twenty acres of his forest. Then my dog decided to chase a young deer around Mr. Drake's property. And now, she was using his lap as a pillow for her wet head. No, this was not how I planned things.

Earlier, when I suggested to Mr. Drake that clear-cutting his stand of aspen was the proper forestry technique, I thought he was going to drop dead on the spot. I'm not exaggerating. His eyes bulged out, and the color of his face turned an interesting shade of purple.

"Are you all right?" I had asked.

He took a deep breath and sputtered something like, "You call yourself a forester? I thought you were supposed to protect the forest, not destroy it. I ask for your professional advice, and you tell me to clear-cut! Well, I never . . . ."

I did not get flustered, or even angry. True, my ethics were being questioned. But I had been through this scene many times since graduating from Michigan State University's College of Forestry in 1976. I calmly responded in my best professional voice, "Mr. Drake, if you would permit me to show you some examples of clear-cuts, you may have a different opinion of my professional advice and understand more of what I am suggesting."

So, there we were driving down the road: Cedar with her wet head on Mr. Drake's lap, him thinking I was a crazed forester, and I mentally reviewing my facts about clear-cutting.

Our first stop brought us to a twenty-acre parcel that had been clear-cut the year before. The new aspen shoots had sprouted over the entire area. It looked like nature's version of shag carpet. Out of the corner of my eye, I could see Mr. Drake looking at the clear-cut with guarded caution. He spoke tentatively, "Yes, I would have to be blind not to see the new forest coming up. But why did you have to cut all of the trees?"

"It is rather simple," I stated.

He shot me a look that said something close to, *Don't be so confident, young man.*

Unflustered, I continued.

"This harvested area was very similar to the forest that you currently have on your property. It was made up of over-mature aspen with some red maple and white birch mixed in. Aspen, and these other species, are shade intolerant, which means they need full sunlight to regenerate and grow."

Cedar started making a very low growl. Mr. Drake was a bit undone by the noise, but I knew all Cedar wanted was to be let out of the truck. When I opened the door, she shot by me. Mr. Drake and I exited the truck with less flare and followed Cedar into the harvested area.

Continuing my lecture, "When the soil around the root system of the harvested aspen is heated up by sunlight, as in a clear-cut, dormant buds located on the root system sprout and send up new shoots, which are new aspen trees. The more sunlight that is present, the more abundant the sprouting is. Also, full sunlight encourages fast growth of the sprouts."

"But what would happen if you just thinned out some of the trees and let the other ones grow?" Colby asked.

"Well, not enough sunlight would reach the forest floor," I answered. "Consequently, the regeneration would be very poor. Also, it was a sure bet that all of the trees in this stand were the same age. Aspen stands mature as one unit. That's the way this species has adapted to nature."

Mr. Drake thrust his hands in his pockets, scuffed the ground a bit with his foot, which immediately drew the attention of Cedar, and said, "I am still not convinced clear-cutting the forest is right."

"It is right if the species present requires full sunlight to regenerate. You see the stand of trees on the side of that trail?"

Mr. Drake nodded.

"That is a northern hardwood stand. Two years ago, we did a selective harvest there. Those northern hardwoods do very well in shade. So, we manage that type of forest by harvesting individual trees in the stand," I said.

Where Mr. Drake had earlier scuffed the ground, Cedar had proceeded to dig a hole about a foot deep looking for a rock. I ignored her, but Mr. Drake looked at my canine workmate with distain or puzzlement . . . not sure which.

"Let me try to explain another reason why clear-cutting your aspen stand is sound forest management," I continued. "You told me earlier you love to see wildlife on your property, and those sightings have decreased over the past years. Well, one reason for not seeing much wildlife is the lack of food and cover. Your mature aspen stand offers little of either. The buds that many animals feed on are way out of reach, and the open forest below provides very little cover. Now, of course, you have many types of songbirds and cavity birds using the mature stand. And they are also important. But by managing the forest properly, you can provide all sorts of habitat for many different forms of wildlife."

Mr. Drake and I settled down on a large aspen that had blown over during the last storm. Cedar, having not reached China, bounded over with a stick for Mr. Drake to toss. I wanted to warn him that once he tossed the stick, it would be back on his lap every several seconds. But I was too late.

With the stick tossing game begun, I continued.

"Aspen, because of its ability to sprout from the root system and thus produce a multitude of young aspen saplings from each parent tree, is an extremely valuable species in terms of wildlife habitat," I said.

Mr. Drake's eyes seemed to brighten up a bit at this. I continued.

"Aspen buds provide the bulk food necessary for deer and grouse to survive the long winter months, when most other sources of food are buried in the snow or nonexistent. Other times of the year, the dense cover provided by the young aspen stands provides protection for deer, woodcock, grouse, turkeys, and rabbits. In addition, birds of prey hang out in adjacent stands hoping to get a sight of a future meal."

Mr. Drake made a very simple statement, which I hear often. "But I always hear that clear-cutting is bad for the environment," he said.

"If it is not done in a proper manner and with the proper species, it is wrong. But as you can see before you, clear-cutting was the proper forestry and wildlife practice here. Clear-cutting, like many forest management techniques, is less man's invention than man's imitation of nature. The benefits of clear-cutting are similar to those provided by wildfire and windstorms. Mature trees are removed to make way for a new generation of growth," I said.

I don't know if Mr. Drake was getting tired of tossing Cedar's stick, or I was boring him. He was staring off into the distance.

"I will be the first to admit that clear-cutting is not aesthetically pleasing," I added. "In fact, it's an ugly sight at first, as are the charred remnants of a forest fire or the skeletal remains of an insect infestation. But by harvesting, we are able to utilize the harvested trees for human needs. And soon, the new forest will begin to thrive, and the whole process is started over. Thus, we have the most important natural, renewable resource: trees."

With my dissertation over, we began walking back toward the truck. I could tell that Mr. Drake was thinking very hard about what I had told him and what he had witnessed himself. I knew he was in a dilemma. But leave it to Cedar to break the ice. She came up behind us with about an eight-foot stick, which caught us both behind the knees at the same time. We both stumbled, which I think was her plan. Golden Retrievers don't smile for nothing.

156

Righting myself, I said, "You know, Mr. Drake, you are not alone when it comes to the clear-cut issue. Many people feel the way you do. But my job as a forester is to explain why in some cases clear-cutting is not only the best choice, it is the only choice. Not all harvesting is done by the clear-cut method. It is only one of many forestry techniques used. But with the species we have in this part of Michigan, this type of management ensures the best regeneration of the forest. Believe me, Mr. Drake, the reason clear-cutting is prescribed is for proper forest and wildlife management."

After I opened the door of the truck, Cedar did her familiar antic. She hung her head, pouted, and dragged her feet. But once back in the truck, she immediately gave all of her attention to Mr. Drake in the front seat. Politely, he raised the console so there was a barrier between them. Cedar finally got the hint and lay down.

It was rather silent as we drove back to Mr. Drake's property. Finally, he broke the ice.

"You have shed a new light on an issue I had some pretty strong feelings about, and it is not always comfortable having your beliefs challenged. I now understand why clear-cutting is used, but I have a hard time thinking of my forest flattened."

"I agree. The area will change. But in nature, all living things mature and die. The trees on your property will die if we harvest them or not. What we will be doing is utilizing the mature trees and establishing a new forest at the same time," I said.

We arrived back at Mr. Drake's property, and I shut off the truck. Cedar popped her head up from the back seat, hoping I'd scratch behind her ears . . . which I did.

Turning to Mr. Drake, I said, "You know, the trees on your property have been here for sixty years and are very mature. In some cases, they are over mature, but they probably won't die in the next few months. Why don't you think about what I have told you and what you witnessed today? Also, I would be more than happy to show you more examples of why in some cases clear-cutting is a good thing."

"That sounds reasonable. I am sure I will eventually follow your advice. But I have to let the concept sink in," he said.

As we shook hands outside, he apologized for his rough comments when I suggested clear-cutting. I told him that was usually the response I got. The word "clear-cut" usually does not bring out the best in people.

And then he said something that really surprised me.

"You really have a nice dog—active, but nice."

As if on cue, Cedar dropped a rock on his foot.

We both looked at her, and I said, "Active? Well, that's another way to look at it. One might also use the word obnoxious."

Halfway There

Michigan, 2005

*S*omehow I had turned fifty-one, which meant that I had spent the last year being half a century old. When I was twenty, fifty seemed ancient. When I was thirty, fifty seemed elderly, and at forty, it seemed old. At fifty-one, it seemed to be all about looking back and reminiscing.

Just prior to turning this milestone, I came up with some goals I wanted to achieve during the year. The whole premise was to think about the challenges I set for myself rather than dwelling on the fact I was rapidly turning into an old man. During the course of trying to achieve these lofty goals, I discovered some things about myself and the times we live in.

First and foremost, my assumption that I was rapidly turning into an "old man" was false. That won't be till I am sixty or maybe seventy. Now, the way I look at it, I have only lived half my life (with any luck). Of course, I have had to make some concessions to being half a century. We all do. But on the whole, fifty was not that bad. As with anything in life, attitude is the key. During the quest of my golden-year goals, I had to remind myself to practice what I preached on several occasions. I am very fortunate to coach the girls' varsity high school soccer team. When things sometimes don't go their way, I always tell my team to control the things they can control and don't worry about what they can't.

Guess what? During the course of the year, I realized I can't control getting older, so I don't worry about it. Or at least, I try not to. I would be lying if I said I enjoyed getting older. But, as the saying goes, it certainly beats the alternative.

The goals I set for my fiftieth year seem very normal to me but probably would seem odd to everybody else, except for my wife. We have been dating a very long time, and she has long since given up being surprised by my antics. In the year of my fiftieth, I wanted to climb Mount Washington again, bike as many miles as possible, backpack more of the Canadian shore of Lake Superior, and run another marathon. I accomplished most of my goals and a few more that just kind of fit the fiftieth theme.

When the year started, I was not real impressed with being fifty. But as time progressed, and I was knocking off my goals, my mindset changed. The turning point was when I reached the summit of Mount Washington in New Hampshire. I had passed several younger hikers on my way up. When I reached the top, I wanted to thump my chest like Tarzan and shout, "Hey, look at me, I can still do this." Thankfully, just prior to me making a fool of myself, I had a thought: Yes, I had reached the summit. But I had to give most of the credit to *my support team*. Without the help of aspirin, ibuprofen, glucosamine, three knee braces, gallons of Bengay, buckets of ointments and creams, ice packs, hot tubs, and two hiking poles, I never would have made it. So, I did not thump my chest and yell, I just took in the grand view and counted my blessings that I could still make it to the top.

Many years ago, when I was much younger, I ran my first marathon. For a week afterward, I was very sore. I had to go down the stairs backwards, because the pain in my legs was so exceptional. And every marathon since, I experienced some form of great discomfort. So why was I so surprised when I was still sore four weeks after competing in a marathon this year? And it was only a half marathon—thirteen miles. The answer is very simple. I (like many men) still think I am eighteen. I will probably still be thinking I'm eighteen while getting my Last Rites. During the race, I was running just behind a fellow. I gave it some gas and caught up to him. We were running at a really good clip, which would have made my time far faster than the previous year.

After several miles of this pace, I said to my fellow sprinter, "We are not in the same age group, are we?"

This comment took several seconds, because I had to say it between gasps.

"Dude, I am twenty," he said as he slowly pulled away from me.

Shortly after this exchange, my back started hurting, and my pace became more age-appropriate.

It never will occur to a guy that he physically can't do something. He would never admit that when he was twenty, he could move that couch from a first-floor apartment to the second floor all by himself, so why not now? Or when he is older, maybe he should order some pizza and have several of his friends over to help. That's never an option.

"Sure honey, I can move that two-ton rock out of the front yard."

Next stop? ER.

The biking on my list of goals was far more pleasant, because it was aspirin-free. I took several long trips through many wonderful parts of northern Michigan. On several occasions, I met my family and we swam and spent the day at the beach as we used to. On these long bike rides, I would listen to public radio on my Walkman and thoroughly enjoy the scenery, music, and commentary. On my second long biking trip, I realized I had been listening to some of the same NPR programs for more than twenty-five years. At least, I had good company in this age thing.

I also had time to ponder the more exciting (foolish) biking trips. One time I was biking from Cheboygan to Mio, and I got sideswiped by a Winnebago. I almost bought the farm on that one. Amazingly, I had no broken bones, but I looked like a piece of skinless chicken from stem to stern. Winnebago 1, biker 0. That one put a scare in my wife. So, I was grounded from biking on the main highways. But I got around that edict by getting a mountain bike, which came with a whole new set of experiences and mishaps.

My canoeing buddies think my wife is a saint, because she puts up with me and all of my escapades. Quite frankly, I would have to agree. In the old days, whenever we had to travel some-where, I would always interject, "Hey, I could ride my bike and meet you there." The distance did not matter. In fact, the greater the mileage, the better. Need to go to the city for supplies? No problem. I would hail, "See ya in Portland," as I wheeled out the driveway. This would leave my wife the chore of driving the ninety miles by herself with a fidgety child. But all of this came to a halt one summer day in the middle of Quebec. We were driving to Michigan from Maine with two very small children. I convinced my wife to drop me off along the highway, drive ten miles ahead, and wait for me. So, I ran the ten miles. But when I caught up to my "happy" family, I was greeted with two wailing children and a wife intent on murder.

I guess the sight of mother leaving father along the highway was quite traumatizing to our offspring. They'd been screaming for over an hour for mommy to "go back and find daddy!"

Maturity does have its upside. While on the annual backpacking trip along the Canadian coast of Lake Superior, I finally had the sense to come in out of the rain. The trail is located right on the shoulder of the coast, which means you hike over rock-strewn beaches, up hundred foot cliffs, and over boulders the size of houses. It is a very rough trail with few places to pitch a tent.

The second day on the trail, when the western horizon of Superior looked as black as a tire fire, I made a mature judgment. It was late in the afternoon, and we had at least two hours of hiking ahead of us along the rugged, exposed shoreline. Along with my son, I had two other lads in my charge. I was certain their parents were counting on my good judgment.

"Lads, we are heading to safer ground. Trip's over," I said as I turned to retrace our steps.

My son was shocked at this announcement, and his expression said it all—my dad is turning around? It was a proud moment for me. I was showing signs of maturity and wisdom. Of course, the next day, I chided myself for being such a wimp. But later, I did feel wiser when I heard that the storm had kept the Canadian Coast Guard busy throughout the night.

The year wasn't all activity, of course. I made some profound observations and pondered several unanswered questions.

Why does hair disappear on desirable parts of the body to reappear as tufts in the most unlikely spots?

Why, when I have at least fifteen pairs of reading glasses, do I never have a pair of reading glasses handy?

And who in the world came up with the idea that at age fifty, one needs to start seeing a family physician? Even though

I now have a very good family doctor, I was content to have the emergency room docs and orthopedic surgeons put me back together for the first forty-nine years of my life. But, oh no! Now you have to have regular checkups. And the first order of business was an eye opener. When we were young, my brother and I loved watching World War II movies. We could not get enough of the action. One of our favorites was "Up Periscope." But not anymore. The term has a new meaning since I turned fifty. Who thought up that test?

My fiftieth year also taught me that memory is a curious beast. Just when we need it the most, it starts to take a hiatus on us. Short-term memory starts to go like everything else. I could be working on a project upstairs and decide I need a particular tool. I trot down to the workshop and stand before my workbench and stare. Not only did I forget which tool I needed, I am not even sure why I came downstairs. Thankfully, some tool or something will usually jog my memory, and I will be reminded that I came down for the Phillips screwdriver. "Ah yes, how could I have forgotten?" Moron.

Another interesting thing happened during my fiftieth year: My dad moved into our bathroom. Every time I look into the mirror, he is staring back at me. I love my dad dearly. But why has his image taken up residence in our bathroom mirror? And we might have a problem brewing. He is sharing our bathroom mirror with my mother-in-law.

But I have come to a conclusion about this half-century thing. There is an upside to living on the cusp. It is all about acting your age. When I feel like it, I can live on the edge with Generation X. Afterward, I can share the doctor's waiting room with my fellow Baby Boomers.

Not acting my age is a good thing.

Nature's March Madness

Michigan, 2002

*W*hat a morning it was! The sky was clear, the snow firm, and the temperature a balmy twenty degrees. I had a very pleasant feeling that this was going to be a perfect day to walk in the bush. What a way to get your work done. Sometimes I can't believe how lucky I am to have picked the profession of forestry. And on that day, I am sure my new companion, Cedar, was equally glad. In fact, out of ten Golden Retriever pups in her litter, she was the lucky one. I can't imagine this bundle of wired nerves and fur sitting quietly inside all day waiting for the master to return. Yes, we were both very lucky.

I pulled into an area between a couple of large snowbanks where I would leave the truck for the day. As soon as the truck rolled to a stop, Cedar started whining. She wanted out, and she wanted out now. Being only twelve weeks old, she had not yet learned the concept of patience. As soon as I let her out, she scampered up the closest snowbank and started yapping at me.

I collected all of the tools I would need for the day's tasks and stuck them into my cruiser's vest. This vest was developed by the Filson Company in the early 1900s and has been worn by foresters ever since. It is a large vest usually made of rugged material such as canvas. There are big pockets to store your compass, notebooks, flagging, and other forestry items. Also, there is a huge pocket in the back, which acts as a backpack. A few weeks earlier, when Cedar was very small, she spent many hours asleep in this pocket while I walked. Into this pocket I stuffed my wool coat, extra gloves, and my lunch.

I planned on mapping and cruising over three hundred acres, which would take me the better part of the day. I looked at my snowshoes and tried to calculate if I would need them. We had recently experienced some thaws followed by a couple of cold days. This melting and freezing had made the snow pack very firm. If the temperature stayed low and the sun did not get too warm, I would be able to stay on top of the snow all day. I would prefer this to wearing snowshoes. Snowshoeing is all well and good for the first three months of winter. But you quickly learn that not having to wear them is far more enjoyable and easier on your knees. I decided to live on the edge and left my shoes in the truck.

Setting my compass to the correct bearing, I headed out to face the day's challenges. Cedar was leaping and bounding in front of me with excitement that only a puppy can display. She had not yet learned to stay out from under foot, so I was constantly stepping on her. An old, brown leaf drifted by her little nose, and she bounded off after it. I gave a whistle and called her, and to my surprise, she headed back to me. Watching her wobble toward me, I would have sworn she was smiling. And why not? She had a lot to smile about, and so did I for that matter. Late winter is my favorite time of year.

During the next few hours, I traversed many beautiful acres.

Without the burdensome snowshoes, I was really flying across the snow. There was about two feet of snow on the ground, which covered all of the brush, downed trees, and many other obstacles. This snow pack made the walking almost perfect, and the traveling was easy. Around midday, Cedar was starting to show signs that she was in need of a puppy nap. So, I found a nice spot for us to stop and take a lunch break. I pulled off my cruiser's vest and removed my coat from the back pocket, placing it on the snow next to a large maple tree. Then I removed my lunch and notebook. I turned to retrieve my coat, but it was too late. Cedar was already curled up in it, fast asleep. She had just walked for four hours, and I was not about to wake her. I figured the sun was warm enough that I could muddle through without the coat.

I placed the vest on the snow next to Cedar and sat upon it using the tree as a back support. As I ate my lunch, I had a perfect view of a snow-laden valley that glowed under the bright sun. The snow, which still remained lodged in the tops of the balsam trees, reflected the sun in searchlight patterns. After a while, I followed Cedar's lead and leaned back against the maple and closed my eyes, feeling the warm sun on my face.

"Man, I love this time of year," I said out loud.

Most people try to flee to warmer climates in late winter and early spring, but I would not want to be anywhere else. Relaxing against the tree, I started thinking of all of the things I like about March in the North. Chickadees were the first thing to come to mind. During the long winter months, they hang around while most other birds head south. In the early spring, their chick-a-dee-dee song is about the only one you hear. Also, they are usually the only birds I can get to land on my shoulder and feed a portion of my lunch. This used to drive

167

my old dog, Prairie, nuts because she felt she was entitled to those meager rations.

I suppose I like the warm sunshine in March as well. After a cold winter, the reflection of the sun off the snow is welcome. Because of the warmth, the snow starts to thaw on the south-facing slopes. This also allows the earth to thaw. Consequently, you can smell the earth for the first time in many months. Small brooks start to fill with the spring run-off, creating beauty and sometimes havoc. Writing my notes in the bush becomes easier because I don't need to wear my mittens. And I hear one of my favorite sounds of spring: the sound of sap dripping into buckets. My fondest memories of March are the years I worked in Vermont. Everywhere you looked, the maples were tapped. On street corners, in backyards, along roadways, and every wood lot in the state. All adding to the drip, drip, drip, on a warm March day.

But I really think the reason I enjoy March so much is the combination of these things—snow, the sound of birds, and the swelling of rivers. Only in March can I enjoy the snow while at the same time hear sounds of life again in the bush. In addition, I, and a close group of friends, can take advantage of the swelling rivers to paddle our kayaks and canoes.

I had half dosed off when I heard another sound of life in the bush. Cedar was awake and was trying desperately to tear the wrapper off my sandwich. I countered with a "NO!" and retrieved my somewhat mangled sandwich. I offered her a small dog biscuit from the pocket of my wool pants, and she was content. Thankfully.

Even with my sunglasses on, I had to squint from the glare of the sun and snow. The surface of the snow was so bright that I felt like I was on an expedition to Everest. And you don't have to be in Tibet to feel the irritation of snow blindness. The feeling of sand in your eyes is the first warning sign.

Out of the corner of my eye, I saw Cedar take off after something. Maybe a small leaf; it did not matter. It was obvious she was well rested and ready to go.

Thus far the day was going as planned. I was now roughly two miles from my truck and would work my way back.

Piece of cake, I thought, repacking my vest. *I will have this job knocked off in no time.*

I set my compass and took my first step to the east. To my dismay, I broke through the snow right up to my middle thigh. Another step and the same. While I had been sitting there thinking how much I enjoyed the sunshine in March, it had turned on me. The sun had warmed the surface of the snow enough so that it would no longer support my weight.

"You bloody fool," I said to myself with each struggling step. "Sure, you wanted to 'live on the edge.' Well, you're going to be on the edge of exhaustion by the time you reach the truck."

It was not the first time I had made this mistake. Once, while working in Maine, I had done something similar. That time, the snow was well over my waist, and it was a struggle to make it out by dark. That event actually made me realize I could get into serious trouble in this profession. After that, I got into the habit of strapping my shoes on my back when in doubt. But today I had been lured into a laziness by the beauty of the March sun. My own "March Madness."

I was really struggling, but my companion was having a ball. She was scampering here and there just checking things out. I think she could sense I was unable to control her scampering, and she took complete advantage.

After an hour, I pulled out my aerial photo to check my progress. I was in the middle of a small opening with a large white pine roughly in the middle. After much squinting, I was able to pinpoint the opening on the photo. I shoved the photo back into my vest and sat down in the snow in disgust. The photo revealed I had only traveled about a quarter of a mile. Watching Cedar explore, I pondered my luck. I could not believe that the conditions had changed so rapidly. I went from complete bliss to pure drudgery in less than an hour. But that is the life of a forester. One minute you are on top of the world enjoying a beautiful sight and the next you are in snow up to your waist.

After a few minutes of much needed rest, I was off. Now Cedar was carrying something indistinguishable. I was not going to even bother. Whatever it was, it had to be frozen. I stopped several times to check my progress on the photo, and each time I was disappointed. But, finally, after almost four hours, I reached my truck. To add salt to the wound, the first thing I saw was my snowshoes propped up in the back. This time I had finally learned my lesson.

"Never leave the shoes behind," I grumbled to myself. Strapped to the back, they are a bit uncomfortable. But nothing like the four hours of torture I had just experienced.

Driving home, I kept thinking how beautiful the day had been prior to lunch. In fact, with the warm sun coming in the window and me being so tired, my reflections started to put me to sleep. But I was saved. Once again, I heard the sounds of life. Glancing behind me, I saw Cedar fast asleep. But her legs were moving as if she were still scampering, and she was sighing little puppy noises.

Smiling, I turned my attention back to the road. Even with the unexpected workout, it had been a good day.

The Dog Days of Autumn

Michigan, 2003

*A*s I crested the hill, I could see the whole river valley below me. There lay the effects of the changing seasons. A few short weeks ago, this valley was lush with as many shades of green as summer could muster. Now, it was as if Mother Nature had painted a giant earth-tone mural across the horizon. The valley was filled with reds, yellows, oranges, and browns. This was a sight to behold. I knew that in scientific terms, the leaves changed colors because the days are shorter, and the growing season has come to an end. Chlorophyll, which is green and helps in the photosynthesis, is present in the leaves during the spring and summer. As the growing season winds down, the chlorophyll breaks down, leaving the leaves their natural color. Also, this natural color depends on how much moisture and nutrients the trees received during the past growing season. But that's rather boring, and I prefer to think that Mother Nature has a bit of the artist in her. Looking down at the spectacular view before me, I knew I was seeing her artistic flare.

Slowly, I wound my way down the valley to my destination.

171

I was to meet two landowners, Don and his wife, Anne, and I was running a bit late. Running a bit late is pretty common for foresters, because you never know how long it will take to do your job. Will you get stuck in some mudhole? Will your snow-shoe break? Is the forest floor covered with brush, so it takes twice as long to walk anywhere?

As I turned into the drive, a pair of dogs ran out to greet me. One was a Basset Hound, with ears dragging on the ground. The other was a Border Collie who bounded here, there, and everywhere. As my truck rolled to a stop, my dog, Cedar, rose from her seat behind me. When she noticed the Basset and Border Collie circling the truck, she became extremely excited. Opening the door was a bit difficult, as Cedar wanted out and the other two wanted in. It was like a scene out of an old Buster Keaton movie. I would open the door, and my dog would try to get out, but the door would close from the weight of the dogs trying to get in.

Through the dog noises, I could hear a female voice yelling, "Nigel! Bailey! Come!" Looking up from the canine trio, I saw Anne rounding the corner of the barn. She was carrying a small ax, which one might use for splitting kindling.

"Did you see it?" she exclaimed.

"Uhh, see what, Anne?" I answered.

"The sign, the sign!" pointing to the end of the road with her ax.

I was so busy trying to dodge Nigel and Bailey that I hadn't noticed the sign. But, there at the end of the drive, was the familiar green and white Tree Farm sign.

"Very nice location, and anyone traveling the road will see it," I said.

Anne beamed with pride and nodded her head in agreement.

172

Anne tugged at my arm, and I followed her through the garden toward a sputtering noise made by an old tractor. There was Don, pipe in mouth, floppy wool red cap on his head, with his hands on the throttle of an old John Deer tractor. A stack of firewood sat next to the bucksaw, which was powered by the tractor. The Basset, Border Collie, and Golden Retriever darted in front of his tractor, giving him quite a start. Don jumped, which caused him to push the throttle forward, and the tractor stalled.

"You dogs! You scared the living tar out of me," he bellowed.

Anne made a coughing noise as if to say, "please don't swear, husband, we have company."

Don looked in our direction, retrieved his pipe, and gave me a warm grin. Trotting over, he said, "Anne said you might be stopping by. Good to see you, young man."

It is always nice to be called young man, especially when you are getting close to fifty. Pumping my hand, I noticed his grip had not softened much since we first met.

Five years earlier, I had received a call from Don wanting some forestry advice and some information about the Tree Farm program. Meeting with Don and Anne around their kitchen table was quite a treat. It was almost like I had traveled back fifty years. They were recently retired and had moved back north to Don's family farm. The furnishings, dishes, cookstove, and appliances had not changed in decades. They were friendly, energetic, and very interested in forest management.

During that first visit, I had explained about the Tree Farm program, which had been started in 1941 by the nation's wood-using industries. The goal was to promote the growing of renewable forest resources on private lands, while at the same time protecting environmental benefits and increasing the public's understanding of a productive forest. The program has since grown to over 64,000 landowners nationwide linked by a common desire to manage their forests effectively.

Of all of the timber harvested in the United States, fifty-eight percent comes from private lands. Tree Farmers help play a very important role in keeping our nation supplied with its wood-product needs. In addition, these Tree Farmers play a valuable role in providing wildlife habitat, watershed protection, and recreational opportunities. I told Don and Anne that to qualify, they had to have a minimum of ten acres and a desire to manage their forest properly. And, as they say, "the rest is history."

Pulling myself back to the present, Anne said, "Follow me." Anne is a wee bit of a lady, but she has a way of capturing the moment whatever that moment might be. So, I followed. Over her shoulder I heard, "We have a lot to show you." And indeed, they did. I followed Anne down an old cow path that led into their maple sugar bush. Don was close on my heels, explaining which trees he had tapped, which gave the most sap, and the stump where he had removed a tree for firewood. Anne led us out of the sugar bush and across a ten-acre field that had been planted to red pine. The soil in this field was very poor, as Don's grandfather had found out. So, these two decided to plant red pine, which does very well in the poor, sandy soil this field had to offer. Looking at the young pines, I was impressed. Their own four hands had planted all of these acres of trees.

As we marched across the field, I had a vision of what we must look like. Short, wiry Anne with her head down in the lead. Me, in the middle, wearing my cruiser's vest and hard-hat. And Don right behind, cap pulled low, leaving a trail of pipe smoke. Bailey was bounding from one side of the field to the other, Cedar was prancing in front of Anne, with her tail swishing the tall grass. Nigel, the long-eared, droopy-eyed Basset was bringing up the rear with his head held high. If not, he would be constantly tripping on his ears. The thought of this unusual entourage brought a smile to my face.

Anne led us into an aspen clear-cut that was harvested four years ago. "Don and I were very hesitant about doing the clear-cut. But you were right. The forest came back like gangbusters. And I now see that aspen does need full sunlight to regenerate. Look at all of those young trees sprouting from the roots! It also created lots of food for the wildlife," she said as if it had been all her idea.

Finally, our merry band ended up in a northern hardwood stand. Don and Anne had been selectively harvesting maple, ash, and beech out of this stand to use in their two woodstoves. It looked wonderful, and I told them so. Don asked: "When do you think we will be ready to harvest some of these larger trees for lumber?"

"Well, by thinning out the poorer trees for firewood, you have allowed the better trees to acquire more food, sun, and water. I think in about five years we should look at a commercial harvest," I answered.

Don and Anne love to cross-country ski and hike on their property. So, located throughout their property, they have built several benches on which to sit, rest, and enjoy their handiwork. One such bench was located nearby, and we took advantage of it.

Don and Anne sat on the bench shoulder to shoulder and holding hands. I could only envision this same sight fifty years earlier when Don was going off to war. I sat across from them with my back leaning against a large maple. Nigel came over and was lying next to me. I could not help myself; I kept tugging on those big floppy ears. I assumed he liked it because he stayed. Looking at the couple across from me, it was obvious they were still in love after all of these years. And that they took a lot of pride in their property. I relayed this to them, and they were quick to agree on the property part but were kind of shy about the two of them. It was funny to see an old married couple still blush.

Then Anne said, "Remember the three P's?" I obviously looked puzzled, because she said, "The first day we ever met you, young man, you said Tree Farmers manage their forest for the three P's."

I nodded and she recited them for me.

"Pride: As a Tree Farmer, we will find great pleasure and satisfaction in improving our forest and being a concerned conservationist, and we have.

"Profit: If harvesting occurs, we will receive income, which we have not yet, but our children and grandchildren will benefit from our sound forest management."

Don butted in: "Don't forget about the maple syrup and firewood, that's a profit."

"Yes, Don, you are correct," Anne said and continued.

"Pleasure: We enjoy our forest either through working in it or just viewing the wildlife and scenery."

"Well, Anne, I must admit I have never heard the three Ps repeated back to me. You and Don took those Ps to heart and have done a right smart job of it," I said, trying to tie Nigel's ears in a knot. Anne leaned against Don and beamed with pride, while Don let out a puff of smoke in agreement.

Nigel, not happy with my knot, strolled off and plunked down next to Cedar and Bailey. I pointed to the trio, and Anne and I laughed. All three dogs were lying down in a row facing us. Their heads were resting on their paws, and their droopy eyes were staring at us. All three expressions were saying the same thing, "Boring! When are we going to do something besides sit here?" Cedar's expression was doubly entertaining, because one of Nigel's big floppy ears was covering her nose like a blanket.

Don chuckled at the dogs, letting out a big puff of smoke, and said, "Just look at those three Ds. Why, they are Devoted, Delightful, Diligent dogs!"

The Note

Michigan, 2012

*U*p to this point, it had been a perfect day, which was very rare this fall. Rainy and cold had been the norm. So, the blue skies and balmy forty degrees were a treat. I opened the truck door to let Cedar into the back. Actually, coaxing would be a better term. After spending hours sniffing, running, jumping, chewing, roaming, and sometimes rolling, she had no desire to jump in the truck for a boring ride. But she finally got in, did several circles around the bed I have for her, plopped down, and let out a long, mournful sigh. I patted her on the head and assured her there were no snakes in the truck, so she could cut out the circling.

I grabbed the handle on the truck's ceiling and hoisted myself up onto the driver's seat. Being somewhat vertically challenged, this task gave me a full upper body workout. I started the truck, turned on the heater, and tuned in the public radio station looking for some soothing symphonic music knowing I needed it. I took the note from the pocket of my wool coat, along with several twigs, a piece of survey tape, and some sort of bone I had wrestled out of Cedar's mouth. I had found the note underneath the wiper blade when I had returned to the truck. I unfolded the note and began to read it again. I was struck by how the person who wrote the note, in such delicate hand, could display so much venom and anger. The message, which was scrolled on an old envelope, called me every name in the book and insulted my profession as well. It was obvious from the tone of the note that the author was adamantly against any form of timber harvesting. I stuffed the note back in my pocket, put the truck in gear, and gunned it. I realized my anger when I heard the tires spinning and let off on the gas.

My next job location was about an hour away, and this gave me plenty of time to stew. I knew I should not get upset about the note. But it was just frustrating for me to spend my whole adult life promoting sound forest management and to have a majority of the public remain clueless.

In a loud voice, I said, "And where do you think the bloody paper came from to write this thoughtful note?" With this outburst, Cedar popped up between the seats. "Sorry girl, just venting a bit," I said, rubbing behind her ear. This had the desired effect on both of us.

A few minutes later, I came to a rural intersection and I saw something waddling toward me down the road. I slowly crept forward, realizing it was a very small, fluffy dog. The off-white ball of fur looked really out of place in this land of hounds, beagles, and mutts, so I stopped to make sure it was not lost or had strayed. I got out and bent down to check to see if the tags would give me a clue of the little canine's residence. Not only were there no tags, there was no collar.

"Darn," I said, "I just became involved."

Picking up the pooch, I was surprised at how light it was. I think it was lighter than Cedar was at birth. The thought of Cedar made me turn around just in time to see her jump from her berth into the driver's seat. The bundle in my hand also witnessed this and began to squirm.

"It's okay, Fluffy. She would not hurt a flea," I said, wondering how many Fluffy was carrying. I also realized I had just given my wayward stray a name. I told Cedar to get in the back, and I placed Fluffy in the passenger seat. Cedar poked her head over the console to examine her new friend riding "shotgun." The two were sniffing each other's noses, and I had to chuckle. Fluffy was standing on the console next to Cedar's head, and the head was as big as the little dog. I let those two focus on passing down family recipes as I drove down the road toward the nearest house.

An hour later, Fluffy had settled in quite nicely, all snuggled up in one of my wool shirts riding "shotgun" because nobody had claimed her. For the short term, I hoped, I was the proud owner of a Shih Tzu. This I had learned from one of the neighbors I had tried to pawn her off on. Something else I learned as I went from house to house, Fluffy did not smell very good. In addition, she only had one eye. At one of the houses, an elderly lady had cooed over Fluffy while brushing the fur off the pup's face. She jerked her head back and said, "The poor little darling has only one eye." Not sure what she meant, I picked up the mop of fur hanging in front of Fluffy's eyes. Sure enough, only one eye peered back at me.

I pulled into a two track and parked the truck. Cedar knew the drill and was alert and ready to explore the next bit of forest. I glanced over at my new traveling companion buried deep into my wool shirt. She was sound asleep, and I had to wonder how long she had been searching for her family. Well, for now, she was going to continue to be a lost soul, because I had work to do. I would try to find her home later. The immediate question was, what do I do with her now? Looking at her, it became obvious: let her sleep. She may very well have felt some sort of security snuggled up in my shirt. I let Cedar out, rolled down my window (for such a small thing, Fluffy sure stunk), and headed into the bush.

Earlier in the week, I had met the owner of this particular forest, and we had agreed that his forest would be healthier and more productive if we removed some of the over-mature, suppressed, deformed, and diseased trees. So, my forestry task at hand was to determine which trees should be removed and then mark them to be harvested later. This is a very thoughtful process, which involves looking at each individual tree.

As I walked through the forest examining the trees, I started to think about the note. Here I was in a tranquil setting and my blood pressure started to rise. "Settle down, lad," I mumbled to myself, "getting all worked up does not help." As I walked and marked, it dawned on me why this particular note, with all of its negative comments about harvesting trees, bothered me so much. The general public thinks that harvesting trees is a bad thing when in fact trees are the answer to many of our environmental problems. Without a question, wood is the most renewable material to build and maintain our civilization. And has been since the beginning of time. There are about seven billion of us inhabiting this wonderful planet. Combined, we use four billion tons of wood per year. In most cases, as soon as a tree is harvested, a new tree is there to take its place. This occurs either by natural regeneration or by planting. If plastic, metal, or concrete is used, the material would come from a nonrenewable source. Every time we use a two-by-four from a North American forest, we can be assured a new tree is growing somewhere to take its place. This is not the case with iron ore, aluminum, oil, coal, or any other resource. The part that really bugs me is the person who wrote the nasty note is one of the millions of people using wood every day. To my way of thinking, if we are the users of trees, we should also be good stewards. This includes managing our forest locally, not wanting our forest left alone, and using someone else's to supply our needs. That is hypocritical in the extreme.

In addition, I want biodiversity. I want all kinds of wildlife to flourish. I work to protect sensitive areas. I want clear, clean water, and most importantly, I want plentiful, healthy forests for my great grandchildren to use and enjoy. In short, every day I go to work, I am an environmentalist. Nevertheless, I and the other professionals who manage our natural resources are most often considered the guys in black hats. This really sticks in my craw.

After several hours of marking and seething, I completed the task and returned to the truck. I glanced inside expecting to see Fluffy snuggled up in my sweater. What I saw was nothing. Bewildered, I opened the door and started looking everywhere and under everything. As a last resort, I even looked in the console. She was gone! Vanished! Not a trace. The only thing she could have possibly done was jump out the window. That seemed highly unlikely, considering she would have had to leap up to get out the window. Nevertheless, that was the only plausible excuse for my AWOL Shih Tzu.

"Great," I said to myself, "here I try to be a Good Samaritan and I end up dumping this two-pound pooch off in the bush where she will not last a night."

With that thought still in my head, I saw Cedar make a beeline for a blown-over tree about twenty feet in front of me. Out from behind the upturned stump, with head held high, strutted Fluffy with Cedar in quick pursuit. The bundle of fur pranced over to me, sat down at my feet, and proceeded to bark at me. Cedar sat down next to her and just kept looking from Fluffy to me as if to say, "Want me to translate?" I think the little beast was either upset about being left alone in a strange truck, or the fall out of the truck. Picking her up, I was happy to find she looked no worse for the wear.

I put Fluffy back on my sweater, and Cedar jumped in behind my seat. When I went to get into my seat, I noticed my new companion was sitting on the console as if she were bred for it. "Hold on, it might be a bumpy ride," I said, scratching her behind the ear. The bumpy ride resulted in her sitting on my lap most of the trip enduring a jealous eye from Cedar.

Earlier, when I had come up empty handed in finding Fluffy's home, I had put a call in to the Humane Society. To my relief, there was a message on my cell phone saying they might know who Fluffy's owners were. A quick phone call back and I had a potential address, which was about three miles from where I had found her. We had a bit of a drive, so I just let Fluffy stay on my lap, pretty certain this was as close I would ever come to having a lapdog. With the console now free, Cedar placed her large head on it and stared at the Shih Tzu on my lap.

"Come on girl, we can show a little compassion. She has had a rough go of it," I said. Cedar was not buying a word of it.

I pulled into the driveway, parked the truck, and got out holding my bundle in my arms. I was just about to knock on the door when it flew open. A large man grabbed Fluffy from my arms, turned, and handed it to a shrieking little girl. The rest of the girl's family was behind her all smiling and trying to pet the returned household icon. I was smiling too. You'd have to have a heart of stone not to be moved by the scene.

The large man turned to me and said, "Where did you find Buck?"

"Buck? Who is Buck?" I said, a little confused.

"Why, that's Buck," he said, pointing at the dog in the girl's arms.

"Buck! Her name is Buck?" I said, surprised.

"Well, she is a he and yes, his name is Buck."

It finally dawned on me that Fluffy's real name was Buck, and I started to laugh. When questioned, I told the family of Buck's rescue, prudently leaving out the leap from the window. They in turn told me Buck had been gone for four days and his owner, the girl now smothering him, was completely despondent. Having lost a dog before, I could really relate. It is a horrible feeling. As I left, I bent down to give Fluffy one last scratch behind the ear; the little girl smiled at me. I suggested Fluffy might want a bath. She pinched her nose and nodded in agreement.

Driving home, I glanced over at my wadded-up sweater lying on the passenger's seat. Next to it was the crumpled-up note. It was then I realized I had wasted a good part of the afternoon stewing over that thing. I took it and pitched it over my shoulder into the backseat. Cedar came up with a start after it landed on her snout.

"Sorry girl, didn't mean to hit you," I said, rubbing her head.

Cedar forlornly looked at my sweater on the passenger seat. As a rule, I don't allow her up front because she usually gets the seat dirty or full of burrs. But her look was rather pitiful.

"All right girl, you can ride shotgun the rest of the way," I said, patting the seat.

Cedar did not hesitate as she leaped over the console. She did a few circles on the sweater and plopped down with a sigh. Her big body hung over the seat, completely covering the sweater. I laughed at the contrast.

"Glad to have known you, 'Fluffy,'" I happily said.

Sometime after I had returned Buck, I got a note in the mail. At first, I was puzzled, then I remembered I had given the father my business card. Sarah, Buck's owner, wrote the note thanking me for finding her dog. Enclosed was a photo with Sarah holding Buck. Each was sporting pigtails, and Buck's one eye was looking right at me. I saved *that* note.

Latitude Attitude

Michigan, 2007

*R*ecently my wife and I attended a wedding in the suburbs of a large metropolitan city. When we first got the invitation, I was pleased that our old friends from college had included us in their daughter's special day. But as the date loomed closer, I was having second thoughts. Several weeks prior to the big day, my wife asked the dreaded question.

"What are you wearing to the wedding?"

Oh boy, here it comes: the suit thing again.

"Ah, I guess I had not given it much thought," I replied sheepishly. Actually, I had just lied to my wife. I had not given it any thought.

"Well, I have, and I think it is time for a new suit," she said.

"What's wrong with my old one?" I questioned.

"Let's see, for starters you bought it for our wedding in 1975," she said, holding up one finger.

"So?" I countered (great comeback).

With two fingers held high, she added, "Do you really want to look like Isaac Hayes or one of the Temptations?"

"Okay, so the lapels are a bit wide, and the color is a tad tacky. But it still fits, kind of," I said, knowing I did not have a bell-bottomed leg to stand on.

As a forester, most of my clothes serve the dual purpose of being rugged and keeping me warm and dry. Hence, my wardrobe consists of a lot of wool, canvas, and flannel. There is the odd polo shirt mixed in. But on the whole, I could not just reach in my closet and be ready for a GQ photo-op.

So, after thirty years of faithful service, my old suit went to Goodwill, and I went to the tailor.

I have a disease my family calls latitude sickness. The symptoms are uneasiness, fidgetiness, short temperedness, and extreme grumpiness when forced to travel below the Forty-Fifth Parallel. In short, their normally good-natured father and husband becomes a very ugly person to be around. The good news is that it does not occur up north. The bad news was the wedding we were to attend was well south of the Forty-Fifth. In addition, the symptoms are intensified when I am around large groups of people in an enclosed space. A mall in the suburbs, for example, is as close to purgatory as I can venture. So, with my disease in full bloom, wearing my new suit, we entered the reception hall with five hundred of our "closest" friends.

For the first hour, things weren't going too badly. I was reunited with fellows from college, trying to remember many names, finally remembering lads after they told a story or two. Our wives were just shaking their heads at what foolish things their mates had done. Then we were all asked to be seated, and my wife and I introduced ourselves to the couple across the table. We chitchatted with the couple for a while about trivial things while waiting for our dinners to arrive.

In the course of the conversation, I was asked what I did for a living. With some pride, because I am proud of what I do, I replied I was a forester working in northern Michigan.

Whoops! Wrong answer. The couple shot each other a horrified look and then turned their intense gaze on me.

"Hmph," the couple said in unison. It was obvious the duo was less than impressed by my choice of vocations.

The gentleman spoke up and said, "We don't believe in cutting trees. We are tree huggers."

My wife had seen this type of reaction before, so she placed her hand on my knee and gave it a rather hard squeeze. It meant, stay cool. I have come to hate the phrase "tree hugger," because it discredits people who are truly concerned about the forest and the environment. The couple then proceeded to lecture me on the evils of cutting trees. In fact, they had just bought a second home in northern Michigan and were very upset when they learned there was logging going on. At this point, my wife realized I was ready to erupt, and maybe it was time for her to go talk with the mother of the bride. As she was pushing back her chair and excusing herself, she squeezed my shoulder and whispered, "Be nice. This is a wedding."

After several more minutes listening about the evils of my profession, I finally had enough.

"Excuse me," I said as politely as my disease would allow, "Do you own a home?"

"Why, we own two homes, one down here, and as I have already told you, one up north," the gentleman replied.

"I see. And is it built out of wood?" I asked.

"Yes," the madam interjected.

"And the furniture . . . is it also made out of wood?"

"Of course," came an unladylike snort from the madam.

"I don't suppose you have books, magazines, cabinets, computer paper, cosmetics, toilet paper, or stationery with your family seal on it lying around the two homesteads?" I said in a rising voice.

"Of course, we do. What is your point?" the gentleman countered.

"My point? What is my point?" I could not believe how daft this couple was. "My point is rather obvious! All of that stuff comes from trees!" I noticed that couples on either side of us were staring at me. Taking a deep breath, to help control the latitude sickness, I calmly said, "With over three hundred million people in the United States, all wanting houses and all that goes in them, don't you think we might have to cut a tree or two?"

The elegantly dressed couple seemed a bit taken aback by my little tirade.

In a calmer voice, I said, "Look, professional foresters are very committed to the health and well-being of our forest. We are a group of individuals who went into forestry because, in one way or another, we loved trees. Members of the forestry profession are the original 'tree huggers,' and we were trained to manage our nation's forest for all of the benefits they have to offer. So, we get a bit testy on the subject of cutting trees. Sorry."

Boy, I sure know how to dampen a party, I thought to myself as I reached for a stale dinner roll. My tablemates decided to excuse themselves and show off their dancing skills. It seemed odd seeing them strutting around the dance floor doing the "chicken." *Well, at least they seem happy.*

Sitting now, slouched in my folding chair, I absentmindedly picked the small paper umbrella out of my wife's drink and started twirling it between my fingers. The new shoes that were required for the new suit were killing my feet, so, I slipped them off. I looked at the umbrella between my fingers and thought, *as a nation, how responsible are we?* We are by far the largest consumers of products made from trees. But for some reason, we think it is a mortal sin to harvest timber. Well, at least in our own backyard, anyway. I truly think most of our society does not even realize the multitude of items they use in their daily lives that are made from trees. Or that milk comes from a cow, for that matter.

Is it really their fault? Probably not. We live in a society so far removed from the land that most of the population does not come in contact with the natural order of things. I was starting to feel a bit guilty about my overreaction to the couple now doing the Hokey Pokey. Latitude sickness! That was it. All the symptoms were present and accounted for. I suppose it is like anything else. Education is the key. If people are not aware of proper forest management and sustainable forestry, they will assume that cutting any tree is bad. So, it is up to us to tell the world that we, in the forestry profession, are truly concerned about the forest and everything that lives and grows in them. It is our job!

Moments later, I had the opportunity to start this education process. A little girl in a white dress and some kind of flora in her hair plunked herself directly across from me.

I smiled, and she said, "I'm the flower girl."

"Ah, I see, well done," I said.

"Why don't you have any shoes on?" she asked.

"Oh, well, you see they were a bit tight," I said sheepishly.

With that she kicked off her shiny black shoes, which sported two big bows. My kind of kid, I thought.

Seconds later, one of the ladies who had overheard my little tirade with the elegant couple came over to collect her daughter. She was probably thinking, "Please stay away from the grumpy old man, honey." So, I was a bit surprised when she sat down and introduced herself.

"I heard you talking earlier, and you kind of got me thinking," she said, firmly shaking my hand.

"About what?"

"Well, I always considered myself a 'tree hugger,' but in reality, aren't we all? We all enjoy trees, yet we cut them down for all kinds of things. Aren't we being hypocritical?" she asked.

"Well, that depends on several things. If we chose to disallow harvesting in our country yet continue to consume vast quantities of forest products, then I would say we are being very hypocritical. Because those products would come from other countries, which probably don't practice sustainable forestry as we do here. Countries with very sensitive ecosystems and little management would be our wood basket.

"On the other hand," I continued, "humans have been using forests as a natural resource from the start. Sometimes greed has gotten in the way, and we have taken advantage of our forests. Up until 1920, forests were generally logged, then abandoned. Now, before a forest is even harvested, foresters will have determined how it will be regenerated. Depending on the forest, regeneration might occur naturally from seeds, roots, or the stumps. If the species needs help, the forest will be replanted. And in some cases, foresters will have determined areas to be too sensitive and recommend no harvesting."

The flower girl was looking bored, so I slid her my paper container of candy, which contained several white candied hearts.

"But isn't conservation a good idea?" the girl's mother asked, reaching for a heart.

"It's a great idea, and it's the whole premise around forestry. Today we have as much forest cover as we did a hundred years ago. Which is about the time the science of forestry was being applied here in America. Our forests are growing nearly four times more wood each year than in 1920. The forest community plants over a billion and a half seedlings a year. If you combine that with natural generation, growth exceeds harvest by thirty-three percent each year. And this is all due to good, sustainable forestry, which I might add, is not the case in many other countries of the world.

"So, my question is, do we want to get our timber resources from our country where the forests are being properly managed?" I asked. "Or do we scream in outrage and proclaim, 'don't cut in my backyard,' and take it from our southern neighbors, where they harvest like we did a hundred years ago? As long as we are having this discussion, it is just as important to talk about recycling as it is conservation. As a society, we consume a lot. And as individuals, we recycle very little. To be concerned about our environment requires personal actions, not just clichés," I concluded.

The mother looked a little befuddled after my rant.

"I can honestly say I never thought about trees in that way. That sheds a lot of new light on the issues. Thank you," she said.

Well, I certainly was not expecting that! Maybe this education thing might work.

"Excuse me," I said to the mother. "May I dance with the young lady?" I looked at the flower girl.

She gave me permission, so the little girl with the wreath in her hair and I headed to the dance floor. The young lady looked up and asked, "Do trees hug back?"

"Sometimes," I said, glancing down at our shoeless feet, realizing my latitude sickness was improving by the minute.

With a Little Help from My Friend

Michigan, 2013

*N*o matter how hard I concentrated, I still could not see any farther than a few yards. The brush was so thick, I had to almost crawl. In fact, I had been crawling a lot that day. But it was very important that I travel in a straight line, because I was attempting to reestablish a survey line. This survey line was between adjoining landowners, and the property to the south was to be harvested soon. So, the line had to be true. They say good fences make good neighbors. I say great property lines make happy neighbors, especially when logging is involved.

To add to the memorable experience of crawling on my belly, it had rained the previous evening. The water was layered on the leaves and grass, waiting for me to soak it up. It was like a car wash, and I was the car. Only I was not that keen on getting that wet that early in the morning. Because of the conditions, my normally hyper dog Cedar was not in her normal state of walking point, checking out anything and everything that might be the least bit interesting. Instead, she was behind me, letting me get soaked while I opened a trail for her.

However, I loved this part of a forester's job. Granted, the conditions were less than perfect, but the company was good . . . except for the smell. You see, earlier in the day, after nine months with a perfect record—which might be a national record for a forester's dog—Cedar had been skunked. Mind you, not badly skunked, but just enough to make your throat sore when she was near. We had just started the survey line when Cedar and a very young skunk came nose to nose. Luckily, the young skunk had not perfected its spray yet, and Cedar just caught a glancing blow. However, any blow from a skunk is unpleasant at best.

For some reason, I have always been very interested in surveying. This is strange, since math was not one of my stronger subjects as a youth. I was far more interested in history than I was in math. Maybe that's why surveying intrigued me so. There is a historical flavor to it, and the property I was working on today was a perfect example of that.

To start the process of reestablishing a survey line, I usually need to do a bit of poking around at the courthouse. There, in the register of deeds office, I go through the old survey notes looking for clues that might help me pinpoint the original line.

If I am lucky, the property may have been surveyed in the last thirty years, and the notes will explain exactly where the corner should be. If nothing can be found, I have to go back to the original notes from the late 1800s. This is a bittersweet pill, because the work is going to be a lot harder. But trying to piece together a little written history is very rewarding. In addition, when I finally locate a particular point on this large planet, I know that the person writing the notes had been at this exact point over a hundred years ago. And maybe they got soaked in the process, too.

The property I was working on this day fell into the "more-work-more-rewarding" category. Earlier, while researching at the courthouse, I was unable to find any clues from the new survey notes. So, I pulled the big, tan, leather book down from its shelf, blew off some of the dust, and started digging for some clues.

These big books hold the original survey notes, and compared to my chicken scratch, the handwritings are works of art. In most cases, and in most counties, a clerk copied the notes with a beautiful flair of the pen. In some townships in Maine, the surveyor did the copying, and they were equally as eloquent. Why their handwriting was so perfect, and mine is getting worse with each year of harsh weather, is beyond me.

I turned to the page explaining the property I was working on and began to examine the notes. The notes were dated August 14, 1906, and explained in great detail about the terrain, timber type, and a small brook that ran one hundred twenty feet from the corner. At the corner in question, a wooden post was driven into the ground. This was a section corner, so a lot of care was given to its location. Many other lines will and would have been run off this corner. The notes explained that the post was fourteen feet from an elm tree that was ten inches in diameter. It was not much of a clue, but with any luck I might be able to find the remains of the elm.

I set out then on my quest, and I was no further ahead now than when I started. I could not find a survey line, corner, or anything that even looked like a boundary. It was getting hotter as the afternoon sun started to turn the wet bush into a sauna. And the smell! Cedar was really getting ripe. I saw a nice tree to lean against, so we took a break. I tried to find something dry to sit on, but it was a fruitless endeavor. As I leaned back against a balsam, I squished into the soil. Every profession has its good points and bad points, right? As my body sunk into the damp earth, I pulled out my aerial photo to see if I could pinpoint where I was.

Studying the photo intently and holding it at an angle as to shed the water dripping from my brow, I could see a small opening I had just passed. I also noticed with interest a field a quarter mile away. The boundary on the north side of this field ran at the same angle as the line I was trying to find. With this little bit of evidence, I cut our soggy break short and headed to the corner of the field.

There I found my first bit of luck, a metal survey stake. If I used the same angle as the field and measured a quarter-mile back, I should be close to the corner I was searching for. As I walked, I had more luck. I could hear Cedar splashing in water. That must be the brook! But when I had covered the quarter-mile to where the corner should have been, there was naught. The brush was so thick, I decided to crawl on my hands and knees again. Trying to go in a straight line while holding a compass and crawling is something they forgot to teach me in forestry school.

As I crawled along, looking for the corner, Cedar took this as an invitation to rumble. Without so much as a hint, she was flying through the air, landing square on my back. This caught me completely off guard, causing me to do a face plant into the wet forest floor. Between the wet, rotting leaves and her wet, skunked fur, the smell was overwhelming. Rolling over onto my back, I struggled to get this stinky, playful canine off me. With a lot of yelling and shoving, she finally got the picture. As she removed herself, she grabbed my cap and jumped into the bush with a very proud look on her face. I remained on the ground for a while, wiping the dirt from my face and looking for all of my gear that was lost in the tackle. Rising, I put my hand on an old, rotting stump for support. Pushing myself up, my hand sunk deep into the pulpy mass. Removing my hand, which was coated in a wet goo, I realized I had finally found the clue I was looking for.

Because of the brush, I had been unable to see it earlier, but now on the forest floor I found the ten-inch elm described in the survey notes. It was not ten inches anymore. In fact, it had grown to about twenty inches before it had died, probably in the sixties, of Dutch elm disease. It was now a pitiful excuse for a stump; but it was my pitiful stump, and I was happy to find it.

I set my compass to the proper angle and measured fourteen feet from the elm to where the corner should be. The entire day I had been carrying a metal detector at a considerable inconvenience to my body. My metal detector is a pole-shaped object about four feet in length. When I carry it, I shove it into my vest with about two feet sticking out above my head. This is all well and good while walking in the open, which I might add is almost never. But, while walking and crawling in brush, the two feet of detector protruding above my head acts like a grappling hook, which grabs and clings to anything and everything. Consequently, it seems I am thrown to the ground several times a day. But even with this risk, it is an important tool. With it, I can scour the forest floor and, hopefully, find metal survey stakes that lay underneath many layers of leaves and dirt.

I retrieved the detector from my vest, turned it on, and started making arch-shaped patterns around where I thought the corner might be. At one point, I got a really strong signal.

"Ah ha," I thought, "there she blows."

I placed the detector next to the stump and started kicking away the dirt near the sounding. Nothing! So, I got down on my hands and knees again and started pawing at the earth with my hands. I was sure this was the correct spot; I kept making the hole larger and deeper. Cedar came over and sat next to me with her head cocked to the side. Even though she is full-grown, she still looks like a puppy now and then. With her head cocked, one ear up, dirt on her nose, and kind of sitting sidesaddle, she certainly looked goofy. Digging is one of her favorite sports, and I was sure she was trying to figure out how to help.

"Clink!" Ouch! I had hit something very hard with my fingernail.

"This must be it," I said in triumph.

It wasn't. It was an old Blatz beer can circa 1960. It was before pull-tabs, because I could see two triangle openings.

I pitched the can over by the stump to retrieve later. I sat back on my heels and grumbled about not finding anything. Cedar, seeing her chance, started widening the hole with great relish. As I sat there looking at my photo, trying to plan my next attempt, the hole got deeper and wider. I glanced at the hole as I got up to retrieve the can, and I thought I saw a rock. Peering again, I saw Cedar uncover more of the rock. Something struck me that this looked odd. *Of course, it did.* It was the top of a concrete survey marker with a metal rod sticking out the top.

I shouted with joy, then laughed because not many people would think this was much of a find. But I did. By finding this corner, I knew I could now run a proper, accurate line.

I sat back down to savor my victory. Cedar strolled over and put her wet head next to my face. I was about to push her away because of the tackle, but I didn't. I knew, and she knew, that had she not jumped on me, I might not have found the elm stump or the corner survey marker. So, I let her lean against me as I stroked her ear. But oh my! The smell of victory was sweet.

Tree Free

Michigan, 1994

It was like a bad B movie. The ending was all wrong. I wanted to reach out and change the channel, but I couldn't. Here was our daughter getting on one of the many planes that would take her half way around the world to India. My wife and I stood and watched the plane until it disappeared into the horizon. Luckily, the moment was so surreal that we had to laugh between the tears. This northern Michigan airport was all but empty, and in the background, a weird combination of music was playing: Asian, Native American, techno-pop, and strings. All good music on their own, but odd mixed together. As our daughter's plane vanished into the clouds, a mellow chant started to play over the intercom. She was off to exotic lands, and the airport's music system was doing its best to accentuate that fact.

On the way home from the airport, I kept thinking of our daughter and the career path she had chosen. At this point in her life, she was very concerned about politics, social injustice, and the environment—a concerned activist, as one of her relatives put it. Hence, she was off to a four-month internship in India. But for some reason, visions of one certain event kept popping up in my mind as we made our way home, a father and daughter trip to the grocery store many years ago.

❧

"Be good to yourself and the environment."

That sounds like grand advice. So why, then, did I feel so agitated when I read it? I was grumbling as I wandered off down the aisle. I knew it was just one more education problem I would have to face as a forester. Here I was on a Sunday afternoon doing some grocery shopping with my daughter, and this product jumped off the shelf and hit me square on the noggin.

"Tree Free," it said, with little green pine trees in the background, and below it read, "Paper Napkins."

I admit as a forester and consumer, the only thing I know about marketing is you should at least try to tell the truth about your product. If that was true, then how in the world could this company make paper napkins and call them "Tree Free?"

I was sure I knew the answer. They used recycled paper, but where did they bloody well think the recycled paper came from? Recycled paper comes from only one possible source: trees, our nation's most important renewable natural resource.

To confirm my suspicions, I asked my daughter to go back and grab the package of napkins. When she returned, she handed me the package and said quietly, "Dad please don't embarrass me."

"Embarrass you? When was the last time I did that?" I asked in mock disbelief.

"How about last week, when you pulled up to the traffic light singing at the top of your lungs, and when you saw my friends, you rolled down the window and sang louder? Or how about last night, when Sarah called and you answered the phone by singing the Canadian national anthem?" she replied.

"So, what's your point?" I asked.

"Just don't read so loud!" she begged.

I assured her I would behave. But the way I figured it, my sole purpose in life was to embarrass my children.

I flipped the package of napkins over so I could read the information about the product.

"Ah ha! There it is. This product is made from one hundred percent recycled paper," I shouted.

My daughter looked at me in despair and said, "What's wrong with that? Isn't that good?"

"Of course, that's good. In fact, it is highly commendable. But they are misleading the consumer. By saying these napkins are 'tree free,' the consumer assumes we don't need to harvest any trees to make this product. Also, people will get the impression we don't need to harvest any trees for the many forest products we use every day. Paper cannot be recycled indefinitely. As paper is successively recycled, the cellulose fibers are weakened and shortened, eventually making it no longer recyclable. That means you still need a continuous supply of fresh raw material to mix in, which in this case means trees. Saying these napkins are 'tree free' is like saying skim milk is cow free," I said.

As we continued our shopping, I realized I might be sending my daughter the wrong message about recycling. Rounding the next corner, I began to explain to her how committed the forestry industry is to recycling, but I cut the corner a tad short and ran into a display of nicely stacked cans of Pringles. The cans went flying in all directions, and my daughter turned beet red as she headed across to the meat aisle, hoping against all hope nobody recognized her. I called for her assistance to help in the restacking, and she slinked over pretending to read the label on a pack of chicken legs.

"Dad, please, you said you would not embarrass me!" she pleaded. I knew if there was anybody from her school within a mile of the store, my daughter would be mortified, so all I could say was "sorry."

While we tried to restack the cans in a somewhat professional manner, I continued my explanation of the forest industry's commitment to recycling. I told her that foresters were bound and determined to leave future generations with productive, healthy, sustainable forests. One of the ways we can ensure that is by encouraging recycling. The demands on our forests are not going to lessen but are going to increase at an alarming rate. It is predicted that our nation's demand for wood may double in the next thirty-five years. Recycling may help us keep pace with the demand. Currently, recycled paper fiber accounts for forty-five percent of the paper industry's raw material. But that also means that fifty-five percent of the raw material comes from newly harvested trees.

We finished picking up the cans and stacking them the best we could. It was obvious I should not give up my day job. The display now looked like a real bad Eiffel Tower. Once more, we headed down the aisle, but this time my daughter was at the helm. With all of the excitement (and potential to be embarrassed), I was really impressed with her next question.

"Dad, can our forest provide that many trees?"

"If we manage our forest right, we should have no problem,' I answered. "Here in Michigan, we are harvesting less than forty percent of the annual growth. So, each year we have more forest, not less. The average American uses about seven hundred fifty pounds of paper every year, and ninety-five percent of the houses built are done so by using wood. So, as a nation, we use a lot of wood. But that is okay. If proper forest management is used, when a tree is harvested, another one takes its place through natural regeneration or by planting. Compare that to plastic or steel. Plastic is made from petroleum and steel from ore. Once it is taken out of the ground, it is gone forever. Of course, as stewards of the land, we should not be wasteful. If we can reuse and recycle, we should."

"What about the rest of the world? Are they doing okay?" my daughter asked.

"Well, not everywhere. Some areas of the world are just scraping by, and they are probably not using the best forest management practices. And if you think about it, that is what we did in the United States as it was settled. We cut the forest and turned a lot of it into agricultural lands just to survive. A lot of that is happening in very sensitive areas like the rain forest of the world.

"But the good news is many forestry groups are concentrating on those areas. They are studying the forest and helping those countries with their forest management needs. A lot more work is needed, but things are starting to take shape."

We managed to make it through our shopping without any more mishaps. I was even able to remove the seven cans of Pringles from our cart without her knowing it. They were stowaways from the display.

As we started out of the parking lot, I noticed one of my daughter's friends and her mother going into the store. I could not resist. Down went the window, up went the radio, and I waved hello as I sang the lyrics to "Born to be Wild." My shopping mate melted into her seat.

After several minutes of silence watching her stare out the side window, I decided to break the ice by saying in an apologetic tone, "I suppose I should have not rolled down the window, eh?"

"Oh, I am used to that. I was just thinking about what you said . . . how much wood we use every year. It just seems like a lot," she said.

"It is a lot of wood. But did you know we have over three times the number of people in the United States than we did a hundred years ago? The timber harvest is actually the same, though. And do you know why?"

She shrugged. "Recycling?"

"Well, that is one reason. But the biggest reason is sound forest management. Forestry in the United States basically started as the result of poor or no management of our forests. There was no long-range planning. Just to supply a growing country with its wood needs was first and foremost. It did not work. Now with recycling, good utilization at the mills, and forest management, we can have our cake and eat it, too."

I was beginning to sound like a broken record.

As we pulled into our drive, my daughter said, "Dad, don't get a big head. But I know you and your forestry friends are really concerned about the forest. Knowing you guys are looking out after the forest makes me not even worry about it. But could you try not to embarrass me so much?"

If she only knew how good it made me feel to hear her say that. Sometimes, it is worth being the father of an easily embarrassed teenager.

A Marked Day

Michigan, 2012

"No, Cedar! Come. Come Cedar, No-No-No! Oh no, not the tail! Please come, Cedar."

"Yelp! Yelp!"

"Dang it! Come here girl. Let's see how bad you got it."

My dog scurried over with her tail between her legs, hanging her head. And from the great Golden Retriever head protruded many long, slender needles. As she approached, she looked over her shoulder as her adversary waddled off into the bush.

"Okay, let's see how much damage you did today," I said as I tried to calm my canine pin cushion.

It did not look good. Luckily, she did not get any in the eye, but that was about the only part of her face that was spared. Cedar had quills up her nose, on her nose, in her mouth, on her tongue, and on her thin, black lips.

Since starting my forestry career in 1975, I had witnessed this event many times. Porcupines carry approximately thirty thousand quills in their arsenal; they usually waddle away the victors. My first Golden, Kipper, had lived to be fourteen and was clueless up until the day she died that each time she got near a slow-moving bundle of thorns, pain and suffering would soon follow. Prairie, my second Golden, figured it out at about age five that she wanted nothing to do with nature's living pincushion. This was only Cedar's second encounter, and I was really hoping she might be a quick learner. But my hopes were now dashed.

It was obvious she was in agony, and she kept trying to spit or cough out the quills lodged in her mouth. Ever since I witnessed my first quilling, I have carried a pair of needle-nose pliers when I go into the field. The barb on the end of the quill acts like a screw and bores itself deep into the flesh at a rate of one-third of an inch an hour. So, time is of the essence. Wolves and other animals have been found dead with snouts full of quills. Cause of death? Starvation. The quills prevent them from eating or drinking.

Cedar was close to frantic, so I knocked her to the ground and lay on top of her. My left arm had her in a headlock, and my right held the pliers. I started with the quills up her nose, then on her nose, face, and lips. These were the easy-to-get-at spots; the hard work was still ahead.

To pluck the quill out, I placed the head of the pliers as close as possible to the tip and gave a quick twisting upward motion. This seems to help release the barb that is on the end of the quill. This process worked quite well, except every once in a while, I got a little too close and I also plucked out bits of fur, skin, and whiskers. To make this whole procedure even more difficult, Cedar was squirming and thrashing like a Brahman Bull, which resulted in more non-quill being plucked.

I decided we both needed a break, but I could not let her go because of the quills still in her mouth. So, I continued to hold her down, seeing the panic and fear in her eyes. I tried to calm her with soothing talk and rubbing behind ears, which she normally enjoys but not today. There was nothing to do except have at her and get the job done. So, the removal process began in earnest. The inside of her mouth had quills lodged on both sides of her tongue and on the roof of her mouth. She struggled and thrashed while I wrestled and plucked. And a half hour and forty-five quills later, we were done.

Cedar was so exhausted, she just lay there panting. Her face was swollen, and droplets of blood told of each quill extraction. I was also a bit gassed and had several quill punctures on my arms and hands. What Cedar needed at this point was some water. I pulled out my aerial photo to see if I could locate any source of water nearby. From the photo, I could see the hardwood ridge I was currently working on. About a quarter of a mile to the north, the photo revealed a dark, wandering line. Conifers always show up dark on the photos. The way the thin band of dark wandered and curved, I concluded it was a brook or stream. There was a good chance the stream might be dry because it was midsummer, and a dry one to boot. But Cedar desperately needed water, and this was by far my best chance of finding it.

"Come on, girl. Let's get you something to drink," I said, coaxing her up. Normally she would be several strides ahead of me checking out all the interesting things a dog can find in the forest. But now she was behind me with her tongue hanging out of a face that looked like it had gone several rounds with Muhammad Ali.

Several minutes later, I could see cedar, hemlock, and balsam ahead of me, and I assumed that was the dark band of trees I could see from my photo. As we struggled through the thick branches, I could hear the sound of moving water. Sure enough, there was a small, clear brook running cold and clean.

Cedar waded in and started drinking very delicately. That was odd, because at her water bowl at home, she creates quite a wake. In fact, we all walk around her when she drinks so we don't get baptized. Her mouth was obviously tender. I lowered my hands into the cool water to relieve the stings I had acquired from extracting the quills.

Lying on my belly, with my hands soaking, I could not help think what a different job I had than the rest of the world. I was pretty certain the lads I went to college with probably were not lying in a bunch of wet wildflowers on the bank of a stream soaking their hands while their coworker was lapping up gallons of water. I guessed this was a forester's version of hanging out around the water cooler.

Then the rest of the gang showed up. Mosquitoes by the thousands descended upon us like bombers over London during the blitz. They were up my nose, in my ear, down my throat, attacking any part of my body that was exposed.

"Break's over, girl. Let's go," I said, pushing myself off the wet bank.

We headed back up the gentle slope. Cedar had a little more spring in her step, so I hoped the worst was over. I had left my cruiser's vest and paint gun hanging in a tree, which I could see on the ridge. Cedar and I had about twenty acres of northern hardwoods to mark before the day was done, and we had already lost some time, so I had to get crackin'.

Marking a hardwood stand is one of the best and worst things about being a forester. The nice side of the equation involves strolling through the woods all day deciding which trees should be harvested and which should be left to grow and prosper. The trees in a northern hardwood stand such as maple, basswood, beech, ash, yellow birch, and cherry can thrive with limited amounts of sunshine. Consequently, you will find all different age and size trees. Deciding which ones should go and which should stand depends on several criteria. Marking the suppressed, deformed, less desirable or mature trees is usually the pattern. Once in a while, a disease or insect invades and you remove the trees that are more susceptible. At the end of the day, I might have marked all different kinds and size trees. By marking the stand this way, you ensure its health and long-term sustainability. And I have the personal satisfaction knowing I just helped give future generations a productive and diverse forest.

The downside to marking a northern hardwood stand is you are usually looking up, which means you don't see the holes, branches, rocks, puddles, barbed wire, old fenders, washers, stone walls, tires, sleeping animals, hornets' nests, discarded bedsprings, or any other of a thousand things waiting to trip you. Not to put too fine a point on it, I fall down a lot. I have many scars on my shins, knees, and elbows directly tied to marking a northern hardwood stand. One of the worst hazards is wire, barbed or otherwise, and I have to admit Michigan is the worst. In northern New England, stone walls were the preferred boundary line choice. Out west, no one cared where the exact boundary line was. But in Michigan, every parcel of land big or small seems to have wire around it. The old wire is probably the worst. In some places, it has fallen to the earth, and in others the trees have grown right around it. I can't see it, nor can my dog. So, countless times during the day, I will hear Cedar yelp, and I will curse as I fall over. But every job has its downside. Mine, literally.

Cedar has mixed feelings about marking timber. When I run a survey line, map a property, or cruise a stand of timber, I walk more or less in a straight line. When marking a northern hardwood stand, you go in a certain direction but you do a lot of roaming back and forth trying to get a good view of the individual trees and their condition. Sometimes, late in the day, Cedar will just sit down and sigh. I am sure she is thinking, "Will you make up your bloody mind? You are going in circles here."

I grabbed my gun and vest, which held four cans of extra paint, and resumed marking. Cedar was still lagging a bit in energy, but I would be, too, if I had had that many needles sticking out of my face. While marking, I listened. Northern hardwoods are home to many varieties of song birds. They spend their winters in the south and summers in the forest of the north. And on this still day, they were all singing their sweet songs. At one time, I was being serenaded by eight different species of birds. Add in the constant drone of the mosquitoes, and it was quite a symphony.

Just as I was relaxing to the music, Cedar cut between me and the tree I was about to mark. Along with painting the trees to be harvested on two sides, I also marked the stump. Before I could stop my trigger finger, Cedar had a big blue splotch of paint on her golden coat.

"Perfect," I thought. If I get pulled over by the law, they will take one look at my dog and throw me in the clink for playing paint ball with a canine

I crossed a small brook lined with stately hemlocks and headed up a small ridge, where my day would come to an end. I came upon a group of large maples and was walking around them, eyes looking upward, when my right foot sank in some soft soil. I felt a slight tremor under foot. Experience told me I better run hard and run fast. Run, Forest, run! echoed in my head.

And I was right. A squadron of bald-faced hornets (large yellowjackets) descended on me before I went five feet. The only part of my body that was uncovered was my neck and face. Within five seconds, I received two stings on the neck and three on the face all the while running through the bush, waving my arms and swatting at my face.

Cedar had not fared much better; I could see her using her paws to rub her nose, and she shook her head violently. During the chase, I must have looked like a fleeing soldier, because my paint gun and hardhat were scattered along my path of retreat. Gathering them up, I was very careful to give the nest plenty of distance.

The rest of the afternoon was mercifully uneventful.

That evening, my wife and I arrived home at the same time from our respective jobs. She was getting out of her car when Cedar and I rolled up behind her. Cedar popped out first, and her tail wagged its usual rapid routine for my wife.

I could hear my wife saying, "Oh Cedar, what happened to your pretty nose and face? And you are so blue.

"And you!" she exclaimed, looking at me. "What on earth happened to you?"

"What?" I said, kind of taken back.

"Your face looks like a blue pumpkin," she said, gently trying to touch my sore cheek.

Leaning over, I glanced in her side mirror.

"Oh my . . . good thing I did not stop at the grocery," I said, trying to rub some of the dried blue paint off my swollen face.

We both turned as we heard lapping. Cedar was standing on her hind legs with her front paws balancing on the birdbath, lapping up water as fast as she could. My wife turned to me with a quizzical glance.

"Just another day at the office, dear, just another day," I said through puffy, blue lips.

Eva's Kip

Michigan, 2013

*A*s any forester will tell you, a truck with a good heater is vital. Southern foresters might argue that an air conditioner is paramount. But I would counter that we northern brethren have a far better chance of losing a finger or toe if our favored device doesn't work. Sometimes we Yankees have the added thrill (or burden) of just trying to turn the key in the door to get our one creature comfort revved up.

Such was the case today. I really didn't realize my hands had gotten so cold until I tried to turn the key in the truck's lock. With my fingers stuck at about a forty-five-degree angle, it was impossible to do any type of motor skill. In desperation, I placed the key between both palms and tried the two-handed method. I realized my ingenuity was in vain when the key slipped from my palms and fell into the six inches of powdery snow at my feet.

"Dang it," I said, falling to my knees to begin the hunt.

Cedar took this as a cue to wrestle.

"Cedar, no!" I said, with a little more anger than intended.

She slinked off with tail between her legs. I felt bad, but I knew the moment she found a stick or rock, all would be forgotten and forgiven.

Unknown to me, as I was frantically pawing the snow looking for my keys, someone had snuck up behind me and was witnessing the event.

"May I help you?" a voice behind me said.

Startled, I let out a yelp as I turned to face the voice. I was a bit confused, because the voice I heard was definitely female, but the attire was not. Before me stood a figure wearing a very long, worn, green, wool coat, knee-high LL Bean mukluks, a furry Russian Cossack cap, and a red-silk scarf wrapped around the neck.

"May I help you?" she said again. Still on my hands and knees, I explained the condition of my hands and the dropping of the keys. As an afterthought, I added who I was and the mission I had been on, which caused my hands to get so cold.

With that, the woman reached out a hand and said, "I was the one who called you. Here, let me help you."

Grabbing her hand, I was helped to my feet.

"I am Eva. I did not think you would get out and look at my forest so soon."

"Well, I was in the area, and it seemed like a nice day for a walk in the bush," I replied, brushing some of the snow off my wool pants.

Out of nowhere came Cedar. I had actually forgotten about her in the hunt for the key. But here she was doing what she was put on earth to do: greet people. I am sure if she were human, her dream job would be the greeter at the largest Walmart in the world.

Thankfully, Eva seemed to be enjoying the ritual. In fact, she was actually laughing at the antics. What with Cedar's goofy grin, high-pitched whine, and the figure eight she does between your legs, when excited, one has a hard time not smiling.

"Okay, Cedar, that's enough," I said, grabbing her collar.

Laughing, Eva said, "There it is."

Looking to where she was pointing with her mittened hand, I saw my keys. Actually, I kept getting glimpses of my keys. Every time Cedar's tail swished to the right, I could see my keys on the left.

"Looks like your dog saved the day with that tail of hers," Eva said as she bent down to retrieve them. After a rub behind Cedar's ears and a "What a good girl," she graciously unlocked my truck.

With Cedar safely secured inside the truck, Eva suggested I join her for a cup of hot tea in her warm kitchen. I wholeheartedly agreed knowing I might sound more professional once my frozen face had thawed out. A few minutes later, I was standing in front of an ancient wood cookstove with my hands wrapped around a steaming mug of tea. Eva had removed her odd assortment of winter garments, and I was surprised to see how smartly she was dressed. From our earlier phone conversation, I had guessed her to be of my parent's generation. Now, I was almost certain of it. Children of the Depression who went on to participate in World War II had a pretty high dress code standard.

Eva gestured to a large pine table, where she had placed a big pot of tea and what looked like a very delicious pie. I felt comfortable that my core temperature had risen enough to venture farther from the woodstove, so I joined her. The heavy chair scraped across the pine floorboards as I pulled it out from the table. To my surprise, a very large, gray cat with light-blue eyes looked up at me from the cushion on the chair.

215

Eva chuckled and plucked the cat from the chair. As the cat was whisked by me, he gave me a look from those light-blue eyes that said, "That is my chair, buddy. Watch your step. I'll be waiting for you."

"What a wonderful place you have here," I said between mouthfuls of pie.

"Yes, it is," she replied with a gentle nod of the head. "My husband and I built it a long time ago," she added. Watching Eva, I could see her mind was a long way away. Then with a slight shake of the head, she said, "Let me go gather all of the information about our property."

With that she bounded out of the chair and disappeared up a flight of stairs. The cat quickly jumped into the empty chair and sat staring at me. I grabbed my mug of tea and did what every other human does when left alone in a strange room—I snooped. I strolled around looking at paintings, books, plaques, photos, and other odds and ends that make a house a home.

I was drawn to a massive stone fireplace that was large enough to fit several well-fed Santas. Over the fireplace was a huge log mantlepiece that held a lifetime of memories. There were old bottles, medals, well-used framed maps, various old woodworking tools, and many photos. One photo in particular caught my attention. The photo depicted a young Marine officer with his arm around a young lady decked out in classic 1940s attire.

"That's Kip and me just before he shipped out to the Pacific," Eva said as she sidled up next to me.

Eva had a very large cardboard box in her hands as I followed her back to the table. Curled up in my assigned chair sat the gray cat. For domestic harmony, I pulled out a different chair. The box that Eva had retrieved contained over fifty years of forest maps, planting records, harvesting results, forest management plans, growth patterns, soil sample results, and many other facts and figures pertaining to their eighty-acre forest. I spent over an hour pawing through the records as if I were an archeologist in some ancient dig. To a forester this was a bloody good read. To most other readers, it would be dull at best.

As I was going through the material, Eva told me that when Kip had returned from three years in the Pacific, with several pieces of shrapnel in his right shoulder, he joined the throngs of GIs who took advantage of the GI Bill and went to the state college. When Kip was overseas, Eva was hard at work on the home front. When Eva heard that her uncle wanted to sell off some of his holdings, she approached him with an offer. As Eva was his only niece, he could not refuse.

Upon Kip's graduation, Eva and Kip moved to their eighty acres and began a new life, new family, and lots of new adventures. For many years they lived in an old hunting camp with no running water or electricity. This was quaint for the two of them, but it soon lost its charm when children started arriving. Over the course of three years, the young family erected a large cabin made from spruce logs harvested from their property. And as many who have built their own home will attest, years follow before it is actually completed.

As I pawed through the stacks of information Eva laid before me, it became clear that by day Kip was employed as an accountant. But by night and on the weekends, he was a would-be forester.

"Wow," I said, "Look at that."

Eva peered over my shoulder to take a look at the photo I had in my hand.

"Mister, I want to tell you, that was a hot day," she said.

The photo depicted Eva in the process of planting a pine

seedling. Behind her lay furrow after furrow of sixteen-inch red pine seedling in perfect rows.

I looked up to see a smile on Eva's faced as it dawned on me that those seedlings now were some fifty feet tall.

"Yes, that's the pine plantation you just walked through," she said with a smile.

I knew that, but seeing it in black and white really hit home. Earlier, I had walked through this pine forest enjoying the shelter that the thick canopy provided. I also noticed the soil underneath was very sandy, and prior to planting was probably susceptible to wind erosion. This was confirmed by an old yellowing article I found concerning wind erosion and pine plantations. Deeper in the box, I found a pamphlet from 1949 titled, "Woodlot Management." So many pages were dog-eared, with sentences underlined in red pencil, that it looked like the owner was studying for a mid-term exam.

"Kip would spend hours studying that pamphlet," she gestured with her mug.

It was obvious he not only studied the material, he put it to use. When I walked their hardwood forest, I was extremely impressed by what I saw. Their forest contained every age of tree possible. There were small seedlings on the forest floor and large trees reaching for the heavens and everything in between. Differing age, size, and species make a hardwood forest not only healthier but more attractive to different forms of wildlife.

At the bottom of the box, there was an article that had its title underlined and circled. I pulled it out, and Eva rolled her eyes when she saw it. I gave her a quizzical look and she grimaced and said, "Kip and I fought like cats and dogs over that." I chuckled because as a forester, I saw many a family squabble over the issue. The brochure boldly stated that clear-cutting an aspen stand was the best form of management.

218

"Well, the article is right, and I see you have done it many times. You have had four different stands clear-cut, and they are doing great," I said.

"I know, I know. Aspen needs full sunlight to regenerate, but it was hard for me to agree to clear-cutting," she acknowledged.

"I know it sounds odd, but with some species, clear-cutting is the best way to ensure its survival," I said reassuringly.

"Yes," she added, "but the idea of clear-cutting always sounds so awful."

"I agree. But you would have to also agree that the young, healthy forest that resulted from those clear-cuts is quite impressive," I said.

After a few more minutes looking at the collected materials, I pushed my chair back from the table and said, "This is one of the best managed forests I have ever seen. You've planted pines. You have thinned your hardwoods, clear-cut the aspen areas, and in the sensitive areas around your swamp, you have done nothing. Your harvesting practices have produced many timber products, provided great wildlife habitat, and most importantly, have kept your forest healthy and sustainable.

"By managing your property so well, you and Kip were also contributing to the well-being of your fellow human beings," I proclaimed.

Eva looked at me with a questioning eye.

"You have provided society with the raw material to make houses, paper, cabinets, and a multitude of other products they use," I added. "You did it in a sustainable manner, never putting your forest or the environment at risk. Quite frankly, I feel we all owe a great deal to people like you."

As I was about to continue with my accolades, the gray cat leapt into my lap, made two circles, laid down, and started purring.

Eva said, "Stormy, what are you doing?"

The cat and I both looked at Eva. Walking toward me, Eva reached out to remove the cat from my lap.

"She is okay," I said, "We have two at home."

"Stormy is a he and sometimes he is quite an annoyance," she said matter-of-factly.

I started laughing and said, "My wife might agree with you."

Eva looked puzzled, so I continued.

"My nickname is Stormy."

Then we both had a good laugh. Eva collected Stormy and sat in the rocker next to the warm cookstove.

Quiet ensued as I took a sip from a fresh mug of tea. Eva tugged on the cat's ears, which he obviously enjoyed from the volume of his purring.

"I wish you could have met my husband. I think you two would have enjoyed each other's company," Eva said quietly.

I did not know how to say it, but after looking at his written material, seeing the house he built, walking through the forest he had painstakingly managed, and hearing the admiration in his wife's voice, I, too, wished I had met Kip.

What I said was, "He sounds like a very wonderful man. It would have been a privilege to have known him."

Eva nodded in rhythm with the rocking chair as she gazed across the room at the picture on the log mantle over the stone fireplace.

In that moment, I realized just how important relationships are and how different they can be. People can have a lasting effect not only on those they love, but also the land they love, long after they are gone.

The Trail Less Traveled

Ontario, 2004

I shifted a little to the right, hoping the rock under my left shoulder might disappear. It did, but now I had a root under my right shoulder. One never expects to be really comfortable while out in the Canadian bush. But this was pushing the limit. My tent was on a slope, rocks and roots were the norm, and it was very hot. The only saving grace was that a pair of barred owls and pack of wolves were serenading us. I was also so fatigued I could not sleep.

This was the sixth and final night of a one hundred mile backpacking trip that my son, two of his friends, and I had embarked on. From the lads' tent, I heard Grover's fatigued voice say, "Stormy, what's that?"

I had to laugh, because in the bush we always use nicknames. As soon as we were back in civilization, it would be "Mr. Stormzand."

"It is only a pack of wolves," I said.

"Oh," was his reply, not sure that was a good thing.

Staring up into moonless sky, I tried to pick out constellations hoping it would lull me back to sleep. Finally, realizing it was useless, I gave up. Rolling over, I grabbed my headlamp and my notebook. For the past week I had been keeping a journal of our trip. I have done this for the past twenty years, keeping notes on all of our canoeing and backpacking trips. With the maps and notes in front of me, I can relive each portage trail and tough ridge in the comfort of a nice chair, sitting by the warm woodstove on cold, winter nights. This trip, I asked the three boys to keep a journal. I wanted to see what their version of our trials and tribulations were.

While trying to get comfortable (even my big toe hurt), I adjusted my headlamp. I flipped to the first entry and started reading.

Day 1

Lads –After driving since dawn, we finally started this trip at 3 p.m. The trail began with a huge uphill climb. Not a good omen. Neither were the fried fish and fries, which was our last real meal earlier. Trail was hard and packs were heavy.

Dad – Long drive but filled with excitement. We sang old rock 'n roll songs to pass the time. Trail started off nice and easy. Only hiked three hours today, as we were all getting our sea legs. Grover was struggling with his pack. I think he was carrying too much water. Camped in a hemlock grove next to a small, muddy pond, which was called Seely Lake. We were very hot, and it was hard to reach clean water for a swim. Had to be careful not to clog water filter due to the mud. Beans and rice for dinner, not bad. Grover lost his map today.

Day 2

Lads – Long, hard day. Crossed a river via a beaver dam. Hiked through "The Crack," a large split in the quartzite rock. Ran into a couple of hikers going the "correct" direction around one hundred mile loop. They said the way we were going was "a lot rougher." Good planning, Stormy. Very fatigued and dehydrated. And we are doing this because?

Dad – Woke the lads at 5 a.m. with small Irish flute. Not sure they enjoyed the melody so early in morn. Very hot day. We hiked from 8 a.m. 'til 7 p.m. in the evening. Near noon, we came down off of a ridge to get water from a small, clear lake. The boys were a bit behind me, and when they arrived, I was alarmed at their condition. They were very pale and just plodding along. I threw off my pack and boots and plunged into the lake. I strongly urged them to follow, which they did. I think they were all about to suffer from some sort of overheating before the plunge. We drank our fill and filtered enough water for each of us to have thirty-two ounces every hour break. Stopped at Heaven Lake around 4 p.m. Swam and filtered more water. We were all gassed, but three hours of hiking and climbing still were ahead of us. Arrived at Rabbit Lake around 7 p.m. Were all in tent and asleep by 8 p.m. Very taxing day. My map came up missing. We need to find more secure pocket for maps.

Day 3

Lads –Woke at 5 with Stormy playing that stupid tin whistle. We were all sore from yesterday's hike. It hurts to breathe. At lunch, we started figuring out our caloric intake for each day. Not good. Figured out we have been living on 750 calories a day. Took an hour break while Stormy climbed to the top of Silver Peak. Passed two hikers, and they told us about a bear and her cub that they encountered on Boundary Lake—our destination for the night. Great. Very hot. No sign of bear that evening. Hit the hay at 7 p.m.

Dad – Climbing Silver Peak "sounded like a good idea at the time." My wife says that is what she is going to put on my tombstone. The view was great, but with the calories I spent getting there, it was not quite worth it. I am concerned about the amount of food I have packed for trip. It would have been fine for our normal canoe trips, but it seems a bit light for this trip. I will start cutting back on my portion, leaving more for the lads. Started eating blueberries off of every bush I came across. The lads seem to be getting their walking legs. Their pace is same as mine. I trained all summer for this, and I don't think they trained one bloody hour. Upon reaching our campsite, I flopped down in a high state of fatigue. Lugie's map is missing. This could get serious. Dehydration, lack of food, and fifteen miles a day is starting to catch up with me. A swim in the cool mountain lake helped to revive me.

Day 4

Lads – Awoke to the tin whistle, what a surprise. Plan on pitching that in lake soon. Very hard climb out of Boundary Lake. We were ready for first break by the time we hit the trail! Trail very tough today. Lots of ups and downs. Ate a "grand" lunch of a half pita bread and tuna sandwich and a couple of candy bites. Arrived at Shigaug Lake late in afternoon. Swimming was best yet. High Mountain Lake with very clear water surrounded by white quartz cliffs. Stormy said tomorrow would be toughest day yet, so we ate "extra" food for dinner. Oh, for a Big Mac.

Dad – Arose at 5 a.m. Brewed some tea and enjoyed the beauty of the lake. A pair of loons kept appearing in and out of the low mist, which hung over the lake. I let the lads sleep in a bit, as they deserved it. This has been quite a challenging trip. Am very thankful I can share it with my son and his friends. Lots of dawdling around camp in morning as we have a shorter day today. Map check before we left. Shigaug Lake was absolutely gorgeous. Since we arrived early, we had lots of time to swim, repair gear, soak feet, and cook. Tomorrow is going to be wicked, so I cooked extra pasta for dinner. Again, we are feeling the effects of our low-calorie diet. I am sure the lads won't let me forget this blunder for a while. After our "feast," I climbed a ridge to get a better view. Watched a young loon going through many different rituals, as its mother watched. Everyone out for the night by 7 p.m. It doesn't get dark 'til 9 p.m.

Day 5

Lads – Today was grueling, taxing, brutal, hot, dehydrating, and fatiguing. Moose Pass was straight up and then straight down. Every little mud hole or trickle we found, we filtered water. Campsite was located on high bluff with no real way to reach water. Tied our shorts to a rope and lowered them into murky water. We then used the shorts to give ourselves a sponge bath. Not very rewarding. Stormy cooked extra chili for dinner. Lots of extra beans. Tent got rather small during the course of the night during the gas attack. Where does he come up with this food? GAG!

Dad – The day did not disappoint me. It was as hard as I had anticipated. To add to the challenge, a pair of hikers told us about a hornet's nest on the trail. They were a little vague on where it was. I led the way looking for it. Found it when I bent down to get some water out of a small brook. Hearing the noise, I scampered away as fast as my heavy pack would allow me. A swarm the size of a basketball gave chase. Would have been a bit dicey, since we are many days from hospital. Started eating my full ration again. I was really starting to feel the effects. I was too tired today to take off my boots. I stopped often to graze on blueberries and take in the wonderful views. Lots of hand-over-hand climbing today. Down to one map. Hopeless in charge of remaining map.

Day 6

Lads – So hot, so tired, and soooo hungry! What we would give for an ice cube. We passed a lady who has only been out two days. You could actually smell the soap as she passed. I am sure she did not have the same experience passing us. Hopeless has worn the same shirt for six days. Rinses it out along with our shorts every night. Very long uphill climb into Topaz Lake. Lugie was a bit wobbly near the end. Stroke has been behind us the last couple of days. He should have trained. We all skinny-dipped at night before we hit the hay. In the tent by 7 p.m. Lugie's water filter clogged up. Great.

Dad – Today was probably the hardest. Everybody's energy level is spent. Just before we started the long uphill climb into Topaz Lake, I came within half an inch of stepping on a massasauga rattler's back. It slithered off into a bush while I contemplated my good fortune. And I thought the bee stings would have caused trouble! A snakebite would really have put a damper on things. Ate most of food since we will be out tomorrow. Mixed up tuna with leftover cracker crumbs for a wonderful cold tuna loaf. A bit salty and dry. The lads were reading the recipes on the back of the tuna package. Bad idea.

That was the last entry so far. So, I switched off my headlamp and laid the journal next to my knife. Finally, I could feel my body relaxing. As I drifted off, I thought to myself how fast a young body can adapt compared to mine. It took these lads less than two days to adapt to the rugged life style. And for me, each day brought a new ache or sprain. This is why throughout history young men are the soldiers and the old men point and say, "The war's this way, gentlemen."

Day 7

We arose early as was our habit. The day was another hot and sultry one. The lads were ahead of me all day until we reached the park where we had started. I had to impress upon them that the trip was not complete until we walked the two miles through the park to our truck. They did not see the wisdom but did it anyway. As we walked, families gawked, young children ran to the other side of the road, and dogs barked. I found this odd until I took a close look at us. We were four bearded, bedraggled hikers who looked like they were in desperate need of a hot meal, a shower, soap, and some sleep. When we finally got to the truck, everyone stripped their gear and fell into the lake. There, we high-fived and congratulated each other on making it. We even had one map left to plan next year's trip. That evening, when we reached civilization, we had as much food as one could stuff into one's body. In addition, we kept the waitress very busy filling our glasses with cold water and ice. The boys actually ate their ice while I used my ice for my feet, hip, shoulder, neck, and knees.

This story is dedicated to Rob Tulk (Grover), who passed away in 2013, just as he was beginning to write his own story. A better lad would be hard to find.

Dressed for Success
Michigan, 2013

*T*here it was again: faint, but I was sure of it. I stopped and cocked my ear toward the sound. Cedar did not see me stop abruptly and plowed into the back of my knees, sending me sprawling forward. We were on the downside of a steep ridge, so I slid a few feet after the impact. Cedar came over and nudged my face with her wet nose just to let me know there were no hard feelings, me stopping and all and not warning her. I could not yell at her. She had no idea what she had done. So, I picked myself up for the umpteenth time and brushed dirt off my face.

About to step forward, I heard it again. Cedar was tugging on a small tree and in the process was making a grunting noise like a pig routing for truffles.

"Shush," I said.

Cedar turned to me with a quizzical glare. She was probably thinking, "Now, there is a new one." Does it mean food? Come? Play? Bad? Up or down?

So, to clarify, I said, "Be quiet."

Cedar again cocked her head in confusion, which meant she stopped tugging and grunting, which produced the intended result. Quiet.

There it was again, I was sure of it.

"A wood thrush! First of the summer," I proclaimed. And to punctuate my proclamation, Cedar barked.

I looked at her and just shook my head and said, "Why do you do that?"

Her response was another bark skyward.

I followed the general direction of her bark until my eyes rested on a broken stick resting about ten feet in the air. That was it. That was what she wanted. In a land of sticks, she wanted one particular stick hanging just out of reach. Knowing full well she would hang around barking for the stick until I was no longer in sight, I decided to give in and shake the tree. She caught her stick as it fell to earth, which would have done any circus dog proud. She pranced ahead of me, shaking her stick as if it were the coolest thing in the world, which in her mind it probably was ... for the next thirty seconds, anyway.

Not long after, she came across a forked stick, and the temptation was too great. For my dog, who is addicted to sticks, a forked stick is the ultimate pleasure. Ever since she was a pup, she goes gonzo when she finds a forked stick. Her current treasure was the perfect size and shape. She latched on to the forked part and started shaking her head and prancing in a big circle. This routine usually reminds me of one of two things. Either she is the canine version of a water witch strutting around with her divining rod, witching for a place to dig a well. Or, she is a wolf on the frozen tundra wrestling with a giant caribou. Either way, it is very comical and entertaining. But, most importantly, she enjoys it tremendously.

Again, I heard the beautiful, throaty song of the wood thrush.

The flute-like sound was off in the distance, and the low clouds and light mist made the melody of the thrush soft and muted. Besides the call of the loon, the song of the wood thrush is my wife's favorite sound. The call of the loon reminds me of Canada and all of the wonderful times my family and I have spent canoeing her many rivers and lakes. The wood thrush melody reminds me of summer evenings sitting outside the sauna or on the porch swing with my family at home. Now, with the kids grown and gone, these sounds sometimes make me melancholy, longing for the days when they were young and close by. However, life moves on. My impatient dog barking at a rock reminded me of this.

Despite the mist, it was turning out to be a grand day. The main reason for my pleasant mood was the absence of bugs. Everything was perfect for a blood fest. It was summer, wet, and humid—perfect conditions. Occasionally, the forestry gods will look down upon us foresters on the ground and have pity on us. Instead of being wet and eaten alive, they only give us wet. In my opinion, wet beats being a blood donor any day. Of course, there are tradeoffs in my profession. I was enjoying a bug-free day, but the mist made everything on the ground very wet and slippery, which meant every step was a potential face plant. Still better than bugs, I concluded. I smiled as the wood thrush sang in the distance followed by Cedar's bark. It was, indeed, a grand day.

As I walked through this small portion of northern Michigan, I was amazed at how different it looked. On my last visit, I was wearing snowshoes, and it was a bitterly cold February day. Two feet of snow blanketed the ground, covering every hole, stump, branch, rock, and wildflower. The trees were devoid of leaves, the air was without a hint of a fragrance, and the woods were completely silent except for the crunch of my snowshoes. Now the foliage was so thick I could barely see my boots. I was surrounded with a virtual bouquet of smells: wet earth, wildflowers, decomposing stumps, bug dope, and a damp, canine companion. The woods were anything but silent. Birds of all varieties were singing their little hearts out with the woodpeckers keeping the beat. And, as always, I had the constant haw, haw, haw, of my dog's panting. Whether it is African hot or artic cold, my dog always pants. The sound is always there; and when it is not, I have to stop and ask why. Normally, Cedar is within a stone's throw of me. When I stop to look through my compass or examine the forest, she stops. Sometimes I think her constant rhythmic panting is a form of sonar, which always tells her where I am and vice versa.

We entered a small clearing, and Cedar bounded ahead, chasing a small, blue butterfly.

"She would chase a thought if given the opportunity," I said to myself.

About half way through the opening, a doe leaped up and bounded off. Seeing this, Cedar abandoned the butterfly and took chase after the doe. I was not too concerned, because she usually only gives chase for a few seconds, then returns. I continued walking, leaving the small opening and entering the cooler forest. Checking my compass again, I strolled off in the prescribed direction. Several minutes later, it dawned on me I was not hearing Cedar's constant pant. I stopped and scanned in every direction for a gold patch of fur in the sea of greens. Sometimes she is near me, and when I stop, she sits down and I can't see her. But usually the sonar is present and I hear her. This time, however, there was not even a ping. After I had scanned the perimeter and was certain she was not there, I started calling her name. After a few minutes, she came slinking toward me, which was not a good sign. Usually this means she has rolled in something exceedingly pungent or met up with a skunk or porcupine. When she came over and leaned against me and did not seem any worse for the wear, I figured she was just apologizing for my inconvenience. I gave her a rub behind the ear and said, "Stay close girl."

The rest of the day was uneventful and routine. So, when five hours later we returned home and Cedar went to greet my wife and my wife said, "What have you done to my dog?" I was a bit puzzled. There on the porch lay a pool of blood where Cedar had been sitting. When I rolled Cedar over on her back, using my best high school wrestling move, I found a wound that was very deep and very long. Being one of those types of guys who will try most anything, personal experience told me this really needed to be stitched up.

"So that's why you came slinking back to me!" I said, trying to figure out how we were going to get her sewn back up at this late hour.

Thank heavens for understanding veterinarians. After many stitches and two bottles of pills, Cedar was declared, "Good to go." The two of us rolled back home exhausted but okay. The next day she tried to act normal, but it was obvious she was a bit off her game. My normal rapid-fire dog was sluggish at best.

Timing in life is everything. As luck would have it, the next day my wife left for a week to visit our daughter. Normally this would not be a big deal, because Cedar is usually with me. However, with her recent injury, things got a bit dicier. I had to attend an all-day meeting, and Cedar had to stay home and "guard the fort," as we say. This, too, is normally not a problem, because she just hangs out. She keeps the deer out of the garden, chases the rabbits back into the woods, and plays spoiler when the cats have spent hours stalking a rodent. All and all, she has a very pleasant day. But upon returning late in the evening, I knew something was wrong when I did not get my normal greeting, which involves a lot of barking and tail wagging. In fact, as I drove down our long driveway, I could not even see her.

As I neared the garage, a little tuft of fur popped up out of a foxhole that would have made any GI proud. I parked the truck and started walking toward her thinking to myself, "This is new."

"What's up girl? Not feeling too perky?" I said as I stroked her head. If she could talk, I am sure her reply would have been, "That's an understatement."

Coaxing her out of her den, I didn't know if her hole was dug due to the heat or some canine instinct to hide from her prey when wounded. Either way, she had dug quite an impressive bunker. I got her on the cool grass, struggled with another wrestling move to flip her over, and examined the wound. I was rather surprised at what I saw. Instead of the wound being all dirty from the foxhole, it was spotless. But next to the wound was an equally large new wound. As a mother will lick her finger to wipe away dirt from a child, a dog will lick a wound incessantly to heal it. In Cedar's case, she was so diligent that her cleaning created a wound as bad as the original injury.

So now I was in a pickle. She would not stop licking. The next day I planned to leave her alone again. Every time I turned my head, she would return to her instinctive cleansing. The vet suggested using a cone collar on her head to prevent her reaching the wound. I tried it, but the results were pitiful. Cedar would just stand outside, shaking and whimpering. Cedar has never been on a leash, has had forty acres to roam, and goes to work every day with me, stomping through the bush. In her eyes, the cone was solitary confinement and the Chinese water torture all rolled into one. It was obvious there was no way I could leave her for ten hours in the heat wearing that device. Therefore, I needed to come up with a new plan. I needed a way to cover the wounded areas and prevent the continuous licking. I tried ace bandages, medical tape, t-shirts, and bandanas with zero success. Then I tried a pair of cut-off long underwear, which worked but would not stay in place. Tape did not work nor did the ace bandage.

I was sitting on our bed scowling at Cedar, muttering to myself, "What am I going to use?" I kind of chuckled, glancing at Cedar because my tailoring of the long underwear gave her the "Capri pants" look. Then it dawned on me: panty hose!

I grabbed a pair from my wife's dresser, then cut and snipped until I had the appropriate tail holes and leg length. Voila! I had it. Calvin Klein watch out. Cedar was a little mortified with the look, but it seemed like it might work.

"Well," I told her, "at least you're a girl dog!"

The next day when I arrived home, she popped out of her foxhole to greet me, and she still had her capri pants on. So, for the next seven days, Cedar and I struggled with the garments, making sure they were clean and not tattered. The woods are riddled with sticks and burrs, which really shorten the lifespan of panty hose. They have not come up with a combat panty hose line yet, but perhaps they should. When my wife returned home, she found out her stocking stock had been severely depleted. In fact, even her exercise tights were gone. However, it was for a good cause.

Three days after her accident, Cedar returned to work with me. This drew several stares from my loggers, as she sashayed around in her panty hose carrying a stick. But I did not care; she was back to normal, obviously no worse for the wear. Thanks to our wonderful veterinarian and my astute fashion sense, we were a team again.

Road Trip with a Twist

New Hampshire, 2006

I am not what you would call a fan of traveling, at least by mechanical means. I consider any form of transportation that does not require the body to move as unnatural. Walking, hiking, running, cycling, canoeing, and kayaking are all natural forms of transportation, and I enjoy them. Driving in a vehicle is not. So, when my daughter asked if I could drive her to Vermont to check out a graduate school, my first response was, "No way!" But as a father, I quickly gave in. But not without one concession: I would drive her out east if she would climb Mount Washington with me. She countered with a promise from me that I would show her where she was born and the houses where we had lived. With a high-five, we sealed the deal, committing to our father-daughter road trip.

A few weeks later (and after a lot of whining), we were off. Driving down the interstate, I leaned over to fiddle with the radio, and I caught glimpse of my daughter huddled in the truck seat sleeping peacefully. Backpacking gear was overflowing from the back seat, and she was using a sleeping bag as a pillow. I hit the AM dial and started hearing stations from the south and east. When I do have to travel, I enjoy doing it in the wee hours of the morning. Traffic is light, I am fresh, and you get a sampling of American radio culture through the AM dial. I caught another glance of my daughter as she dozed.

Man, I thought, *I remember driving her home from the hospital, first day of kindergarten, junior high, high school, down to college, and now to grad school. What on earth happened to the time?*

A flash of eyes brought me out of my reverie as I swerved to the right to miss a deer. So much for reminiscing.

Four hours later, my daughter was wide awake, and I was no longer worried about the wildlife. Wild drivers were now keeping my attention. Buffalo, New York, was not a tranquil place at 8 a.m. on a Monday morning. I drive, at least, thirty-five thousand miles a year. But ninety-nine percent of that is in traffic-free conditions. Certainly, they are not at a breakneck speed with fourteen inches of space on all four sides to call your own. As my daughter read the map, I swerved here and dodged there. I was taught to have enough stopping space between you and the vehicle you are following. Not in city driving! The more space I left meant more cars could pull in front of me.

"These people are bloody nuts," I shouted over the roar of this unsanctioned NASCAR race.

Eventually, the traffic became two solid lanes of metal, plastic, and rubber traveling at eighty miles per hour. As I slowly extracted one hand from the wheel finger by finger, I said to my daughter, "You know, I always forget how many people there really are in the world. It usually takes a trip away from home to remind me how populated this planet really is."

A "whatever" nod came from my daughter. I knew she was thinking that I was about to launch into some kind of dissertation about people, space, consumption, and natural resources. So, I held my tongue for the moment.

Around noon, we hit lunchtime traffic in Albany, New York, and I silently pondered the plight of man and his natural resources. Then, the inevitable happened while we were entangled in a monster traffic jam. That's when I uttered the two words my kids fear the most, "you know??" These are the opening words for an "according to dad" speech.

"There are over 270 million people living in the United States, and I think they are all in this traffic jam," I said with my head slumped against the steering wheel. "Whenever I am around this many people, I am just amazed we have any natural resources left. Each and every one of us using 'stuff' every day, and most of that ending up in a landfill," I grumbled.

"Dad, you are being negative," my daughter reminded me as she shifted a pack to enjoy the view of our current parking lot.

"I know, I am sorry."

Directly in front of us was a car with a bumper sticker that said, *"Cover me! I'm changing lanes."* After several minutes of staring at the sticker, I sat up and said, "Okay, here is something positive. Even though we all use a bunch of stuff every day, the products we use from trees have a life cycle. Think about it. Everything we use that is made from trees has a beginning and an end. As soon as you cut a tree down, Mother Nature takes over. Sunlight hits the soil, which was previously shaded. A seed that has been dormant in the soil now has more sunlight and food, and "presto," it pops up, starting a new forest and new life cycle.

"We use the tree to make anything from paper to a house and in its place a new tree has started," I stated enthusiastically. "Show me a metal post or a plastic crate that can boast about their past and future. Using wood products is actually very environmentally friendly. When we are done using tree products as 'stuff' and they end up in a landfill, it rots into organic matter. Not so with plastic or metal," I concluded.

"Well done," she said. "Do you feel better now?"

"Yes, we are starting to move," I said optimistically.

The next day was much more pleasant. The school was a perfect fit for my daughter, I hiked up a small mountain nearby, and in the afternoon, we drove through Vermont and up into northern New Hampshire. En route, I pointed out where we lived in Vermont and our old house in New Hampshire. I had a rush of emotion when I saw our old house. It was the first house my wife and I had owned, and it certainly was a fix-er-upper. Except for the house, which was built in 1820, everybody was young when we lived in New Hampshire. That evening we got a hotel in North Conway and prepared for the most important part of our road trip—climbing Mount Washington.

I awoke early and peered out the hotel window only to see drizzle and clouds. Perfect weather for a climb to the summit of the highest mountain in the Northeast, which has claimed one hundred and thirty-four lives. I brewed us some tea using our backpacking stove and tossed my daughter a granola bar. She looked at me with a face that said, "Eggs and toast would be better. But I know you are in your hiking 'zone,' so this will do."

Thirty minutes later, we took our first steps toward the summit. We started at Pinkham Notch and were headed for Tuckerman's Ravine. There, we would reassess the weather. I had climbed this mountain many times when we lived nearby. But I was twenty-four years younger, and I really did not take the time to see all of the beauty along the way. As we wound our way up the trail, we passed stands of sugar maple, yellow birch, beech, and ash—the same species you will find in most northern states. As we hiked up in elevation, the tree species became very different, and the temperature dropped. We left the hardwood forest and entered a boreal forest made of balsam fir and black spruce, the type of forest you would find across Canada and northern Minnesota. After two hours of climbing, we reached Tuckerman's Ravine. My daughter's knee was really bothering her, so it was decided she would wait there for me.

As I was emptying my pack of the nonessentials, my daughter read a big yellow sign out loud.

"The area ahead has the worst weather in America. Many people have died from exposure. Turn back now if the weather is bad."

Glancing my way with rain dripping off her nose, she gave me a look inherited from her mom, and I said, "What?"

"Dad, are you really going to try to reach the summit in this weather?" she asked.

"I have seen worse up here. In fact, the last time I tried making it to the top, I got into big trouble. But that is a story for a different time," I said, tossing her the water bottle.

"Won't you need this?" she asked, looking at the bottle.

I pointed to a small waterfall at the head wall of the ravine and said I would be okay, thinking to myself of the last time I was here—October 10, 1981—and how it was frozen and very dangerous.

My daughter sighed and mumbled, "And mom thinks you have matured."

"I think she just means my gray hair and wrinkles," I said with a grin.

As I struggled up the head wall of Tuckerman's Ravine, I glanced down to the valley where I had left my daughter. The view was fantastic when I could see it through the swirling clouds. I had just reached 4,000 feet, which brought me into vegetation made up of arctic-alpine species: lots of lichen and very small, stunted shrubs. The temperature had dropped twenty degrees since leaving my daughter, so I pulled on my extra shirt.

I crested the head wall and had a major flashback. This is where I was twenty-three years ago when a cloud cover engulfed me, and I could not even see my feet. For many hours, I wandered along this ridgetop trying to find a safe route back down. When I finally emerged from the clouds, I was a mile off course, wet, tired, and shaken by the experience. Today, however, it was only raining, and I could make out the summit between the clouds.

Now with the summit within a half mile, I noticed there was very little vegetation. With the clouds swirling around and the bare rock, it seemed very bleak. I lost sight of the summit for about five minutes but kept following the cairns, which are piles of rocks put in place by previous hikers.

After four hours of hiking, I finally reached the top and was rewarded with a glorious view into Maine for about thirty seconds. Without warning, the wind started blowing. Not quite as strong as the world record two hundred thirty-one miles per hour recorded up here on April 12, 1934, but certainly strong enough to get my attention. In addition, the summit experiences hurricane-force winds every third day. So, I was up top for about three minutes before I started my trek down. The weather to the west looked very bad, and I had no desire to go through a repeat of my last trip. It took me two hours to descend to where my daughter waited. As I descended, the temperature got warmer and the vegetation got thicker, but the rain got heavier.

I came upon her huddled under a small spruce tree trying to sleep in the rain.

"Have a good rest?" I asked as I nudged her boots.

From underneath her yellow raincoat, I could see she was in no mood for my humor. Wet, cold, tired people seldom are.

As we headed down the mountain to our truck, I said, "Look at the bright side. We have two hours of walking, all downhill, and no traffic."

My daughter stopped, turned, looked at me square in the eye, and said, "Next time we make a deal, I want all of the details."

I said, "Hey, I drive you to Vermont and you climb a mountain with me. That was simple enough, wasn't it?"

"Details," she said as she slogged her way down the wet, steep, rough, dangerous, long, tiresome, trail.

"Details?" I asked. "I suppose this would not be a good time to tell you there is a road to the top on the other side?"

Just Short of a Dozen
Michigan, 2014

"Bad dog! bad dog!" I thought I heard as I was startled from sleep. I did not recognize the voice, which made it even more confusing.

There it was again, followed by the screen door slamming.

By now, I was conscious enough to recognize the voice shouting "bad dog" as my wife's. She assumes that when she is scolding an animal (in this case our dog, Cedar) she will make a stronger impression if she becomes a baritone. Funny, I thought, rolling out of bed, I don't remember her using that tactic on the kids.

"Troubles?" I asked as I placed my hand on her shoulder, scaring her in the process. Jumping perilously close to the woodstove, which she had been loading, she squeaked out a "where did you come from?"

"What's all the yelling about?" I asked, trying to comfort her.

"Your dog (Cedar is always my dog when she has done something wrong) just ate eleven unbaked, whole-wheat rolls off the counter," she said with uncontrolled anger. "The ones I was supposed to bring to the potluck tonight!"

Oh boy. Double jeopardy for Cedar, I thought. Not only did she eat the unbaked rolls, she left my wife in the position of being pot-less at the potluck. Not an enviable position for man nor beast.

"Where is she now?" I asked.

"Outside and, hopefully, violently sick," she said, gazing in vain into the frig for something miraculous to appear for the night's event.

I knew she did not mean that, but she was a bit peeved. I think getting up at two in the morning to take care of the dough might have added to her mood. And since I was the one who accidentally unplugged the bread machine despite the large note taped to the counter warning me not to, I left her to rummage without further comment, deciding to search for Cedar instead.

It was a beautiful fall morning with the sun just starting to shed its rays on the many shades of yellow and gold. There was a very light mist hanging low over the field with the tall milkweed plants protruding through the veil. I was just forming the thought in my mind that this was an idyllic morning when I heard the retching behind me. Turning, I saw a very miserable dog. She looked like she had a hangover on top of being seasick with the dry heaves.

"Well, come here, girl," I said with a compassionate voice.

She slowly waddled over to me with a major-league hang-dog look.

"Well, was it worth it? Eleven unbaked rolls seem a bit much at one sitting. Looks like we both blew it on the roll thing, eh girl?" I said, rubbing her ears.

She grunted, waddled off, and started retching again. Leaving her to her misery, I headed back in the house to see if there was anything I could do before we both headed to work. No, I could not help. No, store-bought rolls would not do. And yes, it was too early to joke about it.

Ever since I became a forester in 1977, I have been fortunate enough to work out of my home. It has been a great run, and I would recommend it to anyone. Short commute, familiar surroundings, easy access to food and drink, and a dress code that is extremely flexible. However, with every good thing there are some downsides. Taking your work home with you has a new meaning. My office is right below our living room, and I can hear my fax and answering machines kick on at the oddest times of day or night. Curiosity gets the better of me, and before long, I am in my office checking on the problem.

But the worst part about working out of my home is the look I get from my loving wife as she pulls out of the driveway on her way to work. I am usually standing on the porch, mug of tea in hand, shabbily dressed, petting the dog. She calls it envious; I rather think it is envy with a tinge of malice. Moreover, today with Cedar and me both making her life considerably more hectic, the look bordered on "wilting."

Several minutes later, after making the long commute to my office downstairs, my wife called on her cell phone.

"I think you should call the vet, because I am afraid of the yeast in the unbaked rolls," she said with real concern her voice. I agreed to call the vet, realizing Cedar had already been forgiven. The first phone call suggested I force some diluted hydrogen peroxide concoction down her throat. This resulted in a lot of gagging and more miserable looks from my canine friend. The second phone call encouraged me to watch and see if the rolls would reappear by any means. They did not.

The third call resulted in me making a rather speedy drive to the vet's office. Cedar was quickly whisked off for an x-ray, leaving me in the waiting room still unaware of the expanding powers of yeast. I was soon to be educated. The x-ray showed a giant mass of expanding guck that I promptly learned was extremely dangerous. This was made quite clear by the look on the vet's face and the tone in her voice. Cedar had to have her stomach pumped, which was rather tricky at this point due to the gas and expansion of the eleven unbaked rolls. It seems that if Cedar had snarfed the rolls down after they had been baked, she would have only suffered a burnt tongue and gut ache.

That's my Cedar, I thought. *Go big or go home.*

Cedar was led off with a whimper and a look of remorse to the surgical area. I could not see the pumping but I could hear it. First, I would hear a gurgle, then a plop followed by a splash, which went on for a very disturbingly long stretch. During this time, a couple came in with an elderly black lab. Without any hesitation, he wobbled right over to me. As I bent to pet him, I heard one of his owners say, "That's amazing; he never goes to men." If nothing else, I have always been a dog magnet.

I put my head closer to his, and while I rubbed his ears, I said, "Well, old lad, what are you in for today, eh?"

When his owners did not answer, I looked up and I could see in their face what the answer was. Feeling just horrible, I went back to my rubbing and murmured a few kind words into his aged, floppy ears. What a morning this was turning out to be.

With the pumping complete, which yielded a bucket full of guck, I was informed that Cedar would have to be watched for a few hours. And before I left, could I come to her cage and calm her down a bit? I eagerly replied. She whimpered, wagged her tail, and nuzzled her head in my hand. As I was rubbing her ears through the cage, the couple who had just lost their dog passed by. It was obvious they were distraught, and boy, did my heart go out to them. It is amazing how we can get so attached to our canine friends and how much they become part of our family. We also have two cats, and although they don't greet me with nearly as much enthusiasm as Cedar does (no living creature does), they still are part of the family.

As luck would have it, I had just enough time to visit a property nearby that I had been helping the landowner manage. We have had several harvesting projects over the past ten years, and I always like to check on the progress of the forest. The first harvest occurred on the extreme north side of the property, which allowed me a nice walk through a northern hardwood stand. The leaves were drifting down almost like large snow-flakes, settling on the forest floor in an array of colors. There was not a breath of air to stir them, so the forest floor was a mosaic, with each tree displaying its individual color at its base.

This area of the property was also next in line to be harvested, so I was mentally examining the trees. The trees in this stand varied greatly in age, which is what you want in a northern hardwood stand. This coming winter, I was going to mark the trees that needed to be harvested. I would be thinning out the suppressed, deformed, diseased, and less desirable trees along with some of the over-mature trees. There is a misconception that harvesting the larger trees and leaving the smaller ones is proper forest management. Sometimes that is true, but more often that is not the case. By just removing the larger trees, you are probably also removing the most valuable higher quality trees. This method of harvesting results in leaving the sup-pressed, deformed, and lower-quality trees, resulting in a forest of diminished quality and poorer health. If marked and har-vested properly, a hardwood stand will have trees of all ages, high quality, and the ability to provide a financial income for generations. Today's term for this sound forest management is called "sustainability."

Reaching the northern boundary, I walked into the thick aspen stand, which we had clear-cut five years earlier. Aspen needs full sunlight to regenerate suitably, and the regeneration was extremely thick. Walking east through the new, healthy forest, I kicked up several grouse, which benefited from the habitat created by the clear-cut. I was heading down a valley toward a harvest we did ten years ago when it dawned on me that I was woefully lonely. My partner was not with me. She had not chased after the grouse, or splashed in the brook we crossed, or brought me countless sticks and rocks to throw as we navigated the forest. As I came into the red pine plantation we had thinned ten years ago, I was thinking about Cedar and how she had better pull out of her predicament or else. The "what else" part would be very miserable for me. The pine plantation was in excellent shape, having responded well to the thinning. We had removed every third row, and the remaining rows took advantage of the extra water, nutrients, and sunlight. I hoped my friend would fare as well.

Glancing at my watch, I figured I would be a bit early getting back to the vet, but I was very anxious to see how my coworker/friend/family pet was doing. Upon arriving, I was greeted by a smiling staff who produced three x-rays showing Cedar's stomach prior to the pumping, just after, and now. She had made it. The skilled hands and quick thinking of our vet had saved her life, and I was enormously grateful. Even after paying the bill, which made those unbaked whole wheat rolls extremely valuable, I was still tremendously thankful. Moreover, I think Cedar was equally as ecstatic as she leaped into the seat of the truck. She was moving quite well, I thought, for someone who had just gone through such an ordeal. As we pulled out of the driveway, Cedar positioned herself in her official spot. Not quite shotgun nor quite in the back seat—kind of halfway between so she could take a nap if needed but always on guard.

I had one appointment left in my very long day, which was with a landowner several miles away. Arriving at the property, I noticed the landowner was waiting for me near the barn. He was a very tall, lean-looking man with a well-worn canvas jacket. The way he was slouched against the wall of the barn, I did not get the impression my late arrival had impressed him. Bounding from the truck, I stuck out my hand and started my apologies about being late. He grabbed my hand and said it was not a problem. From the look on his face and the pressure in his handshake, I was not convinced. I was really taken aback by his appearance, which was like something out of a John Steinbeck novel. I have dealt with many landowners in my thirty years as a forester, and sometimes a red flag goes up, which tells me to tread lightly. Usually my gut reaction is "spot on." I did not quite have a red flag flying in this instance, but it was at half-mast.

Returning to my truck to grab my hardhat and compass, I opened the door. Before I could stop her, Cedar bolted out and bounded up to Leon (name is changed to protect the innocent), my John Steinbeck character. I clinched the door handle not knowing what the reaction would be. To my relief and surprise, Leon lowered himself to one knee and cradled Cedar like a newborn lamb. She whined with joy and he cooed to her like she was his long-lost child. Relieved, I closed the door and joined the reunion. Leon stood up with a gleeful look on his face and a pleasant tone in his voice. My red flag was lowered, and the three of us headed to his woodlot.

It was a typical farm woodlot: forty acres of trees surrounded by eighty acres of fields. Over the generations, firewood, maple syrup, lumber, and squirrels had been taken from within its borders. Now Leon was looking for advice on how to manage it for future generations. As we walked, I explained what exactly he could do to ensure the health and sustainability of his forest. Cedar bounded ahead chasing a stick that Leon had thrown. When we stopped, she dug and dug until she found a rock for Leon to throw. After an hour, we stood on the edge of the forest looking at several deer in a small pasture. As I expected, Cedar gave chase and returned in her usual amount of time—about fifteen seconds. Panting, she proceeded to dig another hole.

"Cedar," I shouted, "At least act like you just about died today. Settle down!"

Hearing a huff, I looked up and saw the scowl on Leon's face, and the flag was back up at half-mast. After several minutes of explanation about the unbaked rolls, his face relaxed a little, and we made our way back to my truck. Shaking my hand, Leon thanked me for my advice. He grabbed Cedar by both ears, gave her head a shake, and planted a big wet one on her forehead. Cedar leaped in the truck, took up her position as copilot, and we were off. In the rearview mirror, I saw this quiet man take up his position leaning against the barn, hands in pocket, with the Dust Bowl look once again on his face.

Arriving home, we were greeted by my wife, who grabbed Cedar the instant she left the truck. She gave her a very long hug while at the same time telling her how worried she was and how thankful she was. Cedar scurried off to find something for us to throw, and we hugged each other. We stood there watching her, our goofy dog, and we were both very grateful for her and our wonderful vet.

"Hey, maybe you should bake some rolls for the vet? You know, for saving Cedar's life?" I asked, heading into the house.

Then the vision of the bucket of guck, which represented the eleven unbaked whole-wheat rolls, entered my head, and I said, "Or maybe a card would be more appropriate."

Not too many mornings later, I heard a cough, a gag, and "No-o-o-o!" come from downstairs. Then came the desperate voice.

"Mark, Cedar has been skunked!"

I buried my head in the pillow and wondered if Leon might want a dog.

Boundary Waters

Minnesota, 2001

A mournful groan came from the bathroom of this Norman Bates motel. Then I and everyone else in the small room heard a gasp and those fateful words, "Oh NO!!"

I entered the cramped bathroom not knowing what to expect. What I saw was both hysterical and bewildering. Grover (his nickname) was staring into the toilet where the top to his water bottle bobbed, repeating "Oh no," over and over. It was obvious I had to take control of the situation and do what any leader would do. I plunged my hand into the stained bowl to rescue the bobbing top. I threw the top in the equally stained sink, turned to Grover and blurted out, "What are you doing?"

We had all come equipped with water bottles with built-in water filters in the tips. The tip had to be sucked on to draw the water through the filter. That thought, now that Grover's filter just took a bath in a toilet, had Grover near nausea knowing he had a ten-day trip ahead. His almost tearful explanation was that he was prying the top off the bottle, and it flew into the toilet.

By this time, my son and the other members of our expedition were crammed into the doorway trying to see what was causing the commotion. When it dawned on them what had happened, the laughter was loud enough to hear all the way back to Michigan. I was probably the loudest.

As the lads harassed Grover, I went to work sterilizing the top as best I could. It was in my best interest to have a healthy canoeing partner, so I doused it with alcohol and boiled it in water. Even in the wilds of northern Minnesota, water needs to be filtered. Beavers carry a parasite, and when humans drink the water that beavers live in, which is almost every lake and stream, they run the risk of getting "Beaver Fever." I have had it, and it rates right up there with a root canal as things to avoid. We all had the same kind of water bottles, and even though I assured Grover it was fine to suck on the "tidy bowl" top, I took out my knife and made a nick in mine. I certainly was not going to suck on his water bottle, sterilized or not.

After the attention-grabbing start to the morning, we piled into the pickup and traveled the final hours to the starting point of our great adventure. My son and his two friends had just graduated from high school and were about to enter a new phase of their lives. Over the years, my son's two friends have heard the yarns about our wilderness canoeing trips. They had never gone on a trip like that, and it seemed very adventurous to them, despite my son's warnings. So, it was decided that upon graduation, we would take an inspiring canoe trip into the wilds of northern Minnesota. In addition to our group, a good friend of mine and his son joined us for the plunge into the wilderness.

Arriving at our put-in, we disembarked, unloaded the canoes and our waterproof packs. Since we had many long portages, I had drilled into the boys' heads that weight is the devil.

Consequently, we had all of our gear, including food for a week, packed into one pack apiece. My friend and his son were not quite as spartan, having several extra bags. But having canoed with Cookie for so many years, I knew the extra bags usually contained a few creature comforts (mostly extra food that tasted better than the usual freeze-dried stuff.). Now that I think of it, my family was usually more than willing to carry Cookie's extra bags.

We set the timer on the camera and stood, paddles in hand, at the edge of the lake, posing for our team picture. I have several dozen of these photos, and just a glance will fill my head with many memories. We also safely tucked away extra car keys. It is really hard to explain the anxiety one feels after returning from ten days in the bush only to discover that you cannot locate your keys. After much rummaging, they are usually located at the bottom of a pack among the wet socks and granola bar wrappers.

Now we were off, and our spirits were soaring. For the graduates, it was the beginning of a great adventure. For my friend and me, it was a chance to be with our sons in the wild and tackle all of its challenges. Even my son was excited. Having done trips like this since he was a wee lad, he was thankful to have some friends along. Even the gray skies and the prediction of three days of rain could not dampen our spirits yet.

Our three canoes traveled through Lake 1. My paddling partner, Grover, noted that Lake 1 was not a very glamorous name for such a beautiful lake. I pointed out that Minnesota had over ten thousand lakes within her border, and they probably ran out of names after several thousand. From above, the patterns our canoes left on the calm surface of the lake must have seemed a bit erratic. Cookie and his son, Koko, had not paddled in a while, and Koko, being in his early teens, knew best. My son and his paddling partner, Hope, fared slightly better due to my son's experience. I was able to keep my canoe on a steady course because my partner had no experience and was very receptive to instructions from his elder. Earlier, he had lost the coin toss that landed him in my canoe. He was a good sport about it, but I knew he would have rather been in another canoe. However, as they serpentined down the lake eating our wake, he seemed a little more pleased to be with the old man.

Paddling a canoe in the rain is not for everyone; it always evokes a variety of emotions for me. If it is a warm day and you have a warm bed waiting for you, paddling in the rain is almost pleasant. The rain drops make a wonderful pattern on the water, which is rather transfixing, and the sound is soothing. However, drop the temperature a bit, add a breeze, and throw in a wet campsite, and the pleasure level drops considerably. Luckily, it was only a light rain and a warm one to boot. So, our paddle through Lake 1 fell into the "not-so-bad" category.

The first portage of any trip usually forces the members of the expedition to get organized rather quickly. A portage is the process of getting your gear and canoes from one body of water to the next. It can be as short as a few meters or as long as many miles. I am guessing that a lot of marriages, partnerships, and friendships have been tested to the limit on portage trails. My wife refers to portaging as backpacking with a canoe on your shoulders. In short, it is not the most pleasant task in the world. And as I get older, with more aches and pains, I am slowly starting to see her reasoning. But if it were not for portages, the woods would be thick with other canoers. There is nothing like a nice, hard portage to separate the wheat from the chaff.

As we approached our first portage, the experts in the group naturally took over, with my son in the lead. He easily landed the canoe parallel to the bank to allow for easy in and out of gear and passengers. While this was going on, our canoes circled off shore—like the landing craft waiting to beach during D-Day. Once all canoes were unloaded, the sorting out began. It also became obvious who stuck to the "light packing" rule. Usually we like to have one pack per person with an extra bag for food. In addition, all loose objects such as sunglasses, water bottles, maps, sun block, and cameras should be tucked away. Per usual, all canoes were ship shape except for Cookie's and Koko's. There was so much loose stuff on the bottom of their canoe that I wondered if a pack had been dumped. Alas, it hadn't. They just like to make the first portage a secondary packing zone.

I like to grab a pack, paddles, and any loose object and walk the trail first to see if there are any problems. These pitfalls could be bees, bears, holes, wet spots, downed trees, mud, or many other surprises. Occasionally, the trail just disappears, and you have to wander around the bush looking for it. I would rather do that with a pack than a canoe on my shoulder. The second member of the team usually grabs a pack also. In my youth, I would carry a pack and canoe and make the trip once. But age and good sense have convinced me to go back for the canoe.

A curious thing happens on that first portage, and I have always been amazed by it. Whether it is a ten-day trip with fifty portages or a day trip with two, the same phenomenon occurs. Whatever you pick up and carry that first portage is what you will carry every time. It is the same phenomenon as sitting in the same spot at dinner or a staff meeting. And I do it as much as the next person.

Our first portage was uneventful except for the fact that

Hope and Grover had never portaged a canoe before. They quickly realized that no matter how you pad the yoke or what angle you carry the canoe, your shoulders and neck are going to scream in protest.

"Don't fret lads," I said, coming up behind them. "You'll soon get used to it."

A grunt came from each of their canoes. I chuckled at this and had a major deja vu. When my son was around twelve, he was already larger than me and could easily lift more than I could. Throughout the winter, he had flaunted this fact. I just smiled because I knew my life would be easier come next summer's canoe trip. That year's trip was a real test, and it was his first step into canoeing manhood. A lot of complaining came from under his canoe that summer.

When you are walking through bush with a canoe on your shoulders, several things happen. Not only is your peripheral vision gone, because you have a canoe as headgear, but you also have no depth perception. Soon your balance is skewed due to the seventy-pound canoe cutting off circulation to your eyes. Then there is the little matter of where to put the canoe when the pain in your shoulders gets too great. Also, all sorts of flying insects converge inside an overturned canoe. Some sort of invisible invitation goes out into the woods. Since both hands are keeping the canoe from falling off your shoulders, you are powerless to keep those same flying insects from biting the daylights out of you. This is not even mentioning all of the trees and rocks that the canoe runs into, resulting in concussions reverberating down your spine to your feet. If the trail is sufficiently long, most people swear off portaging forever.

Lake 2, 3, and 4 were pleasant paddles with fairly short portages in between. We also encountered several spots where we had to unload the canoes and lift them over beaver dams and logjams. These lift-overs are almost more of a hassle than real portages. Typically, you are precariously balanced on a bobbing log trying to unload the canoe at an uncomfortable angle. Injury is always a concern, and the thought of trying to get a hurt comrade out of the outback is not something you want to contemplate as you work to get your stuff around a "small" obstacle.

By the end of the first day, we had passed through four lakes finding ourselves at a wonderful campsite. In reality, most people would not have called it much of a campsite at all. However, your standards and expectations change when you paddle and lug a canoe all day. A somewhat dry piece of semi-flat ground, relatively rock-free, looks like a Holiday Inn. Add a bit of shade, good swimming, and easy access, and we are talking Hilton.

As evening rolled around, we all commented on how odd the sky looked now that it had quit raining. We were soon to find out what that sky really meant. About two in the morning, I was awakened by a very low grumble. This continued for the next several hours, which really confused me. Was it the Duluth airport, a mining operation, or a NATO exercise? Just before dawn, I got my answer. During the next series of rumbles, my tent filled with a faint light.

"Oh my," I said into the fading light.

"Dad," I heard from the tent next to me, "Has that been a thunderstorm all this time?"

"I'm afraid so, son," I said. "Looks like we are in for a bit of excitement."

The storm finally hit around eight, and our perfect campsite was seriously lacking in anything one would call cover. For the next four hours, we were hit with wind, hail, rain, and the threat of lightning. We hunkered down in our tents hoping our weight would keep them from blowing into the lake. Not until two in the afternoon were we able to start paddling again. The humidity was appalling as a light rain fell in the ninety-degree temps, but it was good to be moving again.

We had to cover a lot of water to make up for our six-hour rain delay, and we all knew it. We paddled and portaged hard until about eight, which gave us one hour to set up camp, swim, sort gear, and eat. Our camp consisted of three brightly colored tents. I was in a solo backpacking tent, which resembles a large ziplock bag. But not being a giant among men, it suited me just fine.

At exactly nine, no matter where you are in the boreal forest, squadrons of mosquitoes will find you. Off in the distance, you start to hear a faint murmur, which turns into a sound like a far-off jetliner. At that point, you have about three minutes before thousands of blood-sucking mosquitoes descend upon you. The first time this happens, you are completely taken off guard as the tranquil, peaceful evening turns into the Battle of Britain. Several nights of this, and you quickly become battle hardened. At the first murmur, you head for the tent and batten down the hatches.

About midnight, the same low rumble as the night before awakened me. Moans came from the other tents, which drowned out the murmur of the mosquitoes. Sure enough, we got a repeat performance of a Minnesota monsoon. Once the heavy rain started, my son and I both realized one of the canoes had not been turned over. This prompted both of us to bolt from the relative safety of our thin nylon tents to roll the canoe over. If we hadn't, it might have been disastrous, because this particular canoe was designed to be light, and the thin fiberglass shell easily could have snapped under the weight. We were both completely soaked as we retreated to our tents, prompting some colorful comments toward the purple tent.

Cookie and Koko, the owners of the canoe, were nice and dry in their snug, little abode.

The thunder, lightning, hail, and rain that accompanied the storm were even more intense than the night before. At one point, I thought I was on an island. This was confirmed when my flashlight revealed flowing water on either side of my sleeping pad. Without hesitation, I grabbed everything in the tent and stuffed it in my sleeping bag, making the hot night even hotter. If the water level in my tent stayed below three-quarters of an inch, I might remain dry. It did, but in the morning, I was shocked to find a three-quarter-inch mud slick covering the inside of my tent. When I took everything out of the tent, there was a perfect design of my pad with mud surrounding it. I scraped out the mud, threw the tent in the lake, and spread it out over our packs to dry as we paddled. It dried nicely, because our drizzly weather of the past turned tropical with temps in the high nineties and not a cloud in sight. Adding to the enjoyment was the humidity. Considering what had befallen us thus far, everybody's spirits remained surprisingly high. However, we were all about to be tested.

From an early age, I always encouraged my son to read the topographic maps on our annual canoe trips. Luckily, he took an interest in it, and he became very good at it. Handing over the important job of navigation to my son was genius on my part. He took ownership in the trip, and to this day I can call him and ask him how far a particular portage was and the name of a certain lake. The real upside for me was I did not need to locate my reading glasses every time we needed a course correction or a question arose as to how much farther we had to paddle. This freed me up for the important task of sightseeing, gawking, daydreaming, or staring at the patterns created by our wake.

This admiration for my son's navigational skills came to a sudden end on the third day of our trip. (It has since been restored.) Coming to the end of a long, narrow lake, it was decided by the two map keepers, my son and Cookie, that the portage trail we were to take was on the right side of the inlet. Never questioning I jumped out of my canoe, hefted a pack, and started up the not-so-well used trail. As I slogged along, I was alarmed by the amount of water in the trail. I knew it had rained a lot recently, but this seemed a little excessive. After about a half hour, I was starting to question if indeed this was a portage trail at all! Normally in the Boundary Waters Canoe Area, the portage trails are pretty well used, and some thought goes into laying them out.

A little bit further, and I was almost up to my thighs in muck, with leeches squirming in my wake. Finding a downed tree, I slung my pack over a branch and headed back to confirm with my comrades. I found the heavy-laden group huddled on a small island in a sea of muck. Grover had lost his boot in the mud, and they were trying to figure out how to retrieve it.

I confronted the two map keepers and expressed my doubts about this being the right portage trail. After a lot of head scratching, swatting of bugs, and leech picking, it was agreed that maybe we had no clue where we were. I suggested that I would continue ahead a little farther to make sure. With map in hand, I waded back to my pack, slung it over my shoulders, and pressed forward. As I slogged ahead through the Mekong Delta, I kept thinking of my brother and his tour in Vietnam. As unpleasant as my situation was, at least nobody was shooting at me.

After about fifteen minutes, I came to a lake, and upon hitting its shore, I threw off the pack and dove right in. Mud oozed out of my shorts, body, boots, and socks. Cookie came up behind me, laid down his load, and joined me for a bath. We floated on our backs for a while and watched the leeches squirm away. While we were floating, we decided the trail we had been using was probably a well-used moose trail. So, after leaving the cool lake and our packs on the shore, we headed back to the boys. The boys had successfully retrieved the boot and were very pleased when they learned we were retreating. Once back in our canoes, it only took a few paddle stokes down the northern shore to find the very visible portage trail. After a rather easy portage, we spent the next hour trying to find the cove in which our two packs lay.

Thereafter, it became a group decision before we headed off in any direction.

During this portage foray, I was starting to get the impression Grover might be getting a little dehydrated. He seemed a bit wobbly on his feet, and his usual "I-am-an-18-year-old guy-and can-carry-anything attitude" was starting to wane.

"Grover, have you been drinking enough?" I asked.

He replied with an unconvincing "you bet." Obviously, the dunk in the toilet was really getting to him, sterilization or not.

The next day we got an early start hoping we might get some tough portaging in before the heat and humidity became overbearing. The night before, my son had figured that we had four long portages covering approximately three miles. Since we double-carried (making two trips instead of one), the time spent on the trail was tripled. Three miles first trip, three miles return, three miles back. The good thing about double-carrying is you get to have a load-free walk going back for your remaining gear. It also gives you an opportunity to collect the gear you dropped. Since stuff is sometimes hastily shoved underneath straps or shoved into pockets, the portage trail is sometimes a virtual warehouse of collectibles. I have found water bottles, sunglasses, maps, flashlights, books, food, hats, raingear, and many knives along portage trails. And I have lost my share of such important stuff. We canoeists like to think of a portage trail as a giant swap shop. The weirdest thing I ever found along the trail was a shrunken head on a key chain. Try to convince your fellow travelers that voodoo is not a bad omen.

It was on the return trip of our first portage that I learned some startling news. Neither of my son's two friends was prolific in water sports. When they told me, I was struck with the incredible irony of it. Here we were in the middle of the Minnesota bush, on a canoe trip; I was entrusted with their lives. And they couldn't swim!

Sitting down on a rock, I said, "You've got to be bloody kidding me. Don't you think this is something you should have shared with me in the planning stage?"

They both just shrugged and laughed like any eighteen-year-old boys would do. In the end, the joke was on them, because no matter how shallow the water, how small the pond, or how hot the day, they were required to wear their life vests. In addition, I took every advantage to rock the canoe, point out the extreme depths of the water, tilt the canoe WAY over when filling my water bottle, and even stand up once in a while to stretch my legs, which is taboo in a canoe.

One hot afternoon, we were in the middle of a large lake and the conversation among the three canoes was about something cold to drink. For the past week, we had been drinking filtered lake water, which ran from tepid to hot. So naturally, something cold sounded good. As Grover was talking about ice cubes, I wiggled myself over the stern of the canoe, gave a shove, and landed in the lake. Even before I popped up, I could hear the panic yells from the two non-swimmers. Swimming under the canoe, I surfaced by the bow scaring Grover in the process. Calmly I said, "Hand me the water bottles." In complete amazement, he handed me the bottles. Then I did my best Flipper dive and headed to the bottom. I passed through several thermal layers before I reached a rock ledge; there, I stopped and filled the bottles. Surfacing, I handed them to Grover and swam to the other canoes to retrieve their bottles. In the swimmers' eyes, I had just done a nice gesture. However, to the two non-swimmers, I had just gone to Mars and back.

The next several days were hot, humid, and still. We paddled, swam, picked leeches, portaged, told guy jokes, talked about the boys' upcoming university days, fished, laughed, fixed blisters, and discussed the virtues of everything from duct tape to the universe. We filtered countless gallons of water, applied sun block, looked for the bottle of biodegradable soap (which was always missing), tried to pretend the food we were eating was good, studied the maps, and in my opinion had a jolly good time. The only thing that was going to spoil this wonderful trip was the tow. Because the last lake we were to paddle was so long, Cookie had arranged with an outfitter to give us a tow. This involved being picked up by a fishing boat and having our canoes towed the length of the lake to where our vehicles were parked. I was against it from the first thinking we were wimping out. Naturally, I grumbled about it the whole trip.

On the last day, we arrived at the designated island several hours before the scheduled rendezvous and decided to spruce up a bit. My son had been wearing one pair of shorts the entire trip. He obviously took my speech about packing lightly seriously. They had held up fine until the last cannonball into the lake, resulting in a split from stem to stern. As he was coming out of the lake, a group of six canoes hailed us. They were all girls also waiting for a tow and could they share our island?

"Sure," we said, "Room for all."

For the next two hours, my son was plastered up against a large rock wall not daring to move and praying their tow would arrive before ours. He was immensely relieved when it did because if it had not, he would have had to bare himself to the world. As it was, we dug out a few small towels and fashioned a type of Polynesian wrap for him to wear until we reached the truck.

When the tow finally arrived, I was still grumbling. But just after a few minutes of the wind blowing through my hair and the rhythmic thumping of the aluminum hull cutting through the waves, I was astonished to realize I was actually enjoying myself. Cookie was right. This was a very long lake and probably would have taken two days to paddle.

Unfortunately, we all had to get back to our normal lives sooner than we would have liked. In the bow of the boat sat the three college-bound lads laughing like they had when they were in grade school. Watching the boys, an amusing thought kept popping into my head. At the turn of the last century, young men and women were sent abroad just prior to their advanced education to broaden their views of the world. Well, it wasn't exactly Europe, but I don't think these three young men could have learned more about life. In one week, they struggled, laughed, persevered, learned about teamwork, and did their part. This fishing boat was their ocean liner, and the Boundary Waters was their Grand Tour. They had been abroad in a roundabout way.

Glancing back and seeing me, the three boys let out a laugh and raised their water bottles in salute. I gave them a shout and returned the salute. We all drank; by now, the three boys were almost falling off the boat in hysterics. Grover again saluted me, and with his left hand, gestured to the top of his water bottle. A bit bewildered, I returned the salute, and then the horror of it all set in. The top of my water bottle was nick-free, showing no signs of the mark I made earlier with my knife. With this realization, I suddenly became a bit seasick. It was a good thing for him I knew he couldn't swim.

Attack of the Big Bird

Michigan, 2010

*N*ature usually gets what she wants. In fact, even if we humans try, she is undeterred. She can move sand dunes with little effort. Her rivers will cut a course exactly where they please. Insects and animals will adapt to any new situation. Volcanoes, hurricanes, and earthquakes come and go at will. Fires will ravage a landscape. And in no time at all, "Mother" has started the task of turning the scorched earth into a young, lush forest. It starts slowly, with grass and weeds leading the assault. Close on their heels, small, woody vegetation and brush will start to dot the landscape. Eventually, seeds will either sprout from the soil, be carried on the wind, or be deposited by birds and animals. Once a young forest has been established, assorted wildflowers and groundcover will complete the recovery program. Nature is always in control. We can work with her, maybe even coax, nudge, or encourage her. But we will never control her. And that is probably the way it should be.

I was having these unusually deep thoughts one morning while sitting at the kitchen table enjoying a bit of tea, gazing out the window at a large, white birch in the distance. My wife was sitting across from me surrounded by checklists, bills, receipts, and a calculator. She was drumming a pencil against her head as she expertly worked the calculator. I could tell she was in the "zone." I should have felt mildly guilty or at least some remorse, but I didn't. I guess I was just used to the weekend ritual. For some reason, when we first got married, she took over the family bookkeeping. In those days, it was fairly simple. No house, no mortgage, no kids, no tuition, no credit cards, and no money. And as the years came and went, my wife became quite good as the family comptroller. In fact, I was proud and inspired by her dedication, and I frequently told her so. For this, I was usually rewarded with a less-than-endearing look.

I took another sip of tea, which was a bit too large, and I was scalded in the process. I think I heard "serves you right" from underneath the stack of bills, but I was not certain. I am sure all husbands and wives go through this same situation. Somehow the chores are divided up. And when one party is doing their most unpleasant chore, they feel they got the short end of the treaty. But as men through history will attest, when bantering back n' forth as to who does the most, men always lose. Females have the last, best word. Their trump card is "I GAVE BIRTH."

At that point, men just surrender. It's not a fight you will win.

Looking back out at the white birch, I was struck how little of the tree I could actually see. When I first built our house in 1985, I would hold my young son on my lap and make up stories about the big, white birch. Later, I put a rope on one of its large branches, and from the window I watched him swing. But time has moved on. Our son is almost done with college, and the field in which the white birch had been king is now overgrown with trees and brush. I was not surprised. If let alone, most fields will revert back to a forest. It is the natural process, just like the recovery from a forest fire. As I sat enjoying the last bit of my tea, I made my decision. I would reclaim the field and restore the white birch as king of the field.

I pushed my chair away from the table and proclaimed, "Well, I suppose I ought to get at it then."

"At what?" my wife said, peering over the ledger book.

"I am going to brush back the field so we can see the big birch again," I stated.

I could tell from her expression that, in her opinion, this was probably not the most pressing of jobs. In fact, on a list of things that needed to be done around the old homestead, this job did not make it in the top one hundred. So, on my way out, I added that I needed to brush back the field because the garden was being shaded by the encroaching forest. This fact alone raised the project up to at least ninety-nine on the list.

For several hours, I wielded my chainsaw, knocking down the young growth. I know to some people, cutting these young trees would be a form of heresy. But the forest really was taking over our field and starting to shade the garden. Like the farmers and settlers of old, we needed our garden plot. I also had the comfort of knowing that wildlife likes diversity. An open area within our hardwood forest provides grasses, bugs, and habitat for a variety of wildlife. Bluebirds, rabbits, deer, turkeys, and several other types of birds would personally thank me if they could.

Bending over to cut a sapling close to the ground, I had a sense of something watching me. Looking up, I saw nothing. I walked over to another sapling, snipped it off, again having the feeling of being observed. On the third wave of uneasiness, I glanced up before I cut the tree off. What I saw made me jump back, stumbling in the process. I was sprawled on the ground in a state of complete disbelief. Looming over me was a giant bird. Was it a grouse raised too close to a nuclear power plant? Or a turkey on steroids? It looked like a bloody ostrich! Whatever it was, it certainly was not native to northern Michigan. I slowly started to crawl toward my chainsaw, which was idling about three feet away. The bird followed my movements with his very small, beady eyes. I grabbed my saw and leaped up, holding the saw out in front of me like a dueling sword.

Big Bird took a few tentative steps closer. Now that I was standing, the bird still looked down at me, which was unnerving. I said something very intelligent like, "Who are you, and where the heck did you come from?" Then it dawned on me. I knew what this large, brown-feathered hulk of a bird was! It was an emu. A few years earlier, I had been introduced to the species while working on a forest not too far away. The landowner, with whom I was working, raised emus, and he had told me countless facts about the bird.

Now that I knew what I was up against, I felt slightly more comfortable. In fact, so comfortable I shut the saw off, an act I would soon regret. This emu probably stood at least six feet tall and weighed roughly one hundred ten pounds. He was eight inches taller than me, but I had him by at least twenty-five pounds. So, I figured we were about evenly matched. Silly me! I put my saw on the ground and started talking to him like I would my dog. However, he was not impressed. He made a very deep, guttural grunt and jumped about five feet into the air. On the way down, I noticed this fellow had three very large claws, which were pointed in my direction. Between the bird and me stood a maple about three inches in diameter. This maple became the only thing between me and a very testy emu. At first, I thought it was funny. I moved right, he moved left. Each time, he zeroed his beady eyes on my chest, grunted, jumped in the air, and flashed his very sharp claws.

"Okay, what gives?" I asked as I danced to the left. I was awarded with another grunt.

As I moved to the right, I grabbed my saw and tried starting it, which in normal circumstances was not easy. At this particular moment, while I was being chased around a small tree by an emu, fruitlessly trying to start my saw, my wife happened to take a break from the accounting duties. What she saw must have seemed surreal. But being a woman good under pressure, she did what came natural to her. After she finished laughing, she dialed 911. She then had to explain the ridiculous situation she was observing. She prefaced her explanation that this was not an emergency, but maybe the animal control officer should be contacted.

While she talked, I dodged and ducked. The bird's featherless head sat perched on a very long neck, which easily reached on either side of the small sapling. Finally, I was able to start my saw, and I began thrusting at his long, darting neck. Bird was starting to back off a bit, and I thought I had finally gotten the upper hand, when my saw started to sputter, spit, and cough. I had run out of gas!

At this crucial moment, my mind suddenly started playing back all of the information I had learned about my fellow jouster. Emus can run up to forty miles an hour, and each stride is about nine feet long. Okay, so I won't make a run for it. They eat bugs, grains, seeds, and vegetation. But that was in their native Australia, where they had been living for over eighty million years. Who knows what they prefer in cold northern Michigan? They are very protective of their young and show signs of aggression during the mating season. I wondered if my saw had sounded like some mating call or territorial signature. It was useless to me now, so I laid it down. Lying next to it was a young sapling I had cut down, and I quickly picked it up. Now I had a weapon that this emu might recognize: a spear. Like any good combatant, my goal was to make it to a secure location, preferably with a door. I started stabbing at Bird, catching him in the chest. Each time, he let out a grunting noise like he was coughing up a hairball. At one point, I was actually chasing him.

As we got closer to the house, I could see my wife looking out the window. She was talking on the phone, and I could tell she was laughing hysterically. What was so bloody funny, I thought? Instinctively, I had adopted the pose of a great aboriginal hunter. In a crouched position with my spear held over my head, I was ready to strike my ancient prey. What a picture.

About half way to the house, Bird decided that my spear really was not that sharp, and he started chasing me. I was back-peddling, thrusting my spear at his ever-moving neck. Each time I thrusted, he pecked my spear. This guy was good, and it was obvious I was about to lose the battle. Then a miracle happened. My wife opened the door. From the house came my canine protector. Cedar bolted toward me and my dueling partner, barking like she was an entire pack of gray wolves. Bird abruptly turned around on its sharp toes and started toward the field. Cedar was right on its heels, barking and nipping. Then Bird put it into overdrive and looked like the roadrunner as he dashed across the field. Cedar stayed on the perimeter for several minutes barking.

I leaned against my makeshift spear, catching my breath. The whole episode probably lasted five minutes, but I felt like I had just been in a rugby match. Cedar strolled back to where I was standing. Actually, she pranced with her tail and head held very high with pride. She had trained her entire life, two years, to be my protector, and now she had done it.

I heard a suppressed laugh coming from the porch behind me. My wife looked like she had just spent two hours on the set of Saturday Night Live. She had been laughing so hard she had been crying.

"What is so funny?" I asked between breaths.

She composed herself the best she could and said, "Nothing." As she closed the door behind her, I heard another burst of muffled laughter.

Cedar leaned against my leg, so I bent down to pet my savior. Scratching her behind the ears, I wondered if maybe this whole ordeal had been a sign. I made a mental note: starting next month, I will become the apprentice to the family comptroller.

Journals from the Bottom of the Canoe

Ontario, 1998

*M*y paddle slices through the cold Lake Superior water
with amazing ease. On the bottom, thirty feet below, I can see
glaciated boulders the size of buffalo. My hand touches the
water as I place my paddle in for another stroke. The water is
bitterly cold . . . painfully so. Normally this time of year, the
water is considerably warmer. But along Canada's north shore
of Superior, it has been a summer-less summer. Not only is
the water colder, the vegetation is weeks behind schedule. I
time my strokes to match my daughter's in the bow of the
canoe, allowing us to glide through the water silently. Superior
is abnormally calm as we travel along its rugged shore. My
daughter stops paddling as we listen to a woodpecker drum
out a beat on the far shore. I hear a whistle and turn toward
my son and wife's canoe. My wife is pointing to a loon she sees
off in the distance.

"She won again," I say, turning to my daughter.

Since the kids have been old enough to ride in a canoe, we have been bringing them to Canada. When they were young, we would award a loony (a Canadian dollar) to the first person who saw a loon. Most of the time my wife or I would spot the first one but not say a word. Since the kids have gotten older, my wife has gotten her share of the loonies.

Again, I dip my paddle into the clear waters of Superior and watch as the drips fall off onto the smooth, calm surface. I look toward my wife and son and am struck by how fast time progresses. Looking across my bow, I see my son, broad shouldered, pushing the edge of his teens and approaching manhood. It was just a few years earlier when he awkwardly held the paddle and tried in vain to propel the canoe forward. Since the kids have been old enough to paddle with efficiency, we have taken two canoes on our annual canoe trips to northern Ontario. My son canoes with his mother and I with my daughter. To see him now compared to a few short years ago is mind boggling. How can they grow up so fast?

In the stillness, I can hear them talking of trips in the past and the rough spots we have been in. It is amusing now. But, at the time, they were less than perfect. I guess that's one of the reasons my wife and I felt these canoe trips were so important. During the course of the day, we had to worry about tough rapids, long portage trails, staying dry and warm, having enough food, making a fire, and purifying the water. This really brings a group together. And if you happen to be a family, it teaches you to count on each other. Now, not to glamorize this, at the time you may wish you were somewhere else. But when you are home and dry, you remember the lessons. After ten days in the bush, each person takes on a responsibility, and the expedition survives.

Our decision to take our holidays in the Ontario bush was

not always a popular choice among our children. I can still hear the words, "Why can't we be like normal families and go to Disney World?"

In the bow, my daughter shifts her weight; we lean a little to the left side. This is no problem as I move my hips a little to the right. That's what you learn in a canoe: compensate and adjust. At home, as the father, I may not do this as well. But in the bush I am an expert.

My daughter lifts her paddle over her shoulder and points to the sky.

"Do you see it?" she asks.

I look in the direction of the paddle and see the bald eagle sitting on the old, white pine snag.

This is it; I am just about overloaded with emotions. I am sitting in my most favorite watercraft, on the most dramatic water in the world, with my daughter, looking up into the cloudless sky at a bald eagle. Mayday, mayday; emotion overload, emotion overload!

How can this be? My wife and I are too young to have kids that are nearing adulthood. Why, it seemed just a few short years ago when I asked her to homecoming. As I lean to one side to adjust our weight again, I realize that was over thirty years ago.

I lean back on my pack and tell myself how lucky I am to see my life before me—my daughter with the self-assurance and zest for life, my son with his ever-present good nature, and my wife, who actually enjoys these trips. I have always known of my luck, but seeing it all again, in front of me, gives it renewed emphasis.

Again, my daughter shifts to the side. I shift, and she looks back. She then puts her paddle down and rummages in her fanny pack, which is bulging. Out comes the camera, and several shots are taken. Some of the shots won't turn out. But to her young eye, what she sees is interesting. May that always be so.

My son and wife are laughing about something. They are out of earshot, and I can only guess what it is. I suppose he is doing some line from some movie and his mother is joining right along. I still remember the year on a Minnesota lake when the two of them were in the middle of a heated discussion on paddling against the wind; my wife reminded him that she still could pop him one. My daughter and I thought it was quite funny, but their canoe was quiet for a very long time. Eventually (several hours later), they laughed, too.

My partner decides to take one of her frequent breaks and leans back against the food pack and gazes up into the clear Superior sky. Since we are not in a hurry today and the sun is shining, I decide to be the tolerant father. This is not always the case. Most of the time I would gently (or not so gently) remind her that we are "burning daylight." Translated, that means: "I can't believe you want to take another break! We have four portages and nineteen miles ahead of us before we make camp. What are you thinking?" But I, too, lean back and enjoy the rare Canadian sunshine.

Actually, the words Canadian and sunshine don't often go together. Many annual canoe trips were spent huddled around a pitiful fire, longing for some sunshine and summer-type weather. But the north shore of Lake Superior always has its own idea of what summer weather should be like.

Probably the most miserable year we spent was in 1995. I had spent the winter months leaning over topo maps spread out on our kitchen table, trying to find the perfect trip. I had received some grumbling from the troops about the amount of calories that were spent each day during our so-called "vacation." The point was made that normal people are supposed to gain weight on their holidays. We, on the other hand, have a tendency to shed a few pounds on ours. In short, my family wanted me to find a more relaxing trip. So, after many hours staring down at the maps and calculating the miles of portaging, I thought I had it. The trip seemed just the right mix of rivers, lakes, and wildlife, except for one thing: Once into our journey, we discovered it was hard to determine the difference between the rivers and lakes, or for that matter, between a loon and a bear. We had to continuously wipe water out of our eyes just to see. The weather was so ugly, it was hard to tell which was land, lake, or cloud.

After several days as the leader of this ill-fated expedition, old dad made a major decision. We had to cut our losses and bail out. This had never been done, and I wanted to make sure the family knew a lot of thought went into this decision. (Actually, if I hoped my family would ever follow me into the heart of the wilds again, it was prudent to get out of this miserable excuse of a vacation with my head intact.)

So, we turned around and made our exit. The trip back was somewhat more pleasant, because the wind was behind us. We rigged sails in both canoes and moved sharply through the wind and rain back to where we left the truck. With the prevailing winds, we were able to travel the distance in one day instead of two.

As my children move on with their lives, I can only hope they will want to share these experiences with their children. Maybe I can be part of that. Now that they are young adults, they are close to the age where they might think we were smart parents because we took them into the wilds instead of to Disney. Maybe not yet, but soon.

I just hope we don't end up on the Jerry Springer show or Oprah discussing the matter.

Unconditional Love

Michigan, 2015

*I*t was love at first sight. Well, actually, it was love at first nibble. Because that is what this little ball of Canadian fur was doing to my wife's ear. My wife, Gail, had such a pleasant look on her face, which I had not seen in a very long time. I felt my heart soar to see her happy. After a few more hugs of the tiny tail-wagger, Gail gently placed her down to mingle with her littermates. The little pup, soon to be our little Golden Retriever, jumped on the puppy pile that was rapidly forming—fluff balls of cuteness all blending together, sending a smile-tsunami throughout the room.

Back in the truck, heading home, my wife said in a quiet voice, "Do you have any clue why I chose that particular puppy?"

I thought for a moment and replied, "Honestly, I don't."

"I didn't think so; you had your eye on one with the green ribbon," she said.

An instant of clarity overwhelmed me, and I felt such a bloody fool and an insensitive moron.

278

"Oh Gail, I am so sorry; I should have noticed," I said somberly.

True to the fighting spirit she had developed over the past two years, she smiled and said, "You are still such a guy."

"Guilty as charged," I sighed.

As I peered over the steering wheel, I could envision the scene less than an hour ago. There was this little ball of golden fur snuggled in Gail's arms sporting a pink ribbon. And since color pink is the universal color defining breast cancer, it was very fitting that our new puppy would be wearing a pink ribbon. It had been a little over a year since Gail had been diagnosed with breast cancer. We had become very mindful of the color pink and the hope it represented.

We could not have the puppy in our lives for another four weeks. That, we thought, gave us ample time to pick out a name. Boy, were we wrong! We could not come up with a name we both liked for love or money. We joked that we spent more time debating the name of this puppy than we ever did the names of our two children. One evening while we were cooking, a song came on the radio, and Gail started to sing.

"Who is that singing?" I asked.

"Dusty Springfield," she replied.

We both looked at each other excitedly and did a high five. We had the name.

Things happen for a reason. Not sure why or how, but they do. From the moment Dusty entered our lives, she was the perfect pup for the times. Not a perfect pup; not by any stretch of the imagination. She was so far from perfect that her antics sometimes allowed us to concentrate on her and her foibles rather than the everyday struggles a family goes through when dealing with a serious illness. Dusty chewed, scratched, mauled, dug, rolled, and whined. She had just about every bad habit a dog can have. If we did not live on a dead-end dirt road with a one thousand foot driveway, I am sure she would have chased cars as well. Through all of this she had, and has, one saving grace that shields her from owner retribution. She is so bloody cute. To this day, perfect strangers will come up to Dusty and coo over her. And at any drive-through, she becomes an instant celebrity. She hangs her head out my window, and bank employees or fast food workers will gather on the other side of their windows to smile and wave at her. Not just one, but all coworkers in the area will gather. And then they start offering her all kinds of bounty: biscuits to sliced roast beef.

A little over a year after Dusty arrived, Gail's battle with cancer took a dramatic turn for the worse. Our normal upbeat mood was being chipped away every day as we were slowly forced to face the horrible truth of the illness. Of the two of us, Gail was by far the strongest. Dusty, sensing the situation, became calmer and started playing the role of therapy dog. The last several weeks of Gail's life were spent in and out of the hospital. When she was home, Dusty would always be near her. When she was not, Dusty was then glued to me. Gail was able to spend the last week of her life at home surrounded by friends and family. Uncharacteristically, Dusty could be found in the shadows, away from the people. I believe she really sensed the magnitude of the situation, and having a dog underfoot was not appropriate. But when no one was in the room, she could be found lying next to Gail's bed.

My wife and I had been high school sweethearts, and upon her passing, I was completely lost and without a rudder. But I did have a life ring and her name was Dusty. Never in my wildest dreams would I have predicted the importance this one beautiful, frustrating dog would play in my life.

Sensing my grief and sadness, Dusty never left my side. She

would lay just outside the shower door making sure all was well. Never having slept in the bed before, she started a nightly habit of not only sharing my bed, but not being content unless three-quarters of her body was touching mine. But the most amazing thing she would do was sense when I became really sad. I would just have sad thoughts, and she would appear out of nowhere and nuzzle my hand with her nose. Absolutely amazing.

I am one of the lucky few who had the good fortune to experience a relationship characterized by "Unconditional Love." Gail used to call it "Golden Retriever Love." Well, I am here to tell you, she was spot on.

If I have learned anything in life, it is that there is nothing more pure, nothing more worth seeking, than Unconditional Love. Gail gave me that blessing. I do miss it so.

THE END

CPSIA information can be obtained
at www.ICGtesting.com
Printed in the USA
LVHW111208161118
596837LV00001B/28/P